as it is

Volume 1

Rangjung Yeshe Books ✦ www.rangjung.com

PADMASAMBHAVA ✦ *Treasures from Juniper Ridge* ✦ *Advice from the Lotus-Born* ✦ *Dakini Teachings*

PADMASAMBHAVA AND JAMGÖN KONGTRÜL ✦ *The Light of Wisdom, Vol. 1, Vol. 2, Vol. 3, Vol. 4, & Vol. 5*

PADMASAMBHAVA, CHOKGYUR LINGPA, TULKU URGYEN RINPOCHE, ORGYEN TOPGYAL RINPOCHE, AND LAMA PUTSI PEMA TASHI ✦ *Dispeller of Obstacles*

YESHE TSOGYAL ✦ *The Lotus-Born*

DAKPO TASHI NAMGYAL ✦ *Clarifying the Natural State*

TSELE NATSOK RANGDRÖL ✦ *Mirror of Mindfulness* ✦ *Empowerment* ✦ *Heart Lamp*

CHOKGYUR LINGPA ✦ *Ocean of Amrita* ✦ *The Great Gate* ✦ *Skillful Grace* ✦ *Great Accomplishment*

TRAKTUNG DUDJOM LINGPA ✦ *A Clear Mirror*

JAMGÖN MIPHAM RINPOCHE ✦ *Gateway to Knowledge, Vol. 1, Vol. 2, Vol. 3, & Vol. 4*

TULKU URGYEN RINPOCHE ✦ *Blazing Splendor* ✦ *Rainbow Painting* ✦ *As It Is, Vol. 1 & Vol. 2* ✦ *Vajra Speech* ✦ *Repeating the Words of the Buddha*

ADEU RINPOCHE ✦ *Freedom in Bondage*

KHENCHEN THRANGU RINPOCHE ✦ *King of Samadhi* ✦ *Crystal Clear*

CHÖKYI NYIMA RINPOCHE ✦ *Present Fresh Wakefulness*

TULKU THONDUP ✦ *Enlightened Living*

ORGYEN TOBGYAL RINPOCHE ✦ *Life & Teachings of Chokgyur Lingpa*

DZIGAR KONGTRÜL RINPOCHE ✦ *Uncommon Happiness*

TSOKNYI RINPOCHE ✦ *Fearless Simplicity* ✦ *Carefree Dignity*

DZOGCHEN TRILOGY COMPILED BY MARCIA BINDER SCHMIDT ✦ *Dzogchen Primer* ✦ *Dzogchen Essentials* ✦ *Quintessential Dzogchen*

ERIK PEMA KUNSANG ✦ *Wellsprings of the Great Perfection* ✦ *A Tibetan Buddhist Companion* ✦ *The Rangjung Yeshe Tibetan-English Dictionary of Buddhist Culture* & *Perfect Clarity*

MARCIA DECHEN WANGMO ✦ *Confessions of a Gypsy Yogini* ✦ *Precious Songs of Awakening compilation*

CHOKGYUR LINGPA, JAMGÖN KONGTRÜL, JAMYANG KHYENTSE WANGPO, ADEU RINPOCHE, AND ORGYEN TOPGYAL RINPOCHE ✦ *The Tara Compendium Feminine Principles Discovered*

as it is

Volume 1

米

Tulku Urgyen Rinpoche

RANGJUNG YESHE PUBLICATIONS

RANGJUNG YESHE PUBLICATIONS
125 ROBINSON ROAD, FLAT 6A
HONG KONG

ADDRESS LETTERS TO:

EDITOR@RANGJUNG.COM
RANGJUNG YESHE PUBLICATIONS
KA-NYING SHEDRUB LING MONASTERY
P.O. BOX 1200, KATHMANDU, NEPAL

5 7 9 8 6 4

FIRST EDITION 1999

PRINTED IN THE UNITED STATES OF AMERICA

PUBLICATION DATA:

TULKU URGYEN RINPOCHE (1920-1996).
INTRODUCTION BY CHÖKYI NYIMA RINPOCHE, TSIKEY CHOKLING RINPOCHE,
TSOKNYI RINPOCHE, AND MINGYUR RINPOCHE.
TRANSLATED FROM THE TIBETAN
BY ERIK PEMA KUNSANG (ERIK HEIN SCHMIDT).
COMPILED BY MARCIA BINDER SCHMIDT AND EDITED WITH KERRY MORAN.
FIRST ED.

TITLE: AS IT IS, VOL. I
ISBN 978-962-7341-35-2 (PBK.)
1. MAHAYANA AND VAJRAYANA—TRADITION OF PITH INSTRUCTIONS.
2. BUDDHISM—TIBET. I. TITLE.

COVER PICTURE COURTESY OF SHECHEN ARCHIVES
COVER PHOTO: MATHIEU RICARD
PHOTO OF TULKU URGYEN RINPOCHE: SAM HARRIS
PAGE 5; PICTURE OF TULKU URGYEN RINPOCHE

DISTRIBUTED TO THE BOOK TRADE BY
NORTH ATLANTIC BOOKS & RANDOM HOUSE, INC.

Table of Contents

✳

Preface

❋

The teachings presented in *As It Is*, Volumes I and II, are primarily selected from talks given by Kyabje Tulku Urgyen Rinpoche in 1994 and 1995, during the last two years of his life. The audiences to whom these teachings were given ranged from large assemblies gathered in the main temple hall of Nagi Gompa to smaller groups present in Rinpoche's private room. A few of these teachings were given to only one or two people. The nationalities of the recipients were similarly diverse. It is more than coincidental, however, that the same themes pervade all the instructions. Kyabje Tulku Urgyen spoke from what he personally experienced and all his teachings were infused with compassionate realization. His energy and intimacy seem all the more precious in retrospect.

The emphasis in Volume I is on the development stage and practices associated with it. Volume II emphasizes the completion stage and its connected practices.

Rinpoche passed away on February 15, 1996. During the forty-nine day period following his death, Rinpoche's four sons were interviewed about their impressions of their father. Each son is an incarnate lama and a master in his own right. We have included portions of their interviews in this volume, as we feel there is no better expression of Kyabje Tulku Urgyen's qualities and teaching style than these.

Rinpoche always taught from the perspective of the view. While we have sought to remain true to the integrity of his instructions, we have not included teachings in which he directly transmitted the pointing-out instruction. This must be received in person from one of his lineage-holders.

In no way are these books meant to substitute for direct contact with qualified masters. No book is able to do so.

To truly benefit from the depth of the teachings contained here, the reader must have received the pointing-out instruction and recognized buddha nature. *As It Is* is our offering to those fortunate people who have received the pointing-out instruction. For those who have not, it can serve as a taste of what is yet to come. These books are therefore also meant to inspire those who are motivated to seek out qualified lineage holders of the Tibetan Buddhist tradition and request the pointing-out instruction and the teachings connected to it.

We would like to thank all the people who helped make this book possible: the transcriber, Dell O'Conner, our editor, Kerry Moran, the proof-readers, Gloria Jones and Shirley Blair and the printing sponsor, Richard Gere. Finally we would like to add that any errors or inconsistencies are solely our own.

Kyabje Tulku Urgyen Rinpoche often recited the following quote from a tantra as representing one of the foremost ways to attain stability in the practice of Dzogchen. This statement is a summary of our intent as well; please take it to heart.

> *Indescribable innate wakefulness*
> *Depends only upon the practices of gathering the accumulations*
>   *and purifying the obscurations*
> *And upon the blessings of a realized master.*
> *To follow other methods should be known as delusion.*

May whatever merit generated by this book quickly hasten the appearance of the next incarnation of Kyabje Tulku Urgyen Rinpoche. May it help expand the activities of the masters of the Practice Lineage, and may it be a cause for countless practitioners to realize the great perfection in actuality!

—Erik and Marcia Schmidt
Nagi Gompa

Introduction

✻

From "Indivisible Nature," spoken by Chökyi Nyima Rinpoche

Our Tulku Urgyen Rinpoche was born in Nangchen, in the eastern Tibetan province of Kham. He began meditation practice at the age of four. Each day his father, Chimey Dorje of Tsangsar, would give guidance in meditation to his many followers. Tulku Urgyen Rinpoche sat and listened with the others, so that when he was only four years old he had already had what we call a recognition of the nature of mind.

As he grew older, Tulku Urgyen Rinpoche received additional instructions from his uncle, Samten Gyatso, who he considered his root guru. Samten Gyatso was a highly realized being. Not only was he a pure monk, but he was also a practitioner with a high level of accomplishment. Khakyab Dorje, the 15th Karmapa, often praised him. One evening after Samten Gyatso had left his room the Karmapa joined his palms together and said, "In these times, perhaps only Samten Gyatso has a totally perfect realization of the view of the Innermost Essence of Dzogchen." Several old monks from Tsurphu told us this story.

It was from Samten Gyatso that our Rinpoche received most of his Dharma lineage, both empowerments and instructions. Of special importance is the fact that Samten Gyatso often gave him *semtri*, guidance on the nature of mind, and helped Tulku Urgyen Rinpoche to progress and enhance his realization. The view itself, which had been pointed out to him at the age of four, could not in essence be further enhanced, because within the view there is no 'thing' to be further developed. But we still talk about enhancing or deepening the view in terms of one's experience of it. Such enhancement requires oral instructions from a competent master. For Tulku Urgyen, this master was Samten Gyatso, his principal root guru.

In our tradition of emphasizing mind essence, the Dzogchen teachings speak of *Trekchö* and *Tögal*, the view being the thorough cut to primordial purity while the meditation is the direct crossing to spontaneous presence. Tulku Urgyen Rinpoche took the Dzogchen view as the very core of his practice. He was also adept in the Mahamudra tradition. While he was trained in both Mahamudra and the Six Doctrines, he always pointed towards the recognition of nondual awareness as being the vital core, the ultimate practice.

If you add up all the time Rinpoche spent in retreat in Kham, Central Tibet, Sikkim and Nepal, you end up with more than twenty years. In his youth he did a lot of accumulation and purification practices: *ngöndro*, development stage, completion stage, *tummo* and so forth. Later in his life, he would describe his retreats by saying, "I'm just staying here chanting the mani," the mantra of Avalokiteshvara. This is how great practitioners often refer to the practice of simply sustaining the natural face of awareness.

Many of the great masters of this time told me about Tulku Urgyen Rinpoche's high level of realization: not only the Gyalwang Karmapa, but also Kyabje Dilgo Khyentse Rinpoche and Kyabje Dudjom Rinpoche. Many of them are connected to him by receiving empowerments, reading transmissions and oral instructions.

When we spent time with him, he never displayed any attitude or showed any conceit about being a great scholar. As Tarthang Rinpoche said the other day, "Tulku Urgyen Rinpoche was a very hidden yogi. Not only was he learned in the various Buddhist practices, but he was a scholar in the ultimate nature. Yet he hid all his qualities within."

When teaching how to practice, Tulku Urgyen Rinpoche placed the greatest emphasis on how to remain in the composure of the true view. He repeatedly taught all of us the importance of undergoing the different levels of training, stressing the general and specific preliminary practices. He said that the teachings and practices should ultimately lead to a direct recognition of the nature of mind. He always taught this view as the indivisibility of the three great traditions: the Dzogchen view of primordial purity, the Mahamudra view of mental non-doing, and the Middle Way view of holding no mental constructs.

Tulku Urgyen Rinpoche's direct oral instructions inspired admiration, delight in practice, and deep trust and confidence in the teachings among those who met him. His words always helped their minds, in the sense that applying even some of his advice helped reduce disturbing emotions and naturally allowed compassion, love and insight to blossom. This was proven in actual experience by many, many people. This is why his disciples had sincere and whole-hearted love and affection for him. This was the basis for their trust and devotion.

All of us who met and knew him could see that he had a deeply humble character, very gentle and soft, kind and loving to everyone. Spiritual practitioners, of course, had trust and devotion through their Dharma connection. He impressed not only practitioners, however. The other day I met someone who said, "I don't know anything about Dharma, but I do know that he was a very nice man. His death made me so sad; I have lost a really good friend. He was the best friend one could have, easygoing, mild, and reliable, very open-minded. We have lost a very good man." Several people spoke of Tulku Urgyen Rinpoche in this way. He was connected to people in many different ways.

We have heard of the great masters of the past who left this world accompanied by many extraordinary signs. The Buddha also described certain signs that occur during the death of great practitioners. When Rinpoche passed away he was very relaxed. Twice he sat up from a reclining position. At one point he removed most of his garments. We quickly covered him up with blankets and gently straightened out his legs so that he could lie down again. He soon sat up again, exclaiming 'ah.' Shortly after this his vital signs all stopped. Some people die slowly, with rasping, labored breathing. Tulku Urgyen Rinpoche experienced nothing of that sort; he passed away very peacefully.

Having passed away; he remained in *tukdam*, in samadhi. The Dzogchen teachings describe the external signs that occur when someone who has reached a high level of realization of the view passes on.

The best sign is said to be "a cloudless, clear sky above, with dust-free air beneath." This sign, quite extraordinary in the modern and often polluted Kathmandu Valley, definitely appeared in the days following his death.

※

From "The Power of Experience and Realization Blazing Forth,"
spoken by Tsikey Chokling Rinpoche

I would like to tell you about the outer, inner and innermost life story of my father and guru, Tulku Urgyen Rinpoche. I will describe what I have heard with my own ears and seen with my own eyes. Of course I didn't meet him when he was young, but I have heard many stories, and I personally witnessed the latter part of his life. One of his unique qualities was his warmth. His heart was full of great love and compassion. Even by ordinary social conventions, he had a really good character. He had no intentions other than to help beings. He was open-minded, possessing a vast, all-encompassing frame of mind. This was how any normal, worldly person would describe him.

When Rinpoche was a young child he received the pointing-out instruction from his father, Chimey Dorje. Describing this experience later, he commented, "I realized the natural face of mind in actuality."

Tulku Urgyen Rinpoche had an incredible respect for the Three Jewels. He said that among all Buddhist masters, Buddha Shakyamuni was the first to catch his attention by triggering enormous faith and devotion. He was equally moved by the Dharma, the teachings he had been given, and he had a high regard for the sangha who maintain the practice of these teachings.

Among the masters in the Kagyü lineage, he showed great affection for and immense faith in Milarepa. Among the Nyingma lineage gurus, it was Longchen Rabjam. Merely hearing the names of these two masters, he experienced such uncontrived devotion that tears would come to his eyes and the hairs on his body would stand on end.

From his early years, he considered his root gurus to be Samten Gyatso, his father Chimey Dorje, and Kyungtrül Rinpoche, a master from Kham. He also connected with Jamgön Karsey Kongtrül, the son of Khakyab Dorje, the 15th Karmapa. From him Tulku Urgyen Rinpoche received the entire *Rinchen Terdzö*, the great treasury of precious termas.

In addition, Tulku Urgyen Rinpoche considered Rangjung Rigpey Dorje, the 16th Karmapa, his root guru. The kind of appreciation he had for the 16th Karmapa was nothing less than that of being in the presence of the Buddha in person. He never thought of the Karmapa as an ordinary human being in a material body of flesh and blood. Therefore, when the Karmapa asked him to do anything, be it a spiritual or a secular task, he wouldn't hesitate for a second to carry out his guru's wish. This was exactly how Naropa served the great Indian master Tilopa. When Tilopa commented, "Someone who was truly my disciple would jump off this cliff!" Naropa jumped without hesitation. Of course he was seriously injured, but Tilopa restored his body to its former state. Naropa underwent many such trials. Tulku Urgyen Rinpoche was similarly ready to sacrifice life and limb to carry out any wish the Karmapa had. People who knew him closely witnessed this unique devotion.

As for Gyalwang Karmapa, he had the deepest trust in Tulku Urgyen Rinpoche, since he saw him with pure perception as Chokgyur Lingpa or Guru Chöwang in person. Many times, while staying at Rumtek in my youth, I noticed that whenever the Karmapa received a letter from my father, he immediately placed it on the top of his head before opening it. I used to wonder, "Why does he treat a letter from Daddy as being so special?" At the same time, Tulku Urgyen Rinpoche saw the Karmapa as the very embodiment of all the Kagyü masters—Vajradhara, Tilopa, Naropa, Marpa and Milarepa. In this way their relationship was as close as between spiritual father and son. This is what I know from spending time with the Karmapa at Rumtek. When the 16th Karmapa needed a mantradhara (an accomplished Vajrayana practitioner) to perform certain ceremonies, he would insist that Tulku Urgyen Rinpoche do it and no one else.

Among the masters of the Nyingma School, Tulku Urgyen Rinpoche was close to the late Kyabje Dilgo Khyentse. I can best describe their relationship as one of indivisible minds—like father and son. Dilgo Khyentse would ask my father to clarify any doubt or uncertainty, and Tulku Urgyen would use the opportunity to expand the expression of nondual awareness even further. Their mutual respect and pure appreciation was tremendous. Dilgo Khyentse regarded Tulku Urgyen as being Guru Chöwang, and Tulku Urgyen regarded Dilgo Khyentse as Manjushri.

Let me also mention Kyabje Dudjom Rinpoche, the master who was the life-pillar of the Nyingma School of Early Translations for our times. This learned and accomplished person received the empowerments and transmissions for Chokgyur Lingpa's terma Dzogchen Desum, the *Three Sections of the Great Perfection*, from our Rinpoche in Lhasa. Dudjom Rinpoche later said: "Tulku Urgyen Rinpoche is the present heart-son of Chokgyur Lingpa, both in terms of Dharma and of family lineage. He is someone whose power and strength of realization has fully bloomed. In terms of the Dzogchen levels, he has gone through the four visions and has arrived at the final stage known as 'the exhaustion of phenomena and concepts.' In other words, he is someone who has fully perfected the great strength of primordially pure awareness. Such a person is rare indeed."

Likewise, Nyoshul Khen Rinpoche had a deep appreciation for my father. He often commented that in these times it is very rare to find someone with such a deep realization of Dzogchen. In this way, many accomplished and learned masters offered lofty words of praise. But how did Tulku Urgyen Rinpoche behave? He always partook of simple food, wore simple clothing, and had a simple, low seat.

Tulku Urgyen Rinpoche gave instructions to hundreds and hundreds of foreigners, and transmitted the sacred *Künzang Tuktig* to many of them. Often these teachings took place in the form of yearly seminars at which both he and Chökyi Nyima Rinpoche would teach. Chökyi Nyima Rinpoche would introduce the participants to the Buddha's teachings during the seminar, and at the end Tulku Urgyen Rinpoche would give the pointing-out instruction. There were many who experienced a taste of liberation, and many who recognized the nature of mind and gained a profound understanding.

I personally wondered how this could be possible in such large gatherings, as traditionally the pointing-out instruction is given to small groups. I have asked several great masters and this is what they told me: Once the strength of awareness is perfected through the path, certain signs automatically occur; for instance, the 'threefold blazing forth' and the 'threefold magnetizing.' These entail the blazing forth of experience, realization and samadhi. Due to the strength of Rinpoche's nondual awareness, the power of his experience and realization blazed forth and burned brightly. Through this, it became possible for others to experience a taste of the true nature of mind. This reminds me of Mipham Rinpoche's words: "Through the blessings of the realization of the ultimate lineage being transmitted to our hearts, may we obtain the great empowerment of awareness display."

Due to Tulku Urgyen's realization of the ultimate lineage, the expression of awareness as blessings combined with the openness created by his students' faith. This coincidence enabled many of them, regardless of their level or capacity, to recognize the nature of mind in a single instant. This evidently happened for hundreds and hundreds of students. This was Rinpoche's unique way of benefiting beings.

Over the years Rinpoche gave instructions in ngöndro, the preliminary practices, and in *semtri*, guidance in understanding and training in the nature of mind, to local people as well as foreigners. He truly turned the wheel of the Dharma throughout his entire life.

Some people wonder what Rinpoche's main personal practice was. We can only surmise this from his instructions to us. For instance, he would always say, "No matter what you do, no matter what situation you are in—whether walking, sitting, eating or lying down—always suspend your attention within the nature of nondual awareness. That's it!" This was his main practice: to simply remain as naked dharmakaya awareness.

One day, shortly before he passed away, I went in to see him and made this request: "We need to do some ceremonies to support your health. You have to remain for our sake, for the sake of the teachings and all beings." "You don't have to worry about me," he said smiling, "I won't die for a couple of years." Although his body was in quite bad shape and he must have been very uncomfortable, he could truly laugh and joke about the prospect of passing away, without any fear or worry. He was like a true yogi who is joyful and at peace even when on the verge of death—not a flicker of despair or attachment to anything. During his last months I spent several weeks with him at Nagi Gompa. Because of having perfected the view; he never showed any anxiety or fear whatsoever. This was the kind of sky-like yogi he was. I feel lucky to have even met such a person.

Here are some of the essential points he taught us students before passing away. With each passing moment all of us approach death. Not a single person in this world lives forever. Once we are born, our death is assured. Nevertheless, if we practice in a genuine way, it is certain that there will be benefit in both this and future lives. This was one of his main teachings—inspiring his disciples to practice by making them face the fact of their mortality.

Once we were inspired by the reality of death, he would tell us, "Don't regard futile worldly aims as being worthwhile!" In this way he would teach us the four mind-changings: the difficult to obtain freedoms and riches of a precious human rebirth, the impermanence created by the inevitability of death, the causes and consequences of karmic actions, and the painful quality of samsaric existence.

Tulku Urgyen Rinpoche's main teaching structure was the Four Dharmas of Gampopa, which is identical with Longchen Rabjam's Four Teachings. These are turning one's mind to the Dharma, making one's Dharma practice the path, letting the path clarify confusion, and letting confusion dawn as wisdom. In connection with the fourth point—letting confusion dawn as wisdom—he would then usually give the pointing-out instruction.

The pith instructions of Dzogchen form the essence of all Buddhist teachings. Tulku Urgyen Rinpoche gave these instructions in a style that was concise, simple, and comprehensible, with a gentle concern that was warm with blessings. This was the way in which he could communicate the profound essence of the Dharma and point out the nature of mind to many people simultaneously, ensuring that the stream of their being became temporarily liberated. This is the outcome of having reached perfection in the view, and in this he was unmatched.

He would often tell his followers, "Everything is impermanent, and no fleeting thing is worth pursuing. But if we practice the Dharma in an authentic way this will surely help us, both now and later." Practicing the Dharma was his main teaching and testament!

Once I asked him what was the most important practice for myself and other followers. His answer was, "Regard devotion and compassion as the most vital!" He emphasized that devotion and compassion are indispensable to recognizing the nature of mind when one receives the pointing-out instruction. A famous saying goes: "A closed-up person gives rise to no good qualities, just like a scorched seed will never sprout." Once you have the openness of faith which allows you to see the guru bestowing the profound instructions as a buddha in person, then it is possible for the transmission of the ultimate lineage to take place by introducing the nature of realization, and so to recognize nondual awareness without a flicker of doubt. So regard devotion to be of vital importance.

Tulku Urgyen Rinpoche also often used the phrase, 'emptiness suffused with compassion.' He would say, "All sentient beings without a single exception have been, and therefore are, our own parents. Cultivate all-encompassing compassion! In our Vajrayana tradition, devotion and compassion are regarded as the most important."

He also told me that disciples who want to practice the Chokling Tersar, especially the teachings of *Barchey Künsel* and *Künzang Tuktig*, must go through the complete path of the preliminary practices (ngöndro), the main part, and the additional practices. "Simply practicing the ngöndro alone would be enough," he often said, "because the ngöndro is even more profound than the main part. The person who sincerely goes through the 'four times one hundred-thousand practices' will purify physical misdeeds by means of bowing down, verbal misdeeds by means of the

Vajrasattva mantra, mental misdeeds by means of the mandala offerings, and their combination by means of Guru Yoga. The reason is that we need to purify our obscurations and gather the accumulations. While it may be possible to glimpse the nature of emptiness without any purification, due to our past karma and temporary circumstances, this glimpse is rapidly covered up again and forgotten. So don't delude yourselves; please apply yourselves wholeheartedly to the ngöndro practices."

Tulku Urgyen Rinpoche said this over and over again. Once you allow these preliminary practices to take effect by purifying your obscurations, then you will automatically recognize the nature of mind, and your realization of the view will unfold further and further.

Another important point he mentioned was this: "Tell all your disciples to keep their view as high as the sky, but to be as refined in what they do as tsampa (barley flour)." Some practitioners may convince themselves that they have an incredibly high view, so high that they needn't worry about the consequences of their actions. That is definitely not all right. Look at Rinpoche's example: he lived with completely pure discipline. In the same way, no matter how high your view is, you should be equally gentle and courteous to others, never frivolous or crude.

That was one point. Another was, "Tell them that all vajra friends will go towards enlightenment as one group, as a single mandala. Therefore keep harmony within the sangha; be kind to each other and observe the precepts with purity. Then the incredibly profound teachings of Vajrayana will take effect."

These are some of the last points my precious father told me. Beside this I don't have much to say. Let me just add these additional words of his advice: "Look really well into the nature of your minds. This is the essence of all the Dzogchen teachings. Recognize first; decide on that recognition; then gain confidence in that. It is not enough to only recognize the nature of mind; we need to develop the strength of this recognition, and then attain stability. That's it! Practice well so that you become fully trained. Generate even more devotion and compassion than you already have, because this will allow your experience and realization to naturally expand. This is what all your students should be told."

I feel I should tell you, his followers, this as well: Whoever personally received the pointing-out instruction from Tulku Urgyen Rinpoche is extremely fortunate. It's like having the end of the golden garland of the lineage placed in your hand. If you also bring this instruction into experience through practice, then it is certain your guru will continue to behold you from the unmanifest dharmadhatu. The true guru will awaken from within your heart. It is said, "The guru is not outside, but within." This means that you are face to face with the true guru the same moment you recognize the nature of mind. Please understand this!

Finally, to those of you who connected to Tulku Urgyen Rinpoche through his books, I would like to say the following. Don't concentrate only on the words on the pages! Turn your attention onto itself and look into the nature of your mind! In a moment of devotion or compassion, if you simply allow your mind to mingle indivisibly with the guru's, you can truly understand the Dzogchen teachings. That would be truly excellent!

From "A Clear, Cloudless Sky," spoken by Tsoknyi Rinpoche

In mundane terms, my three brothers and I—Chökyi Nyima Rinpoche, Chokling Rinpoche and Mingyur Rinpoche—are of course Tulku Urgyen Rinpoche's sons, but that wasn't our main relationship with him. The predominant thought I had of him was that he was my spiritual teacher, my root guru, and I believe I am speaking for the others as well.

While alive and well Tulku Urgyen Rinpoche gave instructions on his main practice, Dzogchen and Mahamudra, to innumerable people. We also received teachings from him; we regarded him as our guru. Honestly though, even though we knew that he would die one day, even though we understood that everything comes to an end, I personally never pictured the day it would really happen. I was really struck when he actually passed away by the simple fact that even such a great Dzogchen yogi dies—a realized practitioner, said by many other realized beings to have reached the 'culmination of awareness.' If even such a precious master, the guru for so many other great teachers, stops breathing and leaves a material body behind, then what about the rest of us?

Tulku Urgyen Rinpoche had told us several times that the passing of great Dzogchen yogis shows itself in the weather outside. The sign of being liberated into the state of dharmakaya is a clear, cloudless sky.

In the hours preceding his death, Tulku Urgyen Rinpoche did not say or do anything spectacular—he simply relaxed into death. In the early morning after he had passed away, I walked outside. There wasn't a cloud to be seen anywhere, not even a single, tiny wisp on the distant horizon. As I stood and looked out over the valley, which on winter mornings is often covered in fog, I saw no fog or mist. There was no pollution from dust particles; not even the slightest haze covered the sky. I saw only an utterly clear and brilliant sky. This sparkling weather lasted for several days following Rinpoche's death.

Seeing this, I thought, "Our Rinpoche has passed away. Although his passing away takes place on the relative plane, his state of realization is like this sky. Rinpoche's realization is like unobscured space, crystal clear. When we train in meditation, this is the state we should train in. This sky today is a perfect example for Tulku Urgyen Rinpoche's realization, for the state of primordial purity." On thinking this my admiration and appreciation for him and my trust and confidence grew even further. Witnessing the sign of realization that showed itself as an utterly clear sky, just like Rinpoche himself had said so often, gave me more appetite for meditation practice. I felt the confidence that we too can reach the realization that is as unobscured and wide-open as this sky.

I would like to remind everyone, and especially all those who received teachings from Rinpoche, that sooner or later all of us will have to leave this material body. We are not beyond that, no matter who we are. But there is a vast difference in how we meet death, which depends upon whether we have practiced or not. Let's assume that we are Buddhist practitioners, and that we wish to realize Rinpoche's awakened state of mind, the realization of primordial purity. When we supplicate Tulku Urgyen Rinpoche and try to mingle our mind indivisibly with his, we can use the external sky as an example. It's as if Tulku Urgyen's realized mind is like pure space, and it's this sky-like state of realization that we should bring into our practice.

I would like to suggest that all his disciples take unobscured space as their reminder for mingling their minds with Tulku Urgyen Rinpoche. A clear, cloudless sky can become the symbol of Rinpoche for us all. Please continue your practice so as to fulfill his wishes to the highest extent possible. Throughout all his teachings over the years, Rinpoche told all his disciples over and over again that we should apply ourselves to the training. He repeatedly said that nothing lasts, least of all a human life.

Remember, whether or not Rinpoche is among us doesn't affect the teachings he gave us — the meditation practice — in the slightest. Use the sky outside as a symbol for the primordially pure awakened state of mind, the realization of Tulku Urgyen Rinpoche. Practice well. Motivate yourself with renunciation, for just like Rinpoche's, our material bodies must all die. It is not enough to merely chant words like 'primordial purity' — we still die.

One last thing. Five days before he passed away I said to Rinpoche, "You look so well these days! I think you will be fine for a while still." He replied, "Really? Maybe that isn't such a great thing. My father and three uncles all looked very well during their last few months of life, with radiant faces and youthful complexions. Samten Gyatso's white hair turned almost black before he died, and his teeth and nails had more luster and radiance. Maybe that was an inherited family trait, or maybe it was a sign of good practice."

He told me how Samten Gyatso passed away gazing into the sky. I asked, "Did Samten Gyatso remain in *tukdam?*" "He did," Tulku Urgyen Rinpoche replied, "but just remaining in *tukdam* is in itself not that astonishing. Someone who has trained in a contrived or intellectually constructed state of meditative concentration can remain in tukdam for quite a while. The true, genuine way is without any need for deliberate meditation. The very moment the white and red bodhichitta essences join together at the heart, there is an immediate instant of unconsciousness. But that doesn't necessarily last; it can open up again right away, without remaining a closed-in state." Rinpoche clapped his hands together, then opened the palms wide. "That is what is meant by the famous quote, 'In one instant the difference is made; in one instant complete enlightenment is attained.' This is the moment a true yogi is liberated. This is the one moment he can really show off his capacity. Such awakening is not necessarily accompanied by rainbow lights, thunder or spectacular displays. Liberation into the state of dharmakaya is shown as a clear, cloudless sky."

※

From "Equalizing Life and Practice," spoken by Mingyur Rinpoche

In mundane terms, Kyabje Tulku Urgyen Rinpoche was my father, but from the spiritual perspective he was my root guru possessing the threefold kindness. There are different levels of viewing the guru, according to different types of teachings. On the Hinayana level you regard the guru as a spiritual guide, while Mahayana followers perceive him as an emanation of the buddhas. As a Vajrayana practitioner, one should see the guru as the embodiment of the very essence of all awakened ones. Based on this, you receive the four empowerments through practicing guru yoga, following his command with trust and devotion, and observing the samayas of body, speech and mind. This is a very profound approach, and the tantras teach that all the key points of Vajrayana can be condensed into devotion towards the guru. Therefore, in terms of the Dharma, I feel that he was immensely precious and kind.

Tulku Urgyen Rinpoche passed away quite suddenly, but after he died he remained in tukdam for quite a while, longer than the sun was in the sky that day. There are many different levels of tukdam. Some practitioners can remain in tukdam due to their training in mundane shamatha and vipashyana; others because of proficiency in the visualization practices of the development stage. How long the tukdam state lasts also varies, from a couple of days to a month or more. Our Rinpoche remained for just over a day. The end of the tukdam was quite amazing. We saw the two types of bodhichitta liquid, both white and red, flow out of his nostrils, something that is said not to happen to just anyone. I felt it was quite extraordinary. Red drops, deep red like blood, appeared from the left nostril, and a clear liquid, quite unlike mucus, came out of the right one. The tantric root texts explain that the red and white bodhichitta will appear from the nostrils of great masters to mark the conclusion of the tukdam, and this is what happened.

As for the length of tukdam, it is said that a person who hasn't 'perfected the strength of experience and realization' can sometimes remain for quite a while. On the other hand, someone who has already reached perfection in this strength doesn't necessarily remain for that long. Our Rinpoche's tukdam didn't last especially long.

It is my general impression that Tulku Urgyen Rinpoche was not only extremely adept in Vajrayana but also especially accomplished in the essential practice of Dzogchen, the Great Perfection. The journey through the Dzogchen path is marked by stages of realization, each having a certain name, and I have the trust that Rinpoche reached quite a high level. Tulku Urgyen Rinpoche himself, though, never spoke of his realization; he lived very humbly, in the style of a hidden yogi. He always praised other masters while avoiding any mention of himself.

It is often said that one cannot really judge the depth of realization of an emanation of the buddhas and bodhisattvas solely from his or her behavior. Without deep and heartfelt reflection, even the Buddha can be seen as just another human being. In fact, some people even perceived the Buddha as ugly! Our impressions and experiences of someone are often colored by our mistaken perception. On the other hand, someone with pure, unmistaken perception would see the Buddha as a pure, divine being. Personally, I trust that Rinpoche was a deeply realized being. I have heard that both Kyabje Dilgo Khyentse and Nyoshul

Khen Rinpoche said that our Rinpoche wasn't an ordinary person, but someone who had reached the level of realization called 'culmination of awareness.'

Please use the vivid memories of Tulku Urgyen's life and death to remind you of his instructions on looking into the nature of your mind. We should try our best to mingle our mind with his and let be in equanimity. Honestly, the guru's awakened state is already inseparable from our basic nature. Seen from the perspective of ultimate truth, our apparently separate minds are in essence indivisible. This is a reality we need to perceive: we need to "know this to be as it is." Unless this becomes part of our direct experience, the mere fact of our indivisible nature will not help us. The outcome of practice results from training in this, from actually *experiencing* this fact.

Please see it like this: the guru's mind is empty, and our minds are empty too. The guru's mind is cognizant; our minds are cognizant as well. In the guru's mind these two qualities of emptiness and cognizance are an indivisible unity. In our minds as well they are also an indivisible unity. The very moment you acknowledge the reality of this, your mind is said to have mingled with and become indivisible from the guru's mind.

After Tulku Urgyen Rinpoche passed away, the sky was incredibly clear for a couple of days, without a single cloud. Among the various signs that accompany the death of a great master, the tantras mention that the most eminent is a cloudless sky. Vajrayana practices fall into two main categories, those with attributes—development stage—and those without attributes—completion stage. Following the passing of a master who had focused on practice with attributes, visible signs may manifest such as rainbows, unusual sounds and various relics like *dung* and *ring-sel*. But the Dzogchen tantras say that a master whose main practice was beyond attributes will show no other sign but a clear sky. The tantras of both the New and Old, the *Sarma* and *Nyingma,* traditions agree on this. So I feel that Tulku Urgyen Rinpoche's death being accompanied by an unusually clear sky with brilliant sunshine is a most amazing sign.

Also, please remember that it is not only our Rinpoche who passed away. Everyone does; even Buddha Shakyamuni didn't remain. The main task ahead for us is continuing to keep Rinpoche's instructions in mind, applying them, and training in the meditation he taught. Remember, we will leave this life alone and totally naked, unaccompanied by any of our possessions, even if we are a king with enormous wealth and luxuries. At the moment of death, none of our possessions can help us. We cannot take anything along, not even something as tiny as a mote of dust. When the spirit leaves the body, nothing sticks to it. It's like pulling a hair out of butter. In that situation—alone, unprotected and defenseless—what can help us other than the Dharma practice we did?

From this perspective it is so important not to give in to our tendency to be lazy and postpone practice until tomorrow, next month or next year. We can spend our lives thinking, "I'll practice tomorrow or the next day," then our life runs out, and one day it's time to die. In death our only support is our personal practice, so reduce your plans and projects. It's much better, and actually much more practical, to think, "I may die soon anyway, so what's the use of planning to do all these tasks? If I don't practice now, the day will come when I'll be sorry."

By not projecting plans and involvements very far into the future, we will find we are able to practice full-time. Milarepa said, "There is no end to worldly pursuits; they only end when you stop." As long as we are involved in all kinds of actions and dealings, they never end. The only way is to make a clean break, discontinuing all of these preoccupations. When we're caught up in our projects, doing this and that, one thing after the other, we feel, "I'd better do this! Then I'll do that! That will improve my whole situation!" Striving so hard to score small successes, we disguise the fact that we are actually being lazy. Our ceaseless activity and our avoidance of what is really important is actually laziness.

It would be much better to just make up our minds, sincerely and decisively, to stop wasting our time. We need to acknowledge that our minds are fickle and appearances are seductive. It won't do to simply continue in our present fashion. Although these are modern times, we still have incredibly precious instructions at hand that, when applied, enable us to awaken to true and complete enlightenment within this same body and life. But since most of us spend our time in indolence and pointless activities, ignoring the importance of genuine practice, there are only a few truly accomplished masters.

On the other hand, someone who practices wholeheartedly can be enlightened in a single lifetime; there is definitely no doubt about that. It's said that if you apply yourself to the practice in an authentic way during a three-year retreat, you can reach the level known as 'seeing the innate nature in actuality.' With this in mind, I wish to spend the rest of my life focused on meditation practice. I feel that I must really 'equalize life and practice.' This is the deep wish that has sprung up in my heart. I feel that doing so will fulfill Rinpoche's wishes, and it is also what will be of greatest benefit for all sentient beings.

It's said to be best if you can equalize life and practice by casting away all worldly involvements out of deep-felt renunciation for all of samsara. Trust in the Three Jewels and have sincere confidence in the consequences of karmic deeds and the reality of past and future lives. If you can practice in this way your mind will become indivisible from the guru's, and within this lifetime you will be able to 'capture the royal throne of the primordially pure Great Perfection.' The next best is to always act in a truthful and honest way and to live in accordance with spiritual principles. Occasionally take the opportunity to practice more intensively in a retreat situation. At the very least, you should try to re-member as often as possible what your guru told you, and be truthful and honest in whatever you do. Keep a good heart and regularly try to do things that are helpful to others. Cultivate an attitude of love and compassion. Be gentle and kind, and make supplications to the guru. Any of these modes of living will please your guru, and, if you do not reach enlightenment in this very life, then you will either at the moment of death or in the bardo. At least you are assured the attainment of bud-dhahood in one of your future lives. One way or another, you are not far away from the omniscient state of a buddha.

In essence an enlightened master remains unchanged. The process of aging, falling sick and passing away exists mainly in our experience. It is a drama played out for us that takes place in our minds, whereas these events have no tangible substance in his experience. Whether he is dead or alive, the natural state of his awareness remains unchanged. This is not evident to people like us. We look at him and see him as a human being just like us; he needs to eat, move about, go to the toilet, just as we do—so aren't we the same?

Actually, we aren't. Rinpoche's experience of his identity is not linked with a material body of flesh and blood. This is hard for ordinary people like myself to understand, but that's how it actually is. If we train ourselves in devotion while deeply trusting that this is his real nature, then there is no doubt that we will receive his blessings. The vital point is to have trust in and devotion for your guru.

In addition, when you gain full confidence in the consequences of karmic actions, then you cannot possibly avoid a wholehearted commitment to practice. You will naturally want to practice, without any doubts or hesitations. Without this trust in karma and rebirth, it is easy to question the value of spiritual practice. Then however much practice you try to do will only end up leading in the wrong direction. So please gain confidence in the law of karma.

Even though space is endless and the number of sentient beings is infinite, the omniscient knowledge of a buddha sees their life-spans, deeds and attitudes in completeness. Such omniscience is like knowing every single leaf on every single tree in the entire world. At the same time, while perceiving all these different individual states of mind, a buddha holds no conceptual thoughts. That's the kind of attainment we can reach if we practice. It's called the inconceivable nature.

Please keep these points in mind. Continue your practice, ideally by equalizing life and practice, or, next best, by living in accordance with the Dharma. At the very least, give your assistance to spiritual endeavors and help in the teaching of the Dharma and in the maintenance of Rinpoche's monasteries. In this way, do what is meaningful in preserving the Buddhadharma and help to bring benefit to all beings.

1

The Basis: Buddha Nature

✳

The main image of dharmadhatu is that of space—the 'space of all things' within which all phenomena manifest, abide and dissolve back into. This is similar to physical space, which is like a container within which the remaining four elements appear, abide and disappear. These four elements do not come out of any other source; they emerge from space itself. They do not remain anywhere else other than within space; neither do they go anywhere outside of space. In the same way, dharmadhatu is the basic environment of all phenomena, whether they belong to samsara or nirvana. It encompasses whatever appears and exists, including the worlds and all beings. Everything takes place within and dissolves back into the state of dharmadhatu. Dharmadhatu encompasses all of samsara and nirvana—it doesn't include only nirvana and exclude samsara; it's not like that.

External phenomena appear within space, remain within space and disappear within space again. Is there any place where earth, water, fire and wind can go that is outside space? Don't they always remain within space? When they disintegrate, isn't it within space that they dissolve? Is there any place at all to go to which is beyond or outside space, which is somewhere other than space? Please understand very well this symbolic resemblance between dharmadhatu and physical space.

The relationship between dharmadhatu, dharmakaya and dharmadhatu wisdom is like the relationship between a place, a person and the person's mind. If there is no place, there is no environment for the person to exist in; and there is no person unless that person also has a mind dwelling in the body. In the same way, the main field or realm called dharmadhatu has the nature of dharmakaya. Dharmakaya has the quality of dharmadhatu wisdom, which is like the mind aspect.

We also need to clearly understand what is meant by the terms 'samsara' and 'nirvana.' Nirvana means the fully realized buddha nature that consists of Body, Speech and Mind aspects. The Body is the essence that simply is. Speech is its nature, the cognizant quality that is vividly present. And Mind is the capacity, which is radiant. These three aspects comprise the basic presence of all buddhas. They are none other than their essence, nature and capacity. All sugatas are of this same identity. In the same way, samsara is the body, speech and mind of all sentient beings, which are the deluded expressions of their essence, nature and capacity. In this way, dharmadhatu encompasses all of samsara and nirvana.

Dharmadhatu is adorned with dharmakaya, which is endowed with dharmadhatu wisdom. This is a brief but very profound statement, because 'dharmadhatu' also refers to sugata-garbha or buddha nature. Buddha nature is all-encompassing: this means it is present or basic to all states, regardless of whether they belong to samsara or nirvana. Remember, 'nirvana' refers to the Body, Speech and Mind of all the awakened ones. Body is the abiding essence, Speech is the vividly present nature, and Mind is the radiant capacity. These three, the Body, Speech and Mind of all buddhas, are also known as the three vajras.

This buddha nature is present just as the shining sun is present in the sky. It is indivisible from the three vajras of the awakened state, which do not perish or change. Vajra Body is the unchanging quality, vajra Speech is the unceasing quality and vajra Mind is the undeluded, unmistaken quality. So, the buddha nature or dharmadhatu is the three vajras; at the same time, its *expression* manifests as the deluded body, speech and mind of all beings.

In the normal sense of the word, 'body' refers to something perishable composed of flesh and blood. 'Speech' refers to intermittent utterances that come and go and eventually perish. And 'mind' refers to thought states and emotions that come and go, come and go, under the power of dualistic attitude, like beads on a rosary. These mental states are also transient. Everyone agrees that the body, speech and mind of living beings are constantly changing, continually coming and going. Still, the basis of our ordinary body, speech and mind is the buddha nature, the dharmadhatu that encompasses all of samsara and nirvana. There isn't a single being for whom this isn't so.

Looking from the pure angle, then, this buddha nature is present in every being, the expression of the victorious ones, just like the rays of light are present from the sun. The light is emanated by the sun, isn't it? If it weren't for the sun, there wouldn't be any light. Similarly, the origin of the body, speech and mind of beings is the expression of the buddha nature that pervades both samsara and nirvana.

It is said that all sentient beings are buddhas, but they are covered by their temporary obscurations. These 'temporary obscurations' are our own thinking. Dharmadhatu encompasses all of samsara and nirvana — not just the awakened state of nirvana, but everything, every single thing. The ordinary body, speech and mind of sentient beings temporarily arose from the expression of the qualities of enlightened body, speech and mind. As space pervades, so awareness pervades. If this were not so, then space would pervade but rigpa wouldn't. Just like space, rigpa is all-encompassing: nothing is outside it. Just as the contents and beings are all pervaded by space, rigpa pervades the minds of beings. Dharmadhatu pervades all of samsara and nirvana.

It is essential to start out with a basic understanding of the profundity of what is meant here in order to be able to authentically practice the teaching of the Great Perfection. Unless we know what is what, at least intellectually, it might seem to us as if sentient beings are disconnected, alien entities, and we have no idea of where they come from, where they belong or what they actually are. They are not disconnected at all. The difference between buddhas and sentient beings lies in the latter's narrowness of scope and attitude. Sentient beings confine themselves to their own limited little area of samsara through their own attitude and thinking.

It is said that the difference between buddhas and sentient beings is like the difference between the narrowness and the openness of space. Sentient beings are like the space held within a tightly closed fist, while buddhas are fully open, all-encompassing. Basic space and awareness are innately all-encompassing. Basic space is the absence of mental constructs, while awareness is the *knowing* of this absence of constructs, recognizing the complete emptiness of mind essence. Space and awareness are inherently indivisible. It is said, "When the mother, the basic space of dharmadhatu, does not stray from her awareness child, have no doubt that they are forever indivisible."

The ultimate Dharma is the realization of the indivisibility of basic space and awareness. That is the starting point, and that is what is pointed out to begin with. It is essential to understand this; otherwise, we might have the feeling that Samantabhadra and his consort are an old blue man and woman who lived aeons ago. It's not like that at all! Samantabhadra and his consort are the indivisible unity of space and awareness.

As you know, the nine gradual vehicles and the four schools of philosophy—Vaibhashika, Sautrantika, Mind Only, and Middle Way—are designed to suit the various mental capacities of different people. The term Great Perfection, on the other hand, implies that everything is included in Dzogchen; that everything is complete. Dzogchen is said to be unexcelled, meaning that there is nothing higher than it. Why is this? It is because of knowing *what truly is to be as it is*—the ultimate naked state of dharmakaya. Isn't that truly the ultimate? Please carefully understand this.

The Great Perfection is totally beyond any kind of pigeon-holing anything in any way whatsoever. It is to be utterly open, beyond categories, limitations and the confines of assumptions and beliefs. All other ways of describing things are confined by categories and limitations. The ultimate destination to arrive at in Dzogchen is the view of the kayas and wisdoms. Listen to this quote: "Although everything is empty, the special quality of the Buddhadharma is to not be empty of the kayas and wisdom." All other systems expound that all things are empty, but truly, the intention of the Buddha is to use the word 'emptiness' rather than 'empty.' This is a very important point.

For instance, in the Prajnaparamita scriptures you find the statements, "Outer things are emptiness, inner things are emptiness, emptiness is emptiness, the vast is emptiness, the ultimate is emptiness, the conditioned is emptiness, the unconditioned is emptiness ..." 'Emptiness' here should be understood as 'empty cognizance.' Please understand this. The suffix '-ness' implies the cognizant quality. We need to understand this word in its correct connotation.

Otherwise, it sounds too nihilistic to simply say that outer things are empty. If we understand 'emptiness' as empty or void, rather than 'empty cognizance,' we are leaning too much towards nihilism, the idea that everything is a big, blank void. This is a serious sidetrack.

The Buddha initially taught that all things are empty. This was unavoidable; indeed, it was justifiable, because we need to dismantle our fixation on the permanence of what we experience. A normal person clings to the contents of his experiences as solid, as being 'that'—not just as mere 'experience,' but as something which has solidity, which is real, which is concrete and permanent. But if we look honestly and closely at what happens, experience is simply experience, and it is not made out of anything whatsoever. It has no form, no sound, no color, no taste and no texture; it is simply experience—an empty cognizance.

The vivid display in manifold colors you see with open eyes is not mind, but 'illuminated matter.' Similarly, when you close your eyes and see something dark, it is not mind but 'dark matter.' In both cases, matter is merely a presence, an experience of something. It is mind that experiences the external elements and everything else.

An appearance can only exist if there is a mind that beholds it. The 'beholding' of that appearance is nothing other than experience; that is what actually takes place. Without a perceiver, how could an appearance be an appearance? It wouldn't exist anywhere. Perceptions are experienced by mind; they are not experienced by water or earth. All the elements are vividly distinguished as long as the mind fixates on them. Yet they are nothing but a mere presence, an appearance. It is mind that apprehends this mere presence. When this mind doesn't apprehend, hold, or fixate on what is experienced—in other words, when the real, authentic samadhi of suchness dawns within your stream of being—'reality' loses its solid, obstructing quality. That is why accomplished yogis cannot be burnt, drowned, or harmed by wind. In their experience all appearances are a mere presence, since fixation has disintegrated from within. Mind is that which experiences, that within which experience unfolds. What else is there to experience? Mind means individual experience. All experience is individual, personal.

For instance, the fact that one yogi's delusion dissolves doesn't mean everyone else's delusion vanishes as well. When someone gets enlightened, that person is enlightened, not everyone else. When a yogi transcends fixation, only the deluded individual experience of that one person dissolves. Please think about this. There is, however, another aspect called 'other's experience' or the 'general experience' of sentient beings.

In all of this seemingly solid reality [Rinpoche knocks on the wood of his bed], there is not a single thing that is indestructible. Whatever is material in this world will be destroyed in fire at the end of the kalpa; there is no exception. This fire then vanishes by itself. [Rinpoche chuckles].

Try to spend some time on *Nangjang* training,[1] and you will discover that all of reality is insubstantial and unreal. By means of Nangjang training, we discover that all experience is personal experience, and that all personal experience is seen as unreal and insubstantial when not fixated upon. In this entire world there is no created appearance that ultimately remains. Seemingly external visual forms do not really remain anywhere. These mere perceptions are dependent karmic experiences. All of relative reality is by definition dependent upon something other, upon causes and conditions, isn't it? When explaining relative phenomena, you have to mention their causes and conditions; there is no way around that. In the end, we realize that their nature is ultimately beyond causes and conditions. What is 'ultimate' cannot possibly be made out of causes and conditions.

Only the authentic state of samadhi can purify or clear up this self-created confusion. More appearances and further fixating will not destroy this. This profound state is present in each individual, if only they would know it! The ultimate nature is already fully present. It is given names like dharmakaya, sambhogakaya, and nirmanakaya. Our deluded state hides this from us, but really it is this which destroys the delusion. Isn't this really amazing! [Rinpoche chuckles.]

Once we attain stability in samadhi, delusion is destroyed, since samadhi dismantles the entire drama of delusion. In other words, this mind has basically created the delusion, but by recognizing the nature of this mind we clear up our delusion, since at that moment no delusion can be re-created. If everyone could just understand this! This is amazing! [Rinpoche laughs.] It is the mind itself that creates this whole delusion, but it is also the mind itself that can let the whole delusion collapse. [Rinpoche laughs again.] Besides buddha nature, what else is there to be free from delusion? Buddha nature is the very basis for delusion. It is also that which dissolves the delusion. Please try carefully to understand this! This is something you *can* understand!

Delusion seems to separate all sentient beings from their buddha nature. But it is this very buddha nature that clears up the delusion. It is basically a matter of recognizing it or not. We speak of those who were never deluded: the buddhas and the hundred sublime families of peaceful and wrathful sugatas, including Buddha Samantabhadra. When failing to recognize, one is deluded. Delusion dissolves the very moment you recognize the identity of that which is deluded.

Delusion is like becoming possessed by a spirit during a seance, when someone starts to suddenly hop around and do all kinds of crazy things. This is exactly what has happened to all of us. Sentient beings are possessed by the 'spirit' of ignorance and the 84,000 disturbing emotions, and they are all dancing around doing incredible things. They have undergone all different kinds of pain and misery for so long, aeons upon aeons. But it is a self-created possession. It is not really something from outside. Buddha nature has lost track of itself and created samsara, but it is also buddha nature, recognizing itself, which clears up the delusion of samsaric existence. The moment of recognition is like the spirit leaving. All of a sudden the possession vanishes. We can't even say where it went. This is called the 'collapse of confusion.'

We have undergone so much misery—oh my! Spinning around on the wheel of samsara, we have suffered so much trouble! Roaming and rambling about among the six classes of beings, of course we have suffered! [Rinpoche laughs] A yogi is like a formerly possessed person whom the spirit has left. While 'possessed,' this mind thinks and acts in delusion, but the very moment you recognize the nature of this mind— rigpa—the possession immediately vanishes. [Rinpoche laughs.]

2

The Four Dharmas of Gampopa

❈

Before receiving teachings, let's motivate ourselves with the precious enlightened attitude of bodhichitta. Form this wish: "I will study the Dharma and correctly put it into practice in order to establish all my mothers, sentient beings as many as the sky is vast, in the state of liberation and the precious, irreversible supreme enlightenment."

I would like to present a teaching called the 'Four Dharmas of Gampopa,' which is identical with four instructions given by Longchen Rabjam. The first of these is how to turn one's mind towards Dharma practice. Included within this is the four mind-changings. The second Dharma is how to ensure that one's Dharma practice becomes the path. This includes teachings on the preliminary practices of the four times hundred thousand. Within the third Dharma, how to make the path clarify confusion, are the teachings on development stage, recitation, and completion stage. And within the fourth, how to let confusion dawn as wisdom, are teachings on how to gain certainty, realization of the natural state by means of the three great views. It is said that the ground is Mahamudra, the path is the Middle Way and the fruition is the Great Perfection. These Four Dharmas of Gampopa contain a complete path for an individual to attain full enlightenment within one body in one lifetime.

All of us here right now have obtained what is extremely difficult to obtain—the precious human body endowed with the eight freedoms and ten riches. It is something that only happens once in a hundred aeons. It has happened for us now, this time around. While we are alive in this body, it seems as if it were so easy for us to be humans. It doesn't appear to have required any effort. Honestly, though, a human body is extremely difficult to achieve and necessitates enormous merit from former lives. It is only due to our former meritorious karma combined with pure aspirations that we now have a precious human body.

Our present situation is like having found a wish-fulfilling jewel. Please don't let it go to waste. Time is quickly running out; we are all mortal. The reason why it is impossible to attain a material state of perfection in this lifetime is because nothing lasts. Everything is impermanent; everyone dies. If the moment of death were a total end, like water drying out or a flame being extinguished, it would be fine — death would be of little consequence. Unfortunately that doesn't happen. The consequences of our karmic actions follow us after death just as our shadow follows our body. The unfailing law of cause and effect requires that we experience the results of what we have done. The places where we experience the ripening of our karma are called the six realms of samsara. This situation has gone on since beginningless time and we are still not liberated.

Reflect on the meaning of these four topics I have just mentioned: the difficulty of obtaining a precious human rebirth, the fact that nothing lasts, that we are all mortals, that everyone is governed by the consequences of karmic actions, and that there is no place within samsaric existence with permanent happiness. Those are called the four mind-changings. They are extremely important to take to heart, because they are not fiction or fantasy. They are facts; they explain the circumstances and conditions that we live under within samsaric existence.

It's not impossible to understand that we do die, nor the details of what follows. We are all really just standing in line for that, waiting for it to happen. We need to face these facts in a very realistic way. Before starting to practice the precious Dharma, it is very important to take these to heart. That was the first of the Four Dharmas of Gampopa: how to turn one's mind to the Dharma.

The second, how to make sure that one's Dharma practice becomes the path, contains the preliminary practices of the four times hundred thousand. Through the four mind-changings we develop the wish to be liberated from samsaric existence and attain the precious state of enlightenment, not merely for ourselves, but for all beings. We have become ready to take refuge in the Three Precious Ones. The Buddha is the completely and perfectly awakened state of omniscience. The Dharma is the path that leads to that, the teachings. The Sangha are all the masters who have upheld, propagated and made the teachings flourish from the time of the Buddha up until our kind personal master with whom we have managed to connect. To take refuge in these with full trust and confidence ensures that we have the possibility to also become awakened ones ourselves. Taking refuge and seeking guidance under the Three Jewels is what opens the way to becoming enlightened. That is the first of the preliminary practices.

Connected with this, as a branch, is the development of bodhichitta. Without bodhichitta, we cannot proceed on the Mahayana path. The understanding that all other sentient beings are in fact our own mothers and fathers from past lives provides a very important basis for our progress. Every little insect that we meet, without a single exception, has been our own mother and father—not just once, but many times. And all of them are on the wrong track. They want to be happy, but do not know how to accomplish this. To develop bodhichitta means to form this most courageous resolve: "I will personally take responsibility to lead all sentient beings to the state of enlightenment!" This bodhisattva vow is what makes the difference between a Hinayana and a Mahayana follower. To take this vow is called generating bodhichitta. Taking refuge and developing bodhichitta are therefore the very essence of the path.

When we do a *sadhana*, we can practice the three vehicles—Hinayana, Mahayana and Vajrayana—simultaneously. Whenever you do a particular deity practice, you always start out with refuge and bodhichitta, the Hinayana and Mahayana elements. There is no way around that. The deity itself, the recitation of mantra and visualization, is Vajrayana practice. Thus, it is impossible to practice Vajrayana without also being a practitioner of Hinayana and Mahayana. The three vehicles are invariably practiced in that same sitting.

The practices of all three vehicles are also contained in the preliminary practices. The first practice is taking refuge and developing bodhichitta. That is followed by Vajrasattva visualization and recitation, which is an actual Vajrayana practice. Vajrasattva practice is structured as the four remedial powers, the first of which is the power of support—to visualize the buddha Vajrasattva. The second is the power of the applied antidote, reciting the hundred-syllable mantra of Vajrasattva and imagining the downpour and purification by means of nectar. The third is the power of remorse for past misdeeds and evil actions. The fourth is the power of resolution, promising ourselves to never commit any negative action again. The Buddha taught that practicing the Vajrasattva recitation while remembering these four remedial powers purifies all our negative karma, even if it is as huge an amount as Mt. Sumeru.

After the Vajrasattva recitation comes the mandala offering, which ensures that we will not have obstacles on the path of practice. In this practice we are creating conducive conditions by gathering provisions that we can bring along—the accumulation of merit and wisdom. There are three levels of mandala offering: the outer mandala, the offering of the external universe; the inner mandala, the offering of the content of sentient beings; and finally the innermost mandala, the offering of ultimate thatness, corresponding to the three kayas. Taken together, these three levels are called "gathering the accumulations of merit and wisdom."

Next is guru yoga, the fourth of the preliminaries. Guru yoga is often said to be even more profound than the main part, because in it we receive the blessings from an unbroken lineage of masters. These blessings come from the dharmakaya buddha Samantabhadra all the way down until our own root guru. It's like the pipe connecting your house to the main water source, which allows water to come out whenever you open your own faucet. The unbroken lineage of enlightened masters connected to you through your personal teachers is like that water pipe. Through this we can receive the blessings of the Buddha, Dharma and Sangha, and of the three kayas in our own practice.

When we truly apply ourselves to the preliminary practices, we can remove obstacles on the spiritual path and create all the conducive conditions for quickly realizing the ultimate fruition. That is exactly what is meant by the second of the Four Dharmas of Gampopa: how to ensure that one's Dharma practice becomes the path.

Some people regard themselves as exclusively Mahayana or Vajrayana practitioners. Others say they only follow Theravada, that they don't know anything beyond that. But talking in this way only exposes one's lack of understanding. The three vehicles are not meant to be separated at all. We can practice all of them simultaneously—in fact, we need to in order to have a solid foundation. Without really applying ourselves to the four mind-changings and taking refuge, we have no real foundation from which to connect to the Buddhist teachings. Similarly, if you want to drink tea, you need a place to put the cup. You need a table, which is the same as the foundation of the Shravaka or Hinayana teachings. You also need the cup to contain the tea, which is the Mahayana attitude. And you need the tea as well—otherwise there is nothing to drink, and you do need a drink. Vajrayana teachings are like the liquid poured into the cup.

In the same way, in order to become enlightened we first need to connect to the Three Jewels. Taking refuge involves entrusting ourselves; that contains the Hinayana teachings. After that, what is the use of being the only one who is enlightened while all our mothers roam about in samsara? That would be totally shameless. It is said that the Hinayana orientation is like the little puddle of water contained in the hoof-print of a cow, while the Mahayana attitude is as vast as the entire ocean. Everyone needs to be enlightened—not only ourselves. Thirdly, without the very profound teachings of Vajrayana including deity, mantra and samadhi there is no way we can achieve full enlightenment in this same body and lifetime. Thus, we need all three vehicles together: Hinayana, Mahayana and Vajrayana. There is no point at all in regarding oneself as some kind of superior practitioner who doesn't need 'low' or 'inferior' teachings. Such an attitude would be very unrealistic.

Ensuring that one's Dharma practice becomes the path means purifying the obscurations and misdeeds that create obstacles and block the path to the attainment of complete enlightenment. There is a profound reason to practice the preliminaries, even though some may think of them as unnecessary. It is through the preliminary practices that we are truly able to clear away obstacles and make our Dharma practice become the path of enlightenment.

Having cleared away obscurations and gathered the accumulations of merit and wisdom, we reach the third Dharma of Gampopa: how to let the path clarify confusion. Confusion here is understood as that which obscures our innate nature and prevents enlightenment. Everyone has buddha nature, all sentient beings without a single exception. Unfortunately, we don't know what we possess. We have fallen into confusion and we are wandering in samsara. Imagine a wish-fulfilling jewel that has fallen in the mud and has become encrusted in dirt. The jewel first of all needs to be acknowledged. Then it needs to be cleaned. Once this happens, it can be utilized. We are all wish-fulfilling jewels but lack the knowledge of what we actually are, and thus the ability to make use of that and actualize it. We need to clean away the dirt that covers our basic state, the wish-fulfilling jewel. The way to do this is through Vajrayana practice.

The most eminent and profound way to do so is by the three principles of Vajrayana practice: deity, mantra and samadhi. By training in the development stage consisting of deity, mantra and samadhi, we actualize what we already are. To properly practice development stage, we need to let go of any ordinary, materialistic world view. Don't chant the lines for the deity while thinking, "I am in this world, in my ordinary house, in my ordinary body." We need to first dissolve everything into profound emptiness, then visualize the celestial palace, the throne of the deity and all the other details. Through this profound training in deity, mantra and samadhi, we are able to let the path clarify confusion.

Remember, in practicing the development stage we are not imagining that we are something that we are not. Everyone possesses the enlightened essence that is endowed with the three vajras, the three aspects of enlightenment. The way to acknowledge that fully is through deity, mantra and samadhi. Development practice is simply knowing the nature of things *as it is*. Training in this is like knowing the jewel to be the wish-fulfilling jewel that it actually is. It's not like we're imagining an ordinary stone to be a jewel. A stone will never possess the value or qualities of a jewel, no matter how hard we visualize. There is incredible profundity in the development stage practice.

Now let's look at the fourth Dharma of Gampopa, letting confusion dawn as wisdom. Even though what is going to be said now will sound very high, I haven't made up anything by myself. I don't have the ability to make up my own teachings or to invent some new, profound path, not at all! Even if I could, there would be no point in doing so, because people wouldn't be interested. I would rather repeat the words of the Buddha and the great masters of the past.

All sentient beings without a single exception have buddha nature, from the dharmakaya buddha down to the tiniest insect. There is no real difference in the quality or size of this enlightened essence between individuals. However, buddhas and fully enlightened bodhisattvas have cut the movement of dualistic mind at the very beginning. That is how they are different from sentient beings. Buddhas and bodhisattvas' expression of mind takes the form of compassionate activity. This activity, through emanations and re-emanations, appears in all samsaric realms in order to teach other beings.

Sentient beings, on the other hand, have fallen under the power of dualistic thinking. An ordinary person's attention strays according to any movement of mind. Suddenly there is the confusion of believing in self and other, subject and object, and this situation goes on and on repeating itself endlessly. This is samsaric existence. The buddhas and bodhisattvas were successful in getting up on the dry land of enlightenment. But we sentient beings became bewildered, and are now in the unsuccessful, unsatisfactory state we all find ourselves in. We are still in the ocean of samsara; we have not yet gotten our heads fully out of the water. We have roamed about in one confused state of experience after the other, endlessly. At the same time, we haven't lost our buddha nature. Our buddha nature is never separate from our minds for even a single instant. Though we are not apart from it we do not know it, and thus we wander in samsaric existence.

Now is the time to free ourselves from samsara. Unless we do it in this lifetime, it is not going to happen all by itself. We have to take care of ourselves. Right now we have the ability to receive teachings and practice the Dharma. Isn't this the right time? Wouldn't that be better than continuing to act like an animal, concentrating only on eating and sleeping and letting the time run out? Why not take your future into your own hands?

It is possible to realize our nature because we have experienced the great kindness of a fully enlightened one's appearance in this world. The Buddha not only appeared, but he imparted the precious instructions on how to realize our own buddha nature. And these teachings on how to realize our enlightened essence have been made available through an unbroken lineage of great masters.

'Confusion arising as wisdom' means to realize that the buddha nature pervades all sentient beings. We have not lost it; it has never been apart from our mind for even a single instant. This buddha nature is always present, and the only thing that conceals it is our own thinking. Nothing else obscures it. The essence becomes obscured by the expression. It is the same as the sun shining brilliantly in the clear sky. The only thing that obscures the sun are the clouds. And the clouds themselves are created through the manifestations of the sun—the light and warmth. They don't come from any other place. The heat from the sun makes water evaporate and forms the clouds that obscure the sun. Likewise, the expression of our own attention takes the form of the confused thinking that obscures us. In other words, we are obscuring our own buddha nature, and now is the time to clear up this confusion.

We are fortunate enough nowadays to have at hand wonderful teachings that show us how to recognize our own nature and obtain liberation from samsaric existence. If we choose to remain obscured by our actions and emotions, we don't know what will happen next. We live one day after the other. If we are going to die tomorrow, we are ignorant of that today. We are really as stupid as an animal. From another angle, we are even more stupid than an animal, because we *can* receive teachings on how to practice; in fact, we may already have done so. If we don't apply them we are far more stupid than an animal. Animals can't really help it; they are not in a body that can receive teachings. But unfortunately we human beings who have been introduced to the spiritual path can waste this precious opportunity. That would be incredibly sad!

Due to the kindness of the Three Jewels, we now have the fortune to receive the teaching through which we can allow confusion to dawn as wisdom. Confusion here means believing something to be what it is not. To be confused is the same as to be mistaken. How do we turn confusion into wisdom? First we need to understand what confusion is. Confusion is taking what isn't for what is. It's the opposite of knowing what is to be as it is. In Tibet there is a drug called *datura*, which, when you take it, makes other people appear as if they had fifty heads or thirty hands. We know that this is not possible in this world; this is an example of confusion.

Within our buddha nature are three qualities of enlightened Body, Speech and Mind. The unchanging quality that is like the openness of space is called vajra body. The unceasing quality is called vajra speech. The unmistaken quality, the capacity to perceive even without thought, is called vajra mind. These three—vajra body, speech and mind—are inherently present as the nature of all sentient beings. All we need to do is to recognize this. Even though we have the three vajras, we don't know it, and thus continue to wander in samsara. Ordinary confusion covers up our innate three vajras. Our physical body of flesh and blood covers the vajra body. The words and sounds we utter, which are interrupted and intermittently created, obscure the unceasing quality of vajra speech. And our train of thoughts that comes and goes, and endlessly arises and ceases from moment to moment, day after day, life after life, is exactly what obscures the unmistaken quality of vajra mind. What is necessary now is to recognize our own nature, instead of going on being confused.

3

Buddha Nowhere Else

❀

Our main guide and teacher, Buddha Shakyamuni, gave a tremendous amount of teachings. To put them all down in writing would fill thousands of volumes of scriptures. But they all are mainly concerned with one thing: how this mind is and how it behaves—how it *really* is, and how it only seems to be. Everything that the Buddha taught involves this subject. If we want to go into great detail, we can say that the Buddha gave 84,000 different sections of the Dharma to counteract the 84,000 different disturbing emotions he observed in sentient beings. Still, we can condense all these teachings into a single point: teachings on how mind seems to be, and how mind really is.

Because the Dharma adapts to the capacity of all different types of people, you can say that there are nine vehicles, nine levels of teaching. People differ: some are sharp-minded, some are of average intelligence, and some are dull-witted. Each of these categories can again be divided into three types, so that there is a total of nine types, and thus nine levels of teachings, nine vehicles. For those who have the least capacity, the buddhas teach the vehicles for shravakas, pratyekabuddhas and bodhisattvas. For the medium type, the buddhas teach the three outer tantras: Kriya, Upa and Yoga. For the highest capacity, the buddhas teach Maha, Anu and Ati.

There are two main ways to approach the Buddhadharma: the way of a scholar or the pandita's way, and the way of the *kusulu*, meaning a simple meditator. The scholar's way involves complete comprehension of what the Buddha taught, which requires a perspective on the whole body of teachings. Scholars need the details of everything in all of the nine vehicles, starting with the aggregate of form and continuing all the way up until the state of complete omniscience, the enlightened state. A scholar needs to gain complete comprehension about how everything works in relationship with cause and effect.

In contrast to this is the path of a kusulu, a simple meditator. For this type of person, the main point of the Buddha's teaching involves nothing more than understanding the difference between recognizing and not recognizing mind essence. Not recognizing is samsara, while recognizing is nirvana or liberation. It's from this perspective that we say that all of the Buddha's teachings are simply about the mind.

So, how is this mind, really? In essence it is empty, one hundred percent so. There is no doubt about this; it is empty and has primordially been so. The analogy often used here is that of space. Space is primordially empty; there is no maker or creator of space. The mind as it really is is empty. How it appears, or seems to be, is that there is a nature that cognizes. This cognizant quality of empty mind is ever-knowing. Whatever takes place can be known, whether it is samsara—the path—or nirvana. These two aspects are called the real and the seeming. The real is empty. The seeming is that there is a 'something' that experiences whatever is.

The essence of mind includes the three kayas of the buddhas. You can say there is the buddha which is empty essence, the buddha which is cognizant nature, and the buddha which is the all-pervasive capacity. Rather than being three different types of buddha, they are indivisible. And this indivisibility is itself the svabhavikakaya, the essence body. This indivisible nature is present in every single being as the continuity of one's mind. If we recognize this indivisible nature as our natural face, we don't need to seek a buddha elsewhere. If you do end up seeking a buddha in some other place, there isn't any to find! This is what is meant by the famous line, "Although my mind is the buddha, I fail to see it."

This buddha nature is present in everyone, just as oil is naturally present in a sesame seed. Squeeze a sesame seed and you'll invariably get a tiny bit of oil. Likewise, this buddha nature is present in everyone, from Buddha Samantabhadra down to the tiniest insect. It's our karma and disturbing emotions that determine how we end up in these different physical bodies, these different incarnations.

The extent to which we can comprehend this makes an incredible difference. Some people, by simply hearing one sentence of this teaching, will immediately understand. Others don't get the point, they don't comprehend, no matter how much is said. Whether one understands or not is dependent upon what particular body supports and what particular type of mind-set this buddha nature is connected to. But buddha nature itself is the same in everyone, with no decrease or increase, change or alteration between individuals. It is not that one person has an eminent buddha nature while someone else has a low-grade buddha nature. It is not that Buddha Samantabhadra has a really wonderful buddha nature, while a dog or a pig has an inferior buddha nature, or maybe none at all. There is actually no difference whatsoever between their essential buddha natures.

Our task is to recognize and realize our own buddha nature. However, if we are in a body that is incapable of this, we can't do so. Even the strongest animals, like elephants and tigers, have no way to realize their own nature. Among the six classes of sentient beings in samsara, only human beings can recognize their buddha nature; only humans have the capacity to understand the meaning of the teachings. We may be living in a dark age, but we still have the ability to recognize our own nature.

An old prediction has it: "When the age of degeneration is rampant, the Vajrayana teachings will spread like wildfire." When the three poisons are ablaze in peoples' minds, it is easier to acknowledge their antidote, which is the recognition of buddha nature.

Among the three realms—the realms of desire, the realms of form, and the realms of formlessness—it is in the realms of desire that the three poisons are most acutely present in being's minds. In the realms of form and formlessness there are hardly any disturbing emotions. Without disturbing emotions, the remedy, the recognition of mind essence, has no real force.

I'm only telling you this to give you the background story. The point I'm trying to make here is that everything is included within the seeming and the real. As for the real, remember that mind is primordially empty. It is original wakefulness that is empty in essence, cognizant by nature, and all-pervasive in its capacity. This original wakefulness, *yeshe*, is not a blank void; it is cognizant. It has the ability to know. When we talk about the real, the original, *this* is what it is. Original wakefulness empty in essence is the dharmakaya of all buddhas. Original wakefulness cognizant by nature is the sambhogakaya of all buddhas. Original wakefulness is also all-pervasive in its capacity. The innate capacity in which being empty and cognizant are indivisible is called the nirmanakaya of all buddhas. These three kayas form a single indivisibility, the svabhavikakaya, which is our own mind. This original basic reality present in oneself—as opposed to the seeming—is exactly what we call buddha nature.

Mind is also 'the unity of experience and emptiness.' You could say that the seeming and the real are a unity as well, in that mind is the unity of experience and emptiness. Exactly how this is possible is described like this: "Intrinsic mind essence is dharmakaya; intrinsic experience is the radiance of dharmakaya." It's like the sun and the sunshine, like the body and limbs, like the sky and clouds. The seeming is the expression of the real in the very same way. Right now, we experience the elements of earth, water, fire, wind and space as external to ourselves. They appear to us through our five senses, don't they? The seeming presence of that which experiences is mind. Without mind, would there be anything that appears? To what would these appearances manifest? Because mind experiences, you cannot deny that there is appearance. To say there are no appearances is a lie. You cannot deny the seeming reality of appearances, because what experiences is mind. But remember, this mind is empty.

All appearances are empty, in that they can all be destroyed or extinguished in some way. Water dries up, evaporates, disappears. Solid-seeming objects can be destroyed by fire, and the flames themselves eventually burn out and are extinguished. The whole universe vanishes at some point, destroyed by seven fires and one immense deluge. In this way, all appearances are ultimately empty.

Mind is also ultimately empty, but its way of being empty is not the same as that of appearances. Mind can experience anything, but it cannot be destroyed. Its original nature is the dharmakaya of all buddhas. You cannot actually do anything to mind—you can't change it, wash it away, bury it, or burn it. What is truly empty, though, is all the appearances that appear to the mind. Because all these appearances are ultimately empty and will vanish completely, we really don't have to worry about them or analyze them too much. They're really just a magical display, just like when demons conjure up some magic to fool you. All appearances are a magical display, experienced only by mind. In fact, we can say that the experiencing of appearances is the magical display of mind.

The three kayas are primordially present in one moment. They are not something that can temporarily be made or manufactured by anyone. Self-existing wakefulness is the realized state of all buddhas from the very beginning; it is primordial. Self-existing wakefulness is in all beings; it simply needs to be known. Our chance to do so comes when it is introduced to us by a qualified master. Our inherently present wakefulness is not something we'll find in the future, nor something we had in the past. It's present right now. And it's something that we don't have to accept or reject. Don't do anything to it: don't adopt it, don't avoid it, don't entertain any hope or fear about it, don't try to change it or alter it or improve it in any way. It is not necessary at all.

Recognizing self-existing wakefulness is not the same as looking at the thinking mind, which means simply to notice what is occurring in one's mind: "Now I am happy, now I am sad." And after noticing, we get involved again in whatever is taking place within our confused thinking. Sentient beings roam about in samsara in exactly this fashion, by chasing after their own thoughts. When they feel happy, they get engrossed in that and laugh and laugh. When they feel sad, they sit and cry.

What I have been explaining here is the theory, the intellectual understanding. But really, it's necessary to gain some personal experience in what I'm talking about here. Explaining the theory of mind essence is like describing different delicious cuisine—Indian food, Chinese food, or whatever—and explaining what each one tastes like. You get an intellectual idea of what it probably tastes like, but you can hear a hundred lectures and still have only an idea. Once you take a single bite into your mouth and it touches your tongue and palate, you taste the flavor. At that moment, you gain genuine confidence regarding the real taste of that food. That is called experience, when we actually know that this tastes pretty good or that tastes disgusting. Experience is the point at which we know it by ourselves.

To leave the view as mere theory is useless. We hear the statement in Buddhism that everything is empty and devoid of any true existence, from the aggregate of physical form up to and including the state of omniscient enlightenment. This is universally renowned as the main principle of Buddhism. To hear this and to comprehend it is to get the idea as intellectual understanding. Actually, the Buddha taught this not from an intellectual standpoint but out of his own experience that everything from the aggregate of form up to complete enlightenment is empty and devoid of true existence. But the hearer of this might say "All right, the Buddha said everything is empty and devoid of self-entity." And he might go on to think, "Well, then, good or evil are also empty, so what does it matter how I act?" That is a severely wrong view. If merely believing something was enough, then why not think, "I am a fully enlightened buddha"? Would that be good enough? Are you enlightened by simply believing yourself to be enlightened? It's not enough to merely get the idea of the view as a theory.

To receive the pointing-out instruction is to experience mind essence. The experience is like putting the food in your mouth. Without doing that, there's no way to taste it. Once you eat the food, you know whether it's delicious or awful; that is the experience. Experience is the adornment of rigpa. When it comes to rigpa, only experience is useful. To leave it as theory is not going to help anything. If it would, we could sit around and say, "The lama says such-and-such about emptiness, so that's probably how it is," but we would never know for sure what emptiness is. That is called theory. Experience of the view is when you recognize the nature of your own mind.

When giving and receiving the pointing-out instruction, one should first chant refuge and bodhichitta. This teaching is not some superficial teaching; it is the real thing. Even though it is the ultimate teaching, one still chants refuge and bodhichitta. It is thanks to the Buddha, Dharma and Sangha that we can recognize the true object of refuge. The Buddha's words, the Dharma, are written down as texts. And the noble Sangha are the people who have been upholding, maintaining and propagating this teaching until now.

Next, it is the tradition to imagine your root guru at the crown of your head and make a deep-felt supplication. The original father of all buddhas is Samantabhadra, who represents the dharmakaya. The sambhogakaya is called the five buddhas, while the nirmanakayas are the lords of the three families: Manjushri, Avalokiteshvara, and Vajrapani. The transmission line from these buddhas to you is like water flowing from the top of the mountain down to here. If it is not interrupted anywhere along the line, the water will flow right out of your water tap. Similarly, if the lineage has not been broken anywhere, something called 'the single uninterrupted transmission of instruction' comes out of your present guru and is received by you. In this way, the blessings of the three kayas of the buddhas are unbroken as well. This is the reason to supplicate your root guru.

Simply let mind recognize itself, like cutting through the thinking. That is called the view of *Trekchö*, the 'thorough cut.' It's thorough in the same way that a piece of string is cut entirely through into two pieces that are completely disconnected. This emptiness is not something we imagine by meditating; it is naturally and originally so. There is no need to merely think it is empty. Simply remain, without imagining or thinking anything. The moment you think, "Now it is empty," a thought has already snuck in. This is unnecessary. This continual process of forming concepts and being attached is itself the root of samsara. You don't have to think, "This is nice!" or "This is not right!" Be free from even a hair-tip of conceptual thought. This is called recognizing present wakefulness.

Trekchö is also called 'four parts without three.' The way to be free is free from the three parts that are the conditioned thoughts of past, present and future. The fourth moment is the timeless great moment. In it, the linking up of consciousness, sense organ and sense object is cut through. Once this link is broken, the chain of samsara is broken. Self-existing wakefulness needs to recognize itself.

Trekchö, the thorough cut, severs the samsaric connection; there is only the gap of empty air between. Remain without following the past, without planning the future. The Buddha described this moment of recognizing mind nature: "No form, no sound, no smell, no taste, no texture, no mental object." Mental objects are called 'dharmas' in Sanskrit, but the word here doesn't mean the sacred Dharma teachings, it means phenomena.

This self-existing wakefulness, in which there is no thing to see, is exactly what is called emptiness, *shunyata*. There are two different kinds of empty: empty and emptiness. Space is empty. Can space, which is completely empty, see itself? Mind, on the other hand, is emptiness. What we need to see is emptiness in actuality, not something hidden. We need to see emptiness, and that which sees is our cognizant quality. At the moment of seeing emptiness, isn't it true that there is not even as much as a hair-tip to see? This is what Rangjung Dorje, the third Karmapa, meant when he said: "When looking again and again into invisible mind, the fact that there is no thing to see is clearly and vividly seen *as it is*." 'Vividly seen as it is' means in actuality, not hidden. Mind essence in actuality, as it is, is vividly seen the very moment you look. If we, on the other hand, sit and think, "Oh, mind is probably empty like space," that is only imagination. We don't need to do that. We don't have to imagine that mind is empty; it is so in actuality. When you see it as it is, you see it is already empty.

Mind is in essence empty. However, it has a cognizant nature of clearly knowing whatever is at any moment. These two aspects, being empty and being cognizant, are a primordial unity. You don't need to grasp at mind essence as something like you, the subject, knowing that, an object. Empty and cognizant are a natural unity, just as water is naturally wet and fire is naturally hot. There is no need for an observer and something observed, or for the making of the thought, "Now I see it."

That would be holding a concept in mind. Recognize the thinker and the thought vanishes by itself, because a thought has no inherent stability. Every thought is empty; when you truly look at it; it can only vanish naturally. Once you truly discover this, there is no need to look here and there; just let be.

In the moment of experiencing mind essence, isn't it impossible to find any word for how it really is? If you do form words about it—"Now it is empty, now it is cognizant,"—aren't those simply words that crowd the mind? When the whole point is to allow our thinking to dissolve, what is the use of forming more thoughts?

You may have heard this quotation: "Transcendent knowledge is beyond thought, word and description." The moment you recognize mind essence, it is impossible to find words and descriptions for how it is. Allow your thinking to vanish, to dissolve, to simply disappear naturally. In this world there is nothing else that can make it happen. We can blow up all the nuclear bombs we like, and mind will still churn out thoughts. There is only one way to dissolve thinking, and that is to recognize your nature. The thought at that moment vanishes all by itself, without any trace left. Why is this? It is because the minds of all sentient beings have always been primordially empty. The experience of emptiness is not something that all of a sudden happens out of nowhere. The very moment you recognize the essence of your own mind, there is no thing to see.

Honestly, this doesn't last longer than a couple of seconds. Because of our habit of always being caught up in our thoughts, a habit that has continued through beginningless lifetimes until now, there is no real stability there; our realization gets lost quite quickly. The moment we forget, we start to think of a lot of different things. Then once again we notice, "Oh, I got carried away; now I am thinking of all sorts of other things."

The training in recognizing your essence is simply to let be in naturalness. Naturalness here means without any technique, without artifice. Here is a very simple example of naturalness: does the water in the river require someone to push or pull it downstream, or does it naturally flow?. You don't need to do anything to it. The wood that makes up my table here has been crafted into this shape. When it was a tree growing on the mountainside it was natural, unmodified. Then a carpenter took it and worked it into a table. Now it is artificial. We need to avoid shaping our awareness into something artificial. The very moment you recognize, don't worry or judge or speculate about it; don't do anything to it, don't try to improve or alter it. Allow nondistraction to last as long as it lasts, as undistracted naturalness. See clearly that there is no thing to see, without trying to improve or alter that.

People experience different degrees of innate stability in this practice, based on their former training. How long that innate stability lasts is hard to say. It may last a little while, but if there is no former training, it might slip away almost immediately. Don't sit and push very hard and think, "I mustn't be distracted, I mustn't be distracted." Simply allow the instants of nondistraction to naturally take place and unfold. To recognize mind essence doesn't mean to sit and meditate upon mind essence. It means simply allowing, simply experiencing, our empty and cognizant nature to be as it already is.

This is what we actually are: empty in essence, cognizant by nature, able to perceive, with no barrier between these two aspects. This empty quality is called dharmakaya. But we are not only empty—unlike space, we possess a knowing quality. This is what is described as cognizant nature, sambhogakaya. The capacity is the unity of these two, suffused with awareness. 'Capacity' here means being empty or being cognizant cannot be separated; they are an original unity. And 'suffused with awareness' refers to rigpa. The minds of all sentient beings are the unity of empty cognizance, but because they are not suffused with awareness, they don't know this. Although their minds are the unity of empty cognizance as a unity, they are suffused with unawareness, with unknowing. The very moment we recognize our nature as empty cognizance, it becomes empty cognizance suffused with awareness, with knowing.

The difference between buddhas and sentient beings is the difference between knowing and not knowing. 'Knowing' means knowing one's own nature, one's natural face. This present wakefulness that is uncorrected or uncontrived is the true Samantabhadra which has never been apart from you. While recognizing, rest naturally. When this present wakefulness recognizes itself, there is nothing whatsoever to see. *That* is the empty essence — that is dharmakaya. However, along with the realization that there is nothing to see, is some knowing or seeing that this is so. That is the cognizant nature, sambhogakaya. This empty essence and cognizant nature are forever indivisible. That is the unity, nirmanakaya.

In the very moment of recognizing, these three kayas are already seen. There is nothing to block this realization, nothing in between the kayas and your awareness. Knowing this is 'self-knowing original wakefulness,' *rang-rig yeshe*. Unknowing is samsara. To be ignorant is to be a sentient being, but to know is to be a buddha. This teaching is something very precious. To have one's nature pointed out is an incredibly great kindness, and it is only due to the compassion of the Buddha that we have this teaching today.[2]

In short, recognize yourself and be face to face with the three kayas of the awakened one. To let your attention stray, to be caught up in the three poisons, is to stray further into samsara. That certainly happens, doesn't it? The moment we see a beautiful form, we love it. The moment we see something ugly, we hate it, don't we? And if it is something in between, we don't care. These are the three poisons, and they go on and on and on. When we see something we like, we become fascinated and we feel attached, while we feel revulsion towards and don't want to look at things we don't like. Towards something in between we feel indifferent, dull, closed-minded. At the moment of involvement in the three poisons, there is no knowing of one's own nature; the three kayas of the awakened state slip away.

There is nothing superior to meeting face-to-face with the three kayas of the awakened state. Isn't that true? Seeing that there is no thought overcomes or expels any previous thought. When the sun shines, there is no darkness. While seeing, it is impossible for any thought to either linger or to be formed. The delusion is completely dissolved. The awakened state is free of thought. But merely thinking "I want to be free of thought" is not the awakened state. It's just another thought. The same goes for checking: "Is there a thought now, or is it free of thought?" Isn't that just another thought as well? It's necessary to rest totally unmixed with or unpolluted by thought. The awakened state is free of thought, yet vividly awake. If we train in this steadily and gradually, it becomes the fully awakened state, buddhahood.

There is a natural sturdiness or stability in the moment of recognizing mind essence. To understand natural stability, think of a needle compared to a hair. A hair, no matter how thick it might be, is not stable; it moves in the slightest breeze. But a needle, regardless of how thin it is, cannot be bent by the wind. We need to be naturally stable in emptiness. We don't have to imagine emptiness by meditating. If we do this, it becomes an act of thinking—we are just thinking of emptiness. When we forget mind essence, we become distracted, confusion arises. Meditating is conceptual, being distracted is confusion. Instead, be naturally stable in the state of undistracted nonmeditation. This undistracted nonmeditation is not something you have to create. You don't have to hold onto the idea of that. Simply allow present wakefulness to be naturally stable by being free of thought. Be stable not in keeping a thought, but in the absence of thought.

To do so is to experience what we call 'present wakefulness' or 'thoughtfree wakefulness.' 'Thoughtfree' means free of conceptual thinking, yet the knowing or awake quality is not lost. If you want to find out what it's like to lose this sense of awakeness, have somebody knock you out with an iron bar so you can experience unconsciousness! Right now, in the moment of recognizing, we are not unconscious. The awake quality is not lost, and yet there is no thought. If you spend your life practicing like this, eventually thinking will get weaker and thoughts will decrease. But the continuity of thoughtfree wakefulness is not lost. It lasts for longer and longer periods naturally, of its own accord, while the moments of conceptual thinking become weaker and take up less and less time. Finally, you become totally free of thought. Conceptual thinking disappears, and there is only present thoughtfree wakefulness, uninterrupted through both day and night. That is called the buddha-mind.

We need to train in this thoughtfree wakefulness, but not by meditating on it or imagining it. It is primordially present already. Yet this present wakefulness gets caught up in thinking. To get free of thought, simply recognize; recognize your present wakefulness. Don't forget; don't get distracted. That doesn't mean to sit and force oneself to be undistracted and unforgetting. Trying like that only fouls it up. Simply allow your basic state to be undistracted nonmeditation. When all the activities of dualistic mind dissolve, when we are utterly stable in the unconfined empty cognizance, there is no longer any basis for remaining in the three realms of samsara.

Even if our recognition of rigpa doesn't become uninterrupted throughout day and night—even if we only manage to sustain it short moments many times—the value of training in this practice of recognizing mind essence will become fully evident at the time of death. At some point we are all sure to die; no one escapes that in this world. Anyone who takes birth dies. If we manage to recognize at the moment when the breath ceases and we are separated from this illusory body, we can in three seconds perfect the strength of that recognition and stabilize it. It becomes the dharmakaya state, just like space mingling with space. It's just like what happens to the space within a vase that breaks: the space inside and the space outside, which were up until this point divided by the side of the vase, become one. Similarly, the ground state of unconstructed dharmakaya, which is the buddha nature present in everyone, and the path dharmakaya, which is the empty cognizance we have trained in, combine into an indivisible unity.

The process of our spirit disconnecting from the physical body is accompanied by the dissolution of all gross and subtle thought-states or mental patterns. At this point there is nothing covering the basic state of mind at all. This is called the 'ground luminosity of full attainment,' sometimes described as the ground luminosity and path luminosity coming face to face. At that moment, the power of our training in this life can create the possibility for recognizing the original wakefulness. If we haven't trained at all, the basic state won't last longer than a single glimpse. But if we have trained, then at that moment complete enlightenment is very likely. This is stated in a tantra: "In one moment the difference is made; in one moment complete enlightenment is attained." All that is necessary is to allow the recognition of original wakefulness to be sustained for three seconds. The scriptures describe it as the length of time it takes to wave the long sleeve of a Tibetan robe or a white scarf three times in the air. If we can do this, we can attain complete stability during the post-death state.

The ground luminosity is like the mother, while the path luminosity is like the child. Mother and child always recognize each other, don't they? When the ground and path luminosities recognize each other in that split second span of time, however small the degree of familiarity might be, it still will be sufficient to take rebirth in a pure buddhafield, in what is called the 'natural nirmanakaya realms.' There you will behold the face of the Buddha, hear his voice, and overcome the remaining obscurations. If there is a strong familiarity, it is like space mingling with space, and you become of one taste with the state of dharmakaya.

The reason why training in this lifetime can yield such great benefit after death is because in the bardo state our mind is not connected to a body, so it's free of the continual obscuration we experience in our lifetime. Right now, we might recognize our own mind in a brief glimpse, only to have it immediately covered up again. But after death, the obscurations created by the body are not there.

You need to train in these instructions in order to overcome the cognitive obscuration. Through this training, you will eventually reach the irreversible state, called the state of non-regression, no falling back. This is the real, true outcome, the profit earned from all the effort of practice. We should experience some positive result from our practice. This practice will definitely help at the moment of death. Right now, we may train in recognizing and sustaining the natural state, but we are not immediately enlightened, because body and mind are still connected. Still, practice brings many other benefits which occur in this life. For one, we do not fall under the power of the three poisons. As we recognize, strengthen our recognition and attain stability, we are always joyful, regardless of who we are with, and wherever we go, the sun of happiness shines. Otherwise, we're like any other ordinary person: depressed when unhappy and overjoyed when happy. In other words, we are totally unstable. Through this practice, good and bad become equalized, without having to adopt one and avoid the other. Even before death we will be totally at ease.

The real problem is the state of mind of an ordinary person, which is always changing from one thing to another. Sentient beings are totally unstable, but someone who has truly recognized mind essence and stays in retreat in the mountains is completely free of suffering. Even in this lifetime one can be totally free of pain and progress further and further on the path of happiness. There is great benefit from this practice. It's never pleasant to maintain the state of mind of an ordinary person, which is always changing. When unhappy, one is totally overcome by that feeling. Better to recognize the wide-awake empty cognizance and remain like that.

Basically there is nothing to do at all in this practice besides training in being stable. Simply allowing our mind to *be*, without having to do anything, is entirely against our usual habits. Our normal tendency is to think, "I want to do this. I want to do that." Then we actually go do it. Finally, we feel happy and satisfied when it's all neat, all completed, accomplished all by ourselves. But that attitude is totally wrong in the context of this type of practice. There is nothing whatsoever to do. We don't have to construct what is unformed. Anything we try to do becomes an imitation, something made up by our thoughts and concepts.

As a matter of fact, it may feel utterly dissatisfying, extremely disappointing, to allow our original nature to be as it naturally is. We might much rather do something, imagine something, create something, and really put ourselves through a lot of hardship. Maybe that is why the Buddha did not teach Dzogchen and Mahamudra openly—because this not-doing is in some ways contrary to human nature.

Buddha nature is free of the three times of past, present and future, while our mind is under the power of the three times. Wakeful knowing is free of the three times. The three times involve fixating, thinking. Wakeful knowing is free of fixation and thought.

The Buddha realized that different beings had various capacities, so out of great compassion and skillful means he gave teachings that were right for different individuals. Although the essence of all teachings of all enlightened ones is to simply let be in recognition of one's own nature, the Buddha taught a lot of complex instructions in order to satisfy people on all the different levels. Another reason why there are the nine vehicles, the nine yanas, is because people couldn't leave well enough alone. It seems to be human nature to love complications, to want to build up a lot of stuff. Later on, of course, they must allow it to fall into pieces again.

So, to repeat it again: in order to make everybody happy, the Buddha and the great masters taught nine vehicles. The variety of teachings that exist doesn't change the fact that the very essence of the Dharma, buddha nature, is extremely simple and easy. In fact, it's so simple and easy that sometimes it's hard to believe!

If we really apply ourselves to it sincerely, there will come a time when we discover something called 'establishing the natural state.' When you experience this, suddenly it's not so hard any longer. We realize that this fantastic thing called buddha nature, our mind essence, is not out of reach at all. Since it is not something very complex, simply allow that to be regularly sustained. When it is totally easy and simple to recognize your natural face, you have 'established the natural state.'

The general tradition of giving this pointing-out instruction says we need to go step by step. First we complete the reflections of the four mind-changings. Next, we go through the preliminary practices of the four times hundred thousand, and after that the inner yidam practice of deity, mantra and samadhi. And indeed these are all still necessary, even if we have already received teachings on mind essence. Don't have the idea that suddenly all the practices taught by the enlightened ones are unimportant; it is not like that at all.

Since it's not so easy or common to have the opportunity to receive this teaching, I feel that I should shoot my mouth off and give it. Please remember that we can easily receive the other important teachings from various masters, so you shouldn't ignore them. Please be diligent in practice. Really, the difference between buddhas and ordinary beings is diligence.

I'm giving this teaching because I'm very talkative. I can't help it; I have to let it all slip out! When I was young I spent a lot of time with my uncle, Tulku Samten Gyatso, who was also my root guru. I listened in on whatever instructions he gave. Often it would be the pointing-out instruction, and advice on how to really meditate in the simplest way. Afterwards, there might be some people outside his room who couldn't really understand what he had said. They would say "How can it be that easy?" And I would say, "Why do you think it has to be difficult—it really *is* so easy." Then they would say, "But I don't get it." And I'd reply, "What do you mean, you don't get it? Just let be!" I had that kind of attitude because I'd heard what my uncle had said, and I'd just repeat it. Sometimes my uncle would call me in, and say "It seems you are talkative, as well as someone who thinks that it is totally easy. There is no problem with that at all; you are simply that type of person. I think that in the future you will be like this as well—you will be both talkative and somebody who acts like it is really simple!" And he was right.

On one hand, maybe I'm just fooling everybody, making it too simple. But on the other hand, this is really how it is! It is the truth. What is the use of trying to sit and push and struggle, when you can allow the three kayas of buddhahood to be naturally present? Why do we have to strain and contort ourselves into an uneasy posture and an uptight meditative state with some hope that in the future, after a lot of trouble, we may get there? You don't need to go through all that trouble and tension. All you need to do is totally let be and recognize your nature right now.

Because people are different, there is a need for different levels of teachings; we need something that is exactly suited for ourselves. And there are the four liberations: liberation through hearing, liberation through remembering, liberation through understanding, and so forth. Maybe all that I said is not wasted. Maybe there are some who understood what I talked about. Maybe there are some who will remember this teaching and be liberated.

If we really practice what was taught here today, it will eventually be possible to recognize our own nature as unconfined empty cognizance. The pointing-out instruction is the present wakefulness pointed out *as it is*. It is not something in the future, not something in the past, but present right now. You don't have to accept or reject it. Don't do anything to it: don't adopt, don't avoid, don't entertain any hope or fear, don't try to change, alter or improve it. It is not necessary at all.

In terms of training in this practice, there are three steps: recognizing, developing the strength and attaining stability. The most important is to recognize. In this world, is there anything more precious, more profound than the three kayas? That this profundity is present right in ourselves and we can recognize this fact in actuality is the first step.

It's like acknowledging the seed of a flower. It may be very tiny, like the seed of this flower right here originally was. It doesn't look like much, because we don't see the fully manifested qualities of enlightenment in the moment of recognizing. Yet we need to acknowledge this seed as being the seed of a flower. We may not see the colors right now, the brilliant yellow or red or white that will unfold. But by planting this seed, the possibility of a flower will become a reality. We water and fertilize the soil, nurturing the seedling. If we do that, it's certain it will sprout and develop tiny leaves that slowly grow bigger and bigger. The stamen will form, the buds—and finally there will be a flower that fully blooms. All this is unavoidable or inevitable if the right circumstances are supplied.

It's the same with recognition. It's not like we are suddenly fully enlightened right after we recognize for the first time. Rather, the span of time from the moment of one's first recognition until achieving total stability is itself the path. All the different teachings of the Buddha have their own ways of defining stages of the path. But they all involve developing the strength of recognizing your buddha nature.

We need to let this recognition grow. It's like a newborn child: we can't expect a baby born yesterday to be a full-grown man or woman today. The baby needs to grow gradually. In the same way, we need to grow in the recognition of buddha nature, and the only way to do so is by training. Please train in this practice, because this is the way in which we can awaken to complete enlightenment. Although there are many different practices in Buddhism, this is the very heart, the most vital essence of what the Buddha taught. This is what we need to train in to attain complete enlightenment.

Right now, in the very moment of recognizing mind essence, there is an immediate absence of disturbing emotions, of ignorance, of deluded thinking. This training is to simply remain undistracted, because it is this nondistraction that brings us all the way to complete enlightenment. Nondistraction doesn't mean deliberately trying to be undistracted, as we do when we replace normal thoughts with the thought "Don't be distracted." It is simply to not forget. The moment we forget—and we do forget—both the practice and all other things get forgotten, because our attention strays. The key point here is not in keeping undistracted in a conceptual way. It is simply allowing the state of unconfined empty cognizance, which by itself is undistracted, to continue. That is the training.

Try to imagine what it's like when this moment of empty cognizance suffused with awareness starts to last for a full hour, unbroken. The very first moment of empty cognizance already has the potential for full omniscience, as well as the potential for compassion and loving kindness—the potential ability to protect and help other beings, as well as to manifest the activity that functions for the welfare of all. All these qualities are present, but not fully manifest. The longer this duration lasts, the more the qualities become visible, actualized. They don't just appear later on, when realization is fully experienced. When the sun rises in the morning, do we have to wait for it to shine for it to be warm and brilliant? Although the noon sun may be stronger than the dawn sun, all of its qualities are present from the very first moment, though they may not be fully manifested. It's the same in this training. What is essential is to train in order to attain stability.

Please understand that *rangjung yeshe,* self-existing wakefulness, is primordially endowed with all perfect qualities. The qualities of enlightenment are not a fabrication or a product. They are not a new achievement, an unprecedented new discovery, or something that we achieve. They are present from the very beginning. It's like the unchanging brilliance of the sun shining in the sky. It can be obscured by clouds, but these clouds are neither primordial nor intrinsic to the sky; they are always temporary, momentary. What prevents full realization of our innate nature of self-existing wakefulness is the momentary occurrence of thoughts and fixation. Because this occurrence is momentary, it can be cleared away. It's very important to understand this.

4

Existence and Nonexistence

※

Whatever practice you do, please do so while embracing it with the three excellences. The first is the excellent preparation of bodhichitta. The bodhisattva resolve is to form the thought, "I will attain complete enlightenment for the sake of all beings." Engendering that motivation is a superb way to begin one's practice.

This excellent preparation is indispensable for all Buddhist practitioners, because we all have had many lifetimes other than this one. The pure vision of the fully enlightened ones sees that we have been through countless lifetimes. In every one of these, we had a father and a mother. We have had so many lifetimes that every sentient being, without a single exception, has been our own father and mother. Thus, we are connected to all other beings, and to merely wish enlightenment and liberation for ourselves is far too limited. To achieve enlightenment in this way would mean abandoning all our parents.

Please understand that all sentient beings, all our parents, want nothing but happiness. Unfortunately, through their negative actions they only create the causes for further pain and suffering. Take this to heart and consider all our parents, wandering blindly and endlessly through painful samsaric states. When we truly take this to heart, out of compassion we feel motivated to achieve enlightenment to truly help all of them. This compassionate attitude is indispensable as a preparation for practice.

The excellent preparation also includes the taking of refuge. Do we actually have the ability to genuinely help other beings? Do we have the power, the wisdom, the boundless compassion to do so? At present we don't. Who does? Only the fully awakened Buddha actually possesses the power to protect others, as well as the pure teachings on how to attain enlightenment. In addition to these two there are those beings who uphold these teachings in an unbroken lineage. These three, the Buddha, Dharma and Sangha, are the only true protection and rescue for unenlightened beings.

We should regard these Three Precious Ones as our shelter, our refuge, our escort, from now on until complete enlightenment. They embody a reliable and authentic source of protection. To entrust ourselves and place our confidence in the Three Jewels from this point until we ourselves become truly able to benefit others is called 'taking refuge.' Together with bodhichitta, taking refuge is the excellent preparation. Taking refuge essentially embodies all Hinayana teachings, while all Mahayana teachings are contained within forming the bodhisattva resolve.

The second of the three excellences is called the 'excellent main part beyond concepts.' This has two aspects, development stage and completion stage. This excellent main part beyond conceptual focus is a synonym for Vajrayana, the vajra vehicle of Secret Mantra.

Development stage is usually understood as visualizing the support, which is the buddha field and the celestial palace, and what is supported therein—the form of the deity. The palace and deity are considered to be the pure world and pure being. We may think that this is a product of our imagination, but in fact it is an exact replica of the original state of all things. It is how things already are in actuality—also called the great mandala of the manifest ground. Thus, visualization is ultimately not a matter of imagining something to be what it isn't, but rather, of seeing it as it actually is. It is acknowledging things as they already are. This is the essential principle of Vajrayana. Within this principle is contained both development stage and completion stage.

Development stage is not like imagining a piece of wood to be gold. No matter how long you imagine that wood is gold, it never truly becomes gold. Rather, it's like regarding gold as gold: acknowledging or seeing things as they actually are. That is what is meant by training in deity, mantra and samadhi. The body, speech and mind of the deity is contained within the three aspects of Vajrayana practice called development, recitation and completion.

All appearances are the mandala of the deities, all sounds are the mandala of mantra, and all thoughts are the mandala of enlightened mind. The nature of all apparent and existing things—of this entire world and all its beings—is the great mandala of the manifest ground, our basic state. These three mandalas are present as our ground. The practice of a sadhana is based on manifesting from this ground. Sadhana practice is also based on some very essential principles: that the tantras are contained within the statements, the statements within the oral instructions, and the oral instructions within the application of the sadhana itself.

Let me rephrase this vital point. In Vajrayana, a sadhana is the act of manifesting what is originally present in the form of the threefold mandalas of deity, mantra and samadhi. When practicing a sadhana, we are not superimposing something artificial atop the natural state of things. Rather, it is a way of acknowledging our original state, in which the nature of all forms is deity, the nature of all sounds is mantra, and the nature of mind is samadhi. This is the basic principle of development stage. And the differences in profundity between the teachings of sutra and tantra lie in how close the teachings are to the original nature. The closest, the most direct, are the Vajrayana teachings.

What are the reasons for development and completion stages? The profound development stage enables us to attain enlightenment in one lifetime and in one body through deity, mantra and samadhi. And completion stage means that the deity is none other than our originally enlightened buddha nature. Its essence is present as Body, its nature radiates as Speech, and its capacity is pervasive as Mind.

As previously mentioned, our originally enlightened essence contains within itself the awakened state of all buddhas as the three aspects of vajra body, vajra speech and vajra mind. Training in these three vajras is intrinsically contained within the profound state of samadhi, which is none other than one's own nature. That is the starting point or source of the excellent main part beyond concepts.

Deity, mantra and samadhi are the enlightened body, speech and mind. Vajra body means the unchanging quality which is the identity of the deity. The unceasing quality is the identity of the mantra, while the unmistaken or undeluded quality is the identity of the deity's mind. These three vajras are complete in our buddha nature. They are also called dharmakaya, sambhogakaya and nirmanakaya.

These profound methods of Vajrayana—practicing a sadhana, meditating on the deity, reciting its mantra, and training in samadhi—are called a quick path. The essence of this is the nature of mind. But this old man here who lives up on this hill does not want to waste any more of your time. Now I will tell you a few things that you all took the trouble to come up and hear me say.

What I will repeat once more is the unfailing, unmistaken vajra speech of the perfectly enlightened Buddha, which can enable us to attain complete enlightenment in one lifetime. As I mentioned previously, this teaching has been passed through an unbroken lineage of great masters all the way down to my own root guru. While my ears have been very fortunate to receive this teaching, I myself am nothing special. Although I may take great words in my mouth, please understand that I am merely repeating what I have been fortunate enough to receive.

It is very difficult to really learn something or to be educated in it without a teacher. You probably all know this very well, having gone to school so many years. The education we have received is something that we can make use of our entire lives. Even so, our education has not brought us even one inch closer to the state of perfect enlightenment. Our years of effort in school are ultimately of no real benefit.

Because you are all intelligent, I think you can understand why I am saying this. No matter what we do in this life, all the information we gather and all the knowledge we accumulate and all the effort we make to amass wealth through work and business—when the time comes for us to leave this life, all of it is futile and in vain. It will not help us in any way whatsoever. I can easily say this since I am not educated at all! So I can smile and act big about this. Don't be angry, please.

What I'm trying to say is that we may well succeed in becoming extremely rich and gain great material profit. We can buy the most expensive clothes or manage to be famous in this world so that everyone knows our name. That is quite possible. We can pursue these worldly attainments very enthusiastically and think that there is plenty of time to enjoy them while we are in the first half of our lives. However, in the second half of our lives, as we age and become elderly, life starts being less fun. I speak from experience here. It begins to be difficult to stand up and to move around. You get sick more often and you start to ail in different ways. What lies ahead of you is only further sickness and finally death. All these disasters are lined up in front of us, and we will meet them one after the other. What comes after death is not clear to us right now, because we cannot see our next rebirth. We cannot even see if there is anything after this life. When we look down at the ground we don't see any lower realms; when we look up in the sky we don't see any heavens or buddha fields. With these eyes we have now, we don't see that much.

I'm sure that you know about this. You have already received a lot of teachings, and have probably thought about them as well. There is no reason why this old man should go on about this topic. There is a saying where I come from: "Take advice where it is closest; fetch water where it is nearest."

Please consider this: right now, you have a body, a voice and a mind, don't you? Of these, mind is the most important. Isn't it true that your body and voice are the servants of mind? Mind is the boss, and here comes more about mind. The five physical elements of earth, fire, water, wind and space do not perceive. Mind, in contrast, means that which can experience; that which perceives. The five sense organs of eyes, ears, tongue, nose and body do not perceive and experience. A corpse possesses the five sense organs, yet a corpse does not perceive, because it doesn't have a mind. The term corpse means that the mind has departed. We say that the eyes see, that the ears hear, that the tongue tastes, the nose smells and so forth — but it is only possible for this to happen when there is a mind to experience through the senses. The moment what we call consciousness, mind or spirit leaves the body, the five sense organs are still there; but there is no experience taking place through them.

Mind means that which knows pleasure and pain. Of all the different things in this world, only mind experiences and perceives; nothing else. Therefore, mind is the root of all states—all samsaric states as well as all nirvanic states. Without mind there would be nothing to feel or perceive in this world. If there were nothing that feels or perceives in this world, the world be utterly empty, wouldn't it? Mind is completely empty, but it is at the same time able to perceive, to know.

The three lower realms are arrayed according to the degree of pain experienced in each, just as the three higher realms are arrayed according to degrees of pleasure. Everything is based on that which feels pleasure and pain, which is mind. In other words, mind is the basis or root of everything.

Mind is empty, and while being empty, it still knows or experiences. Space is empty and does not know anything. That is the difference between space and mind. Mind is similar to space, in that it is insubstantial, not material. Isn't it quite amazing that something that is insubstantial is also able to experience?

There is mind, but it is not tangible or substantial. You cannot say that there is no mind because it is the basis of everything; it is that which experiences every possible thing. You cannot say really that there is a thing called mind, and yet at the same time you cannot say that there is no mind. It lies beyond both extremes of being and not being. That is why it is said, "Not existent, since even a buddha does not see it; not nonexistent, since it is the basis of both samsara and nirvana."

If we were without a mind, we would be corpses. You are not corpses, are you? But can you say that there is a mind that you can see, hear, smell, taste or take hold of? Honestly, you can continue to search for it exactly like this, scrutinizing for a billion years, and you will never be able to find mind as something that either exists or doesn't. It is truly beyond both extremes of existence and nonexistence.

The absence of contradiction between these two is the principle of the Middle Way—that mind is beyond conflict between existence and nonexistence. We do not have to hold the idea that there is a concrete mind or that there isn't. Mind in itself is natural 'thatness,' meaning that it is an unformed unity of being empty and cognizant. The Buddha called this unformed unity shunyata, emptiness. *Shunye* means empty, while the *-ta* in shunyata, the '-ness' in emptiness, should be understood as meaning 'able to cognize.' In this way, mind is empty cognizance. Natural thatness means simply what is by itself. Our nature is just like that. Just recognize that fact, without coloring it with any kind of idea about it.

If you believe there is a thing called mind, it is just a thought. If you believe there is no thing called mind, it's just another thought. Your natural state, free of any kind of thought about it — that is buddha nature. In ordinary sentient beings, this natural state is carried away by thinking, caught up in thought. Involvement in thinking is like a heavy chain that weighs you down. Now it is time to be free from that chain. The moment you shatter the chain of thinking, you are free from the three realms of samsara

In this entire world, there is nothing superior to or more precious than knowing how to break this chain. Even if you were to scan the entire world, or piece by piece put it through a sieve in an attempt to find something more precious, you'd come up with nothing. None of the buddhas of the past, present and future have discovered an instruction that is more profound or more direct in attaining enlightenment. To ask for teachings on the nature of mind means to understand how to recognize mind nature. I am being very talkative, but I'll try and say it simply now.

The traditional way of receiving the instruction on how to realize the nature of mind involves first going through the training of the preliminary practices of the 'four times hundred thousand.' After that, you would carry out the yidam practice, staying in retreat and completing the set number of recitations. Finally, after all this, this teaching would be given. But nowadays we live in different times. People are so busy that they have no time to actually sit down and go through all this training. We might call it progress in material development, but doesn't it just make us all so much more busy? It's very hard to find students, and if a Buddhist teacher had to run around looking for students, that would be a little awkward. Actually it's a very fortunate circumstance for us all to be together here now, because it's a rare event for people to have enough time to meet together like this.

My root guru told me once that different times were coming. He said, "If you happen to be in front of people who ask about and want to hear about the nature of mind, explain it to them. If they have the karmic readiness, they will understand, and if they do understand, they are benefited. To benefit beings is the purpose of the Buddha's teachings. It's all right."

As I mentioned earlier, when I was young, I often tried to do that. It's like someone pointing out the sunrise. Often people look towards the west and see that the sunlight has hit the mountain top; that's how they know the sun has risen. But actually what they have to do is turn around and see the sun rising in the east. When someone tells them to do so, they turn around and say, "Well, yeah, the sun is actually rising in the east!" That is how I have been teaching, and that is how I will continue to teach now.

So: you have heard that our mind is actually empty, meaning it is not a concrete thing, and that at the same time it is able to perceive, to understand, to experience. When you hear this and think about this, can you trust it? Is it clear? Can you decide on this point?

Our mind is empty, and yet it does think. That it is empty means there is no concrete substance with any definable attributes. And yet, mind does think. Isn't it true that we are always thinking about the past, present or future? And aren't we so busy thinking that we have one thought after the other, day and night, incessantly? This is not something that has suddenly happened. It has been going on for a long time, through countless past lives in samsara. We have been spinning around involved in one thought after another in different realms in samsara. That is the essence of samsaric existence. And if we carry on in the same way, we will be busy thinking one thought after the other until the very end of this life. It doesn't stop there. Of course there is no body in the bardo, but mind continues churning out one thought after the other due to habit. After a new rebirth, regardless of whether it's in the lower realms or the higher realms or the deepest hell, everything is simply one thought after the other. Yet all the time, the very nature of all this thinking is buddha nature—the enlightened essence.

Let me give you an example for the relationship between thinking and the nature of mind. The nature of mind is like the sun in the sky, while thinking is like the sun's reflection in water. Without water, it's difficult for the sun to reflect, isn't it? Water here is the analogy for all perceived objects, for anything held in mind. If you drained the water from a pond, where does the reflection go? Does it run out with the water? Does it stay suspended in mid-air? Holding subject and object, perceiver and perceived in mind, is symbolized by the reflection of the sun in the pond. Without the sun in the sky, would there be any light in this world? No, of course not. And yet, one single sun is able to illuminate the entire world. This single sun is like the nature of mind, in that it functions or operates in many different ways: it has great warmth and brilliance, and through its heat it sets wind in motion. In comparison to this, the reflection of the sun is nothing. Is the reflection of the sun able to illuminate the entire world? Can it even illuminate a single pond?

Our enlightened essence, the buddha nature, is like the sun itself, present as our very nature. Its reflection can be compared to our thoughts—all our plans, our memories, our attachment, our anger, our closed-mindedness, and so on. One thought arises after the other, one movement of mind occurs after the other, just like one reflection after another appears. If you control this one sun in the sky, don't you automatically control all its reflections in various ponds of water in the whole world? Why pay attention to all the different reflections? Instead of circling endlessly in samsara, recognize the one sun. If you recognize the nature of your mind, the buddha nature, that is sufficient.

Understand the difference between buddha nature and its expression, which is thoughts. Thoughts appear in many different types. There is attachment, anger and stupidity; there are the fifty-one mental events, the eighty innate thought states, the eighty-four thousand disturbing emotions. No matter how many different types of content the mind can manifest as, they are all simply expressions of the nature of mind.

The eighty-four thousand different types of disturbing emotions are like eighty-four thousand different reflections of the sun in different ponds of water. If you take the sun and put it in your pocket, you automatically control all eighty-four thousand reflections. Similarly, the very moment that you recognize your natural state, the buddha mind, your enlightened essence—in that same moment, all eighty-four thousand types of disturbing emotions are simultaneously vanquished.

All the different thoughts we can have are either of the past, present or future, so they can be called past thought, present thought, or future thought. The Tibetan word for thought is *namtok*. *Nam* means the perceived forms of the five senses and the mental objects. *Tokpa* means the concept formed about what is perceived. Sentient beings are constantly busy producing *namtok*, making one idea after the other about what is experienced. This thinking of your own mind's thoughts is exactly what hinders and obstructs liberation and enlightenment.

If we try to stop thinking it only gets worse. You cannot shake off or throw away the thinking. Can you throw away your shadow? Can you somehow cut the flow of thought created by your own mind, maybe by detonating a nuclear bomb? Will this stop the mind from thinking? It will kill you, sure, but your thoughts will continue in the bardo and into the next life. Is there anything else in this world that can stop the mind from thinking?

To stop thinking, you need to recognize your essence. It's like seeing the sun in the sky just once—forever after, you know what the sun looks like. If you chase one reflection of the sun after the other, you'll never be able to see all possible reflections. There is no end to that. The sun in the sky is the real sun, and without it, there would be no reflections. Its reflection in the water is only an imitation. In the same way, all thoughts are only expressions or displays of your essence; they are not your essence itself. Without being free of thought, without the thinking having dissolved, vanished, disappeared, there is no way to be liberated or enlightened. There is a saying: "Use the thought as its own antidote."

In the same way, the reflection of all suns comes from the original, real sun. If you recognize the real sun in the sky, there is no need to chase around after all its reflections in this world in order to see the sun.

The most important thing is your empty, cognizant mind. Its natural emptiness is dharmakaya, also called empty essence. Your natural ability to know and to perceive is cognizant nature, sambhogakaya. This being empty and being cognizant are an original unity. The famous statement 'unity of empty cognizance suffused with awareness' refers to your own nature, the essence of your mind.

After having been pointed out your nature and recognizing your essence, you see that there is no 'thing' to see. As I have repeatedly said, "Not seeing a thing is the supreme sight." We need to see that. It is seen the moment you look, and in the moment of seeing it is free, liberated.

This seeing may last no longer than a few seconds, perhaps no longer than three snaps of your fingers. After that brief period of time, we either get carried away by the thought of something, or we become forgetful. This happens to all ordinary sentient beings. From beginningless life-times until now, we have been continuously carried away by forgetful-ness and by thinking.

The moment you recognize, it is already seen. There is nothing ex-tra remaining that you missed. This is not like space looking at itself, because space does not see anything. When your mind, which is cogni-zant, recognizes itself, you immediately see that there is no 'thing' to see. It is already seen in the same moment. At that very moment there is no thought, because the present thought has naturally vanished.

The moment of recognizing mind nature is called ordinary mind, whether you talk about Mahamudra, Dzogchen or the Great Middle Way. When recognizing, don't do anything to it; don't try to correct or improve it; don't alter it by accepting one thing and rejecting another, motivated by hope or fear—don't do anything to it. An ordinary person is involved in conceptualizing with the present thought. Don't con-ceptualize with a present thought. Present thought means wanting or not wanting, with hope or fear. Just disconnect from the present thought;

don't follow it up. The moment you are free from thoughts of the three times, that is the buddha mind.

You don't have to try *not* to think the present thought. We need to train in just letting go of what is thought of; that is the practice. In this letting go there is not even a dust mote to imagine, so it is not an act of meditating. At the same time, do not be distracted from this for even one second. It's like trying to imagine space, because there's nothing that needs to be imagined or meditated upon. Do you need to imagine anything to imagine space?

When we hear "Don't be distracted," we may think that we have to do something in order to be undistracted. People usually think that trying to remain undistracted is some kind of deliberate act. This would in fact be so, if the aim was to maintain a particular state of concentration for a long time. Deliberate action would be necessary in that case. But I am not telling you to do that. The moment of natural empty cognizance doesn't last very long by itself, but that's perfectly okay. You don't have try to prolong that moment; rather, repeat it many times — 'short moments, many times.' This is the training in uncontrived naturalness. Uncontrived naturalness means you don't have to do anything during that state. It's like ringing a bell. Once you ring the bell there is a continuity of sound; you don't have to do anything in order for the sound to continue. Simply allow that continuity to endure by itself until at some point the sound fades away.

At the moment of recognizing your mind essence leave it in naturalness, simply as it is. If you keep striking the bell, the sound is interrupted by the effort. Just leave that recognition be without altering it. That is the way to not lose the continuity. Soon enough the recognition will vanish by itself. As beginners, naturally we will forget after a bit. We don't need to try to prevent that or guard against it with great effort. Once distracted, again recognize. That is the training.

Every level of teaching has its own purpose, and even though the very heart of the Buddhadharma is to recognize mind essence and train in that, still, there are obstacles and hindrances that need to be cleared away and enhancement practices that need to be done. An obstacle is something that prevents us from remaining in the natural state. These can be cleared away by certain practices. There are also ways to improve or enhance our practice and to deepen our experience. These two—clearing hindrances and enhancing—are extremely useful.

Outer obstacles are connected with our environment; inner obstacles with our physical body, and innermost obstacles with our thought patterns. To dispel these, it's extremely beneficial to do the preliminaries and the inner practice of deity, mantra and samadhi. Hindrances need to be removed as they are the result of negative deeds that obscure our nature. Relying on the Buddha, Dharma and Sangha and on the guru, yidam and dakini as support quickly clears away hindrances.

Enhancement practices, for instance, are to develop devotion to the enlightened ones and compassion for sentient beings. Devotion and compassion strengthen the recognition of mind nature. Other practices also further enhance mind essence; however, the Third Karmapa stated the most essential point when he said: "In the moment of love, the empty essence dawns nakedly." In the moment that either devotion or compassion is felt sincerely, from the core of our heart, there is really nothing to obscure us any longer. The more we train in devotion to all enlightened masters, buddhas and bodhisattvas, the more our progress in recognizing mind essence will be enhanced. In exactly the same way, generating loving kindness and compassion for all sentient beings will also help tremendously to enhance our realization of buddha nature.

Let us conclude this teaching by engaging in the last of the Three Excellences, the excellent dedication. As a result of having studied these teachings please dedicate the merit and make aspirations for the benefit of all sentient beings.

5

Experience

✻

The essential practice is about nothing other than realizing your mind. It is only your mind which experiences; there is nothing other in this world that can experience. The five outer and inner elements, comprising the world and your body, don't experience anything. Neither do the five sense organs. Thus, it's this mind that we need to be one hundred percent clear about.

Mind is empty in essence and cognizant by nature. It is not a blank and empty state like the sky. Empty space cannot become enlightened, nor does it experience happiness and suffering. The Buddha has said that mind is like space, but it's not exactly the same as space. Even though our mind is empty like space, we can cognize. The knower needs to recognize his own mind. We then see that there isn't even a hair-tip of something to see. It is as the Heart Sutra said: "No form, no feeling, no perception, no formation, no consciousness; no eye, no ear, no nose, no tongue, no body, no mind." That absence of any concrete substance whatsoever is called dharmakaya. Is there anything more precious in this entire world than dharmakaya?

In the moment of seeing that, there is no 'thing' to see. In this moment that fact or experience is an obvious actuality. The cognizant quality that sees that there is no thing to see is called the sambhogakaya aspect of the awakened state. The mind's absence of any concrete thing, and its ability to know that it is no thing, are indivisible, like water and wetness, fire and heat, sugar and sweetness. That indivisible unity of these two aspects—being empty and cognizant—is called the nirmanakaya. At the moment of recognizing you see that these three are inseparable, and that is the svabhavikakaya, the essence-body. This is what I mentioned before: "Seeing no 'thing' is the supreme sight." In this world, is there anything more profound than being face to face with the three kayas? Recognizing this fact is the essential point of all practice.

Every time we recognize the three kayas, not in a conceptual way, but being face to face with them, the three poisons are not merely pushed to the background; they are totally dissolved. It is like a hair that cannot stay in the fire, or the darkness that disperses the moment the sun rises. Conceptual thinking is temporary. In the perfectly clear sky, there are no clouds. Temporary clouds obscure the sun. This sky is an example for the basic space of our nature, while the sun in the sky represents the indivisibility of basic space and wakefulness. The moment the cloud cover vanishes, the indivisible space and wakefulness that is the natural state of the three kayas is immediately an actuality. Clouds can temporarily cover the sun shining in the sky, but sunshine is always indivisible from the sky. So this sunlit space is an analogy for basic space and original wakefulness, which are and always have been indivisible.

We continue in samsara because we've fallen under the power of conceptual thinking. Recognizing mind nature does away with thoughts. In the moment of recognizing, thoughts disappear. If thoughts were substantial or solid, we would not be able to do away with them, but they are merely empty movements, not stable in themselves. Dharmakaya, like the sun, is inherent to our mind nature. Thoughts are like the light of dharmakaya, its expression, just as light rays are the expression of the sun. Remember the essential point concerning mind nature: that it is the three kayas of the buddha.

The most essential training of Dharma practice is to recognize and be face to face with the three kayas—not merely once, but to grow fully used to that. Every time there is a recognition of the three kayas, the three poisons are absent. They totally dissolve at that point. In addition, the intrinsic qualities of basic wakefulness, the wisdom qualities that are fully present at the moment of recognition, will start to unfold further and further.

Phenomena manifest in both pure and impure forms. Impure phenomena is what is experienced in this world. Pure phenomena is when there is no dualistic grasping. It is becoming accustomed to the inseparable, unobstructed, undeluded dharmakaya, in which all phenomena appearing have no self-nature. If you practice diligently in this way, eventually the buddhafields with all the inconceivable qualities will be known, and your own innate wisdom qualities will manifest. Only confused thinking deludes us and prevents us from pure perception. Impure phenomena is thus the manifestation of our own deluded thinking. Impure phenomena—unaware perceptions—are the same as dream phenomena. Once we wake up from the delusion of sleep, they disappear.

The three kayas of the buddhas, the densely arrayed buddha-fields, are profusely decorated with all the different manifestations of enlightened qualities. Right now these are obscured by our impure perceptions. Just like dreams, however, these impure perceptions don't exist once we wake up. They vanish completely; they are finished. This is the understanding you need to gain.

The moment of recognizing mind essence is the instant that impure experience, the habit of fixating on all things as solid reality, disperses into basic space. What is left is pure experience, pure phenomena. Out of that, all the inconceivable great qualities of enlightenment begin to manifest. The great perspective of the three kayas of buddhahood is a natural outcome of pure experience. Experiencing these qualities in actuality is not the same as simply imagining them. Actually *being* those qualities is not like when you think of deities, their mantras and virtues, all of which are still objects of dualistic thoughts. When we begin to grow more stable in the absence of impure experience and the manifestations of pure experience, all these qualities of deities, as well as all the aspects of wisdom, start to become an actuality.

All the qualities of the sun are naturally present within it. They don't need to be made. It is only the clouds that obscure the sun. Once these are gone, the qualities of the sun blaze forth. Likewise, the qualities of the three kayas are present as the essence of our mind. It is only conceptual thinking that obscures this, like clouds obscure the sun. The key point here lies in the recognition of mind essence. Knowing, we obtain the state of buddhahood. Not knowing, we fall under the power of conceptual thinking, and samsara unfolds like a dream.

The training in recognizing mind essence is this: short moment repeated many times. There is no other way. A short duration guarantees it is actually the authentic mind essence, by itself. Many times ensures we will grow used to it. Attempting to keep long moments of recognition will simply corrupt the natural experience with a conceptual state of mind. We have gotten into the bad habit of constant involvement in the three poisons, which create further samsara. As long as this mind keeps projecting outwardly, samsara will continue. But if we train in short moments of uncontrived naturalness, we arrive at flawless dharmakaya.

We do not need to *make* this uncontrived naturalness. Simply give up thinking of the three times. When the past has gone and the future hasn't arrived, your present wakefulness is right here. We all have this cognizant quality—if we don't, we are corpses! Don't investigate or make thoughts about this present wakefulness. Making thoughts is the act of dualistic fixation. Without these thoughts, we are free of the three times.

This unaltered, unfabricated present wakefulness is the buddha nature, totally fresh. Simply leave your present ordinary mind, without either accepting or rejecting anything. Totally free of hope and fear, let your wakefulness be *as it is*, simply and naturally. Then there is only buddha nature by itself. At that moment, there is nothing other than buddha nature! That is what we need, and we have this right now in our hands. The moment you totally let go, uninvolved in either past, present or future, there is only buddha nature by itself. That is the very core, the very heart, of Dharma practice.

Whatever yidam practice you carry out is complete within the view of Trekchö, in the sense of facing the indivisible empty cognizance which is your basic nature. For example, Chakrasamvara, in essence, is the cognizant quality, while Vajra Varahi is the empty quality. The two of them are indivisible. To be face to face with this indivisibility of empty cognizance is to meet the true inner deity in person. That is not the same as having a vision of the deity as coming from outside. Of course, to experience the latter purifies a lot of negative karma. At the moment of seeing a deity you may think, "Wow, there it is, finally!" And you join your palms together and have great respect and devotion, which purifies negative karma. The vision of course doesn't remain; it eventually vanishes and does not permanently cut through the stream of dualistic thinking.

In contrast, in the moment of recognizing the indivisible empty cognizance that is the inner Chakrasamvara and Vajra Varahi, the stream of deluded thinking is interrupted completely, right there. The continuation of all deluded habits from all countless past lives is instantly brought to a halt. Simultaneously, the continuation of all future delusion is interrupted right there as well. The inner Chakrasamvara and Vajra Yogini is the essential yidam. Having a vision of those by recognizing mind essence is more important and profoundly more effective than having a vision of a deity as being outside of oneself.

Of course, when people have a vision of a deity like Chakrasamvara they are exhilarated. They congratulate themselves and say, "How wonderful, I had a vision of the deity." In that happiness and appreciation is a purification of a lot of negative karma, but the taking pleasure in seeing something is still attachment. The opposite of that attachment is aversion. Thus, having a vision of the deity does not eliminate dualistic thinking. All yidams, whether they are male or female, are included within this empty cognizance. This state is described as 'knowing one liberates all.' When you know this one nature, every state of mind can be liberated.

When you start a session, begin by taking refuge three times in the Buddha, Dharma and Sangha. Next, form the bodhisattva resolve with the wish, "I will do this practice for the benefit of all beings." Then imagine yourself in the form of a buddha. It doesn't matter which one it is—whichever one you like best is fine. Think, "I am this particular deity," and chant its mantra. While chanting the mantra, recognize who imagines this deity, what is it that chants this mantra. 'Recognizing' means seeing that there is no thing to see, in actuality. At that moment you don't have to start formulating a philosophy about how emptiness is. Instead, let it be as it naturally is without doing anything to that state at all. Don't get involved in judging. End the session by dedicating the goodness of this to the welfare of all beings. Everything is contained within this simple way of practice.

If you train in this, you could be a cow herder and still be liberated. If you don't train in this, you might be a great scholar and still remain in delusion. When recognizing mind essence, don't do anything to it. Allow it to be as it is; the moment you get distracted, remind yourself again to recognize. When recognizing, leave it in naturalness. When forgetting, remind yourself. That is the training in essence.

By training thoroughly in this way, discursive thinking will gradually grow less and less, and moments of thoughtfree wakefulness will grow longer and longer. When this nonconceptual wakefulness lasts one hour, you have attained the level of an arhat. When it lasts throughout the day, you have attained the level of a bodhisattva. When it is uninterrupted day and night, you have become a fully enlightened buddha. There is nothing more precious than this.

Once you have truly received the pointing-out instruction and recognized mind essence, becoming enlightened through training is not out of reach; it is in your own hands. You can remind yourself to recognize your mind essence as often as possible. If you train in this way, you can be liberated even if you spend your entire day doing something as simple as grazing cattle. If not—if you know all the words of the Dharma but don't really experience the essential meaning—the moment you depart from this life you will just roam about in confusion. This is the essential point.

There is another thing that I would like to say. The Buddha was totally awakened and saw the three times as clearly as if they were held in the palm of his own hand. The teachings are based on this immense clarity. We don't have to speculate about whether the words of the Buddha are true or not. I am not saying this because I am a Buddhist, but because it is really true. It is not the same as certain spiritual systems taught by unenlightened beings who had some partial insight and gave some portion of the truth, but not the complete picture. Because of not being enlightened themselves and not having this completely unimpeded clarity, they were not able to teach in the same way as a fully enlightened buddha. This is something to bear in mind. I am not being prejudiced here, but it is really true that we don't have to judge the words of a fully enlightened being. They have already been checked thoroughly.

Any questions?

STUDENT: How to not be distracted in this practice?

RINPOCHE: When distracted, the best thing to do is simply to recognize your essence. In that moment, we don't see any concrete thing whatsoever. There is an immediate knowing that the essence is empty. There is something that cognizes that the mind is empty, and this cognizant quality is indivisible from the emptiness itself. At the moment that this is an actuality, you don't need to do anything more. Simply let be in naturalness, until at a certain point you forget, and it slips away. That doesn't mean we have to keep pressing ourselves to continuously recognize mind essence. It's like switching on a light in a room: you press the switch once and the light comes on to illuminate the room. In order for that brightness and light to stay, you don't have to do anything. If on the other hand you keep pressing the switch, something gets disturbed. If in order to see the mind essence you keep saying, "I want to see it, I want to see it, I want to see it," it becomes a deliberate conceptual act. Instead, just let be, just like letting the light shine. At that point there is no other technique you have to use. This is called 'naturalness without technique.' We don't have to try to keep the mind essence. It is seen without fixating.

Mind *is* empty, we don't have to make it empty. It's not that there is something remaining that is left out or is incomplete at this point. We usually understand empty as meaning "there is no thing." If you come into an empty room, there is nothing in the room. The mind is like that empty room; in actuality, it is not some object of sight, sound, smell, taste or texture. In the moment of recognizing, we see that immediately. "Seen in the moment of looking, freed in the moment of seeing."

Do not hold onto the notion that mind is empty. To hold an idea "Now it is empty; now it is empty," is a conceptual construct that we keep in mind. That is not necessary. In the moment of recognizing, you see that mind is empty. At that point allow it to be naturally as it is, without applying any technique whatsoever. That is naturalness without technique. That will last for a little while. Your attention will then stray, and you will at some point notice that your attention wandered off. Our mind is not completely beyond us—we know when we get distracted. Simply recognize what was distracted. Again, the moment you do so, you see that there is no thing to see; and the moment of seeing that there is nothing to see, it is free of thought. And again leave it in uncontrived naturalness for a short while. The mind of all sentient beings is already empty; it is not something that we have to create.

When a thought moves, simply recognize the thinker. The thinking then dissolves. No matter what the thought is about, the thinking and the thinker are empty. A thought in itself is not made of any concrete substance; it is simply an empty thought movement. By recognizing the empty essence in a thought, it vanishes like a bubble in water. That is how to deal with any particular present thought at hand. Once you know how to let the present thought dissolve, any subsequent thought can be dealt with in exactly the same way, as simply another present thought. But if we get involved in the thought, thinking of what is being thought of, and continue it, then there is no end.

It is our thinking that propels us or forces us into further samsaric existence. As long as we get caught up in our own thinking, samsara doesn't stop. On the other hand, any thought is an empty thought, in that it has no concrete substance to it whatsoever. It is very easy to notice this, because the moment you recognize mind essence, the thought dissolves right there. The thought vanishes into your empty essence, into your basic nature which is emptiness. There is no remnant whatsoever. That is the only way to solve the problem. When recognizing your essence, the thought is executed on the spot; it is totally obliterated.

Samsara is created when we let our mind extrovert through the five senses. We focus on an object through our eyes, or through the ears, or the nose, and make thoughts and emotions about this object. It may seem like we have different consciousnesses through the different senses, but actually it is one mind that alternately grabs at objects through the various senses. The traditional example for this is of a monkey in an empty room with five windows, restlessly jumping around and looking out through one window after the other. An outside observer might think there are a lot of monkeys in that room, but in fact there is only one. If you catch hold of that monkey and tie it up, there is no jumping around anymore. In other words, the way to capture the monkey is by dissolving the thought.

Another example is of a fireplace in the middle of the house, with smoke coming out through all the openings. If you throw a bucket of water in the middle, the flames are extinguished, and the smoke simultaneously disappears in all directions. 'Smoke' is an example for the expression of the essence, just as thoughts are the expression of dharmakaya. They are not dharmakaya itself, but they are a manifestation of our basic nature. Just like our basic nature, this manifestation has no concrete substance to it.

The essential teaching is *never* to just recognize dualistic mind. That is what all sentient beings are doing all the time—noticing their feelings and thoughts, and then acting upon them. The meditation instruction is not to perpetuate that; it is more than simply recognizing dualistic mind, dualistic thinking. Rather, it is to recognize the essence of this mind. That is the crucial difference. Being caught up in one's thoughts and acting upon these feelings is the cause of endless samsara. This is being caught up in the expression and not knowing the essence itself.

You may have heard this famous statement by the vajra-holders of the Kagyü lineage: "Intrinsic mind essence is dharmakaya; intrinsic experience is the radiance of dharmakaya." Experiences and thoughts are not dharmakaya itself, the same way that the smoke from the flames is not the flames, but is the expression or manifestation of the flames. Caught up in noticing the smoke, you forget the flames themselves. The principle in the practice here is not to be occupied with the smoke, meaning recognize the essence and don't be caught up in the expression. Recognize that this expression doesn't come from any other place than the essence itself.

Caught up in thinking, we focus on the false, the unreal. Yet the real, the indivisibility of the three kayas, is already spontaneously present as our own nature. The choice simply lies in either not recognizing, which is samsara, or recognizing, which is nirvana. If you don't recognize mind nature, you stray again into the three realms of samsara. Recognizing self-existing wakefulness is the very essence of nirvana. At that very moment of recognition, nothing is concealed in any way at all—your nature is laid utterly bare.

The statement that 'not recognizing is samsara' means that the moment you link your mind up with some object of experience, the immediate reaction is one of the three poisons. Either you like something, or you don't like it, or you remain indifferent. Caught up in these three emotions, people might still claim, "I create no negative karma." But how can there be any negative karma besides the three poisons? The three poisons are exactly what creates the three realms of samsara. Attachment creates the realms of desire. Aversion creates the realms of form. Indifference creates the realms of formlessness. Not recognizing one's own essence and being caught up in the three poisons perpetuates nothing other than the three realms of samsara. It is unavoidable.

If you simply recognize your essence, you are immediately face to face with the three kayas. It is so simple that it's actually incredibly easy. There is no way you could miss it. The problem, in fact, is that it's too easy! It's too close to oneself. Some great masters have said the fault lies in not that it is complicated, but that it is too simple. People don't trust it. They think, "This is just my present state of being awake, so what use is it? It's not very special. I want something astounding, something totally different. Something that is far superior to this present state of wakefulness. Something with amazing lights and great splendor." And they ignore their present natural state of mind and hope that something extraordinary will happen, maybe coming down from above. They are right: this present state is not that special. But by sitting and hoping like that, they turn their backs to the innate three kayas. If you recognize your own mind, on the other hand, in the moment of seeing, there is freedom. You are liberated from any thought involvement at that time. That itself is the essence of nirvana. If however, we ignore that fact and chase after something else—some kind of altered state we believe to be superior to the present nature of mind—it is going to very difficult to ever find the buddha mind.

Right now, the difference between samsara and nirvana lies in recognizing or not recognizing mind essence; that should be clear. The moment you recognize mind essence, the present thought involvement dissolves, vanishes without leaving a trace. You are left with the intrinsic three kayas. It is not that we need to create the three kayas or achieve them. You are recognizing what is already there. On the other hand, if you are caught up in what is thought of, samsara goes on endlessly. In the moment of thinking, recognize the identity of that which thinks, and the thought dissolves. That is so easy!

Recognizing is not the problem. Anyone who is taught to recognize their own mind essence will see that it is 'no thing'; they can identify mind essence. The problem lies in our habitual tendencies from innumerable past lives. Just because we recognize once doesn't mean that recognition stays. There is no stability there; it just slips away again. We have the bad habit or the negative pattern of always grasping towards objects. For so many lifetimes, life after life after life as well as in the bardos between, we have been reinforcing the habit of looking away from mind essence itself. We keep re-creating samsara, again and again. Every time you get caught up again, the training is therefore simply to recognize and dissolve the thought.

Our habit of thinking extrovertedly, focusing only on external objects, is what propels us day and night, life after life, and in the bardo state in between. We have this habit in the dream state as well: our body runs around and does things in our dreams, even though it is not a real body, but a body created out of habitual tendencies. In dreams, we experience loss and gain, enemies and friends, and all different types of pleasure, pain, and so forth. But at the moment we wake up, where are all these entities? They are gone without a trace, not to be found any place at all.

The dream state is created by our own thoughts. Likewise, in the waking state, these same thoughts create this whole drama of life. In the bardo state there is no physical body, but due to habit we still believe that we have a physical body with the five senses. Of course there is no real body there; this physical body definitely doesn't go through the bardo. Neither does it go to the hell realms, the buddha-realms and so on. Our present body is a just a temporary dwelling place, like a hotel.

The man living in this hotel right now is the mind. It's he, rather than the body, who will experience all the different effects of various karmic actions. This body won't feel a thing, because as soon as it dies it is gone—there is nothing there. But the mind continues in these patterns, and it will continue to experience. Still, all this experience is no more real than the dream you had last night. It is the dream-like thinking that goes on experiencing the hell realms, it is only more thinking. The bardo is also just more thinking. And when we eventually enter into a new physical body at the end of the bardo, it is more thinking again, day after day, life after life.

Unless we now bring an end to this thinking by dissolving it, samsara is not going to end by itself. It will go on and on indefinitely, as it has through beginningless lifetimes until now. All the while the essence of enlightenment, the fully awakened state, has been with us always; it has never been separate from us for even an instant. The moment you recognize your nature, you are face to face with the three kayas. These three kayas, intrinsic to our buddha nature, were never lost at any point whatsoever.

The Buddha sees that all sentient beings are dreaming: they are dreaming the six realms, they are dreaming the four places of rebirth, they are dreaming all their joys and sorrows. When we are on the bodhisattva bhumis, we are just about to wake up from the dream. Only the fully enlightened Buddha is totally awakened. Buddhas see that beings are ignorant. Sleep is only a subsidiary of ignorance; the real stupidity is not knowing our own awareness wisdom. Buddhist training is all about first recognizing this basic nature, then training in the strength of recognition, and finally attaining complete stability. That is the only way to awaken from this dream state.

We need to obliterate this deluded thinking, and no material thing in this world can do that. The only way is to recognize the insubstantial identity of the thinker and experience the three kayas indivisibly. There is no other way. No drug, not even the strongest anesthesia, will totally eliminate deluded thinking; it only puts it on pause, bringing it to a temporary halt. The moment the anesthetic wears off, thinking begins again. Drugs also block the enlightened qualities of original wakefulness, the wisdom qualities. Under their influence, there is no wisdom of seeing the nature as it is, and no quality of seeing all that exists. Rather, we are totally obscured by mindlessness. To make oneself mindless and oblivious is not a solution. An anaesthetic that lasted forever would certainly wipe out all conditioned states of pleasure, pain and indifference, but there is no such drug. Every drug has only a temporary effect, which soon wears off.

Instead of bringing the mind to a halt, recognize mind nature with its basic quality of unimpededness. A scripture called the *Ngakso*, the *Ocean of Amrita*, says, "By conferring upon you the empowerment of the unimpededness of Samantabhadra, entwined with the non-arising quality of Samantabhadri"—in other words, by conferring this empowerment of the male and female in union, meaning experience of emptiness indivisible—"may your perceiver and perceived," your grasping at duality, "dissolve into basic space." That is what is necessary.

The Tibetan word *yeshe*, original wakefulness, implies an absence of clinging to subject and object, perceiver and perceived, which is not the case with normal mind. Normal mind is always structured as the duality of perceiver and perceived. Without any duality of perceiver and perceived, there is no way a normal thought can survive; it vanishes. The phrase 'single sphere of dharmakaya' refers simply to this original wakefulness. It is called single or sole, meaning not a duality, whereas the normal thinking mind is dualistic, and is never called single. If this holding onto duality is not dissolved from within, there is the perpetuation of subject and object, perceiver and perceived. Another famous phrase goes: "As long as duality does not become oneness, there is no enlightenment." When recognizing, this duality is dissolved into oneness.

The nature of mind is yeshe, original wakefulness, which in itself is free of duality of the perceiver and perceived. The normal mind of sentient beings is called *namshey*. *Nam* is the objects of the senses; the *shey* is the forming of concepts about these objects. Yeshe is the awakened mind of the buddhas, the nirvana aspect, whereas namshey is the deluded mind of sentient beings. Yeshe means to recognize the nature of mind, while namshey means that the wakefulness reaches out through the five sense doors at the sense objects and holds onto them.

Any questions?

STUDENT: Can you explain a little more about our experience in dreams and the bardo state?

RINPOCHE: In the bardo state, you believe you have eyes that see. However, everything is merely experience, whether it is the bardo or the hell realms or any other place. It is all your personal experience. Just because one believes one has eyes and can therefore see does not change the fact that what one is experiencing is basically mind experience. When you dream at night you see all sorts of different things. Are those things seen with the eyes? You believe you have eyes in the dream, don't you? You walk around and look all over, yet in reality your eyes are closed and you're in bed.

Please understand that all your experience is your personal experience rather than somebody else's. It is *your* experience, and thus is different from the personal experience of others. While we are unenlightened, there is an element of shared or general experience. The mountains, the city, the roads, the sky, the five elements, all seem to unenlightened beings to be as they appear. Right now we have what is called impure experience, which means we are constantly solidifying the content of experience into a solid reality. That is the definition of 'impure.' But it doesn't have to remain like that.

When we are training in this practice of recognizing rigpa and becoming great yogis, everything experienced is to be seen as 'the eight analogies of illusion.' These eight are reflections in a mirror, the moon in water, echoes, rainbows, dreams, city of Gandharvas, mirages, and the magical illusions created by a magician. In other words, we are comparing our experiences and perceptions to something that seems to really be there but in reality isn't. Once that illusory nature is seen in actuality, then the solid character that we have attached to what we experience simply vanishes. That is how a great yogi can move freely through what other people see as solid matter. It is not that he somehow becomes really strong and can force his way through solid matter. Rather, it's due to realizing the unreality or insubstantiality of all things.

This doesn't change how other beings experience. For them, 'reality' still seems solid. The way to reach the yogi's realization is by recognizing rigpa. Once we do that, we have hold of one end of the 'rope.' It is like a huge, heavy 100-meter thick rope that's lying in a lake: there is no way you can lift it out all at once. But if you catch hold of one end of the rope, you can slowly pull in the rest. The 'one end of the rope' is the recognition of rigpa we can get right now from a qualified master. At the other end of the rope lies the state of complete realization.

Who experiences all this experience? For who or for what does all this exists? It is only for mind. Besides mind, there is nothing else that experiences. Thus, everything is a personal experience for the mind which experiences, and all experience is nothing other than that.

We cannot really say at this point that everything is empty, because when we touch something that we experience, it seems solid. You can't move your hand through a wall like Milarepa. In *The Rain of Wisdom*, Gyalwa Götsangpa sings about how all appearances are deceptive. "Everything is like a great magical illusion, trickery. The rock behind my back is transparent." Then he leaned back and made an imprint of his back in the rock. To not only consider matter transparent but be able to transverse it as well, is possible for someone who truly attaches no solidity to what is experienced.

A single yogi's realization doesn't remove the solid feeling that all other beings have. When your personal experience is realized to be insubstantial, it doesn't really change it for other beings. For them, the walls and the mountains are still there. Once we fully realize the state of rigpa by training again and again, the five elements are realized to be as they truly are in essence—the five female buddhas. The five aggregates, the five skandhas, are in their natural state the five male buddhas. At this point, you can truly declare that everything is all-encompassing purity.

STUDENT: How can we take rebirth in a buddhafield?

RINPOCHE: The buddha is dharmakaya; his mind is called dharmadhatu wisdom, and the realm is the dharmadhatu buddhafield. This is what we can become stable in; this is our real home—the realm beyond increase and decrease.

Even though all phenomena of samsara are empty, they are not empty of dharmadhatu wisdom. This all-pervasive dharmadhatu wisdom is our real home. If you want to go to the best place, go there. Next best is to go to one of the buddha-fields of the five buddhas. There you can travel about unimpededly each day, and in the evening you are able to return unimpededly back to Sukhavati. These nirmanakaya buddha-fields are magically manifested out of the aspirations, blessings and compassion of the buddhas. It is possible for us to go to the nirmanakaya buddhafields. If you can become stable in recognizing your own nature, there are many buddha fields you can go to. Once there, I am one hundred percent sure that you won't have to go to any of the six realms of samsara. However, if you want to, you can still return there to benefit other beings.

It's very important not to think that everything is voidness, that there is nothing whatsoever. Actually, there are inconceivable great qualities in enlightenment. If you want only voidness, nothing whatsoever, there is such a state in one of the formless realms, at the highest level of samsara, called 'the summit of existence.' When your experience focuses on the idea that space is infinite or consciousness is infinite, or that there is nothing whatsoever, you can enter a state known as 'neither presence nor absence of perception.' Dwelling on that notion, you can be stuck in that for a very long time.

6

Unity of Development and Completion

※

According to the inner tantras, all development stage practices begin with the samadhi of suchness. Suchness means the real, that which truly is. What is real? It is the primordially pure state, also known as Trekchö. The ultimate point of completion stage is the primordially pure state of Trekchö, which is the dharmakaya, here called the samadhi of suchness. In other words, you begin with dharmakaya. The natural quality of that dharmakaya state is called sambhogakaya. Or, said in another way: essence is dharmakaya; nature is sambhogakaya.

The great state of dharmakaya is space-like emptiness. The expression arising out of the state of primordial purity is a spontaneous presence which includes the two form kayas—sambhogakaya and nirmanakaya. There is a poetic saying,

> *Within the all-pervasive space of dharmakaya,*
> *Sambhogakaya manifests distinctly, like the light of the sun,*
> *While nirmanakaya, like a rainbow, acts for the welfare of beings.*

What that means is our essence, which is a primordially pure emptiness, is dharmakaya. Indivisible from that is the natural cognizance, the spontaneously present basis for experience that is the sambhogakaya aspect. Without departing from dharmakaya, the sambhogakaya aspect unfolds. It is like the shining of the sun and moon. They do not come from or go other places to shine; they do so from within space. When the conditions are right, when there is moisture in the air and the sunlight meets the shade provided by the clouds, a rainbow automatically appears. In the same way, nirmanakaya manifests for the benefit of beings out of the unity of emptiness and cognizance.

The training in the development stage follows this exact same principle. Space is primordial purity, the samadhi of suchness, dharmakaya. From this expanse arises experience, sambhogakaya, which is like the sun shining. When the two of these converge there manifests a rainbow, the nirmanakaya. In this way, the three kayas are like a natural progression.

There is no way to practice development stage separate from the completion stage. In fact, to genuinely and authentically train in development stage, according to the inner tantras, it is necessary to receive the pointing-out instruction. Lacking this, one does not identify exactly what the samadhi of suchness is, which is the basic nature of mind. Without that recognition, the second samadhi of illumination is not present because there is no recognition of the cognizant quality. Then the unity of the two, the third samadhi, which naturally takes the form of the seed-syllable and thus is called the samadhi of the seed-syllable, will not naturally happen.

Without the recognition of the samadhi of suchness, of mind essence, each of the three steps—the samadhi of suchness, illumination and of the seed-syllable—becomes a mental fabrication. The meditation becomes an attempt to imitate the three samadhis, using a mantra to dissolve everything into emptiness, while the visualization is constructed as a mental fabrication. This is not the actuality of the three samadhis.

The samadhi of suchness, the dharmakaya principle, is great emptiness, and it is indivisible from your natural cognizance, from the quality of experience. This cognizance is comparable to light or clarity, and therefore it is called the samadhi of illumination. And yet, it takes place without moving away from the samadhi of suchness, without leaving that behind. Please understand that these two are indivisible. This indivisibility of emptiness and cognizance, often called luminosity, is what naturally manifests as the seed-syllable. In other words, allow this indivisibility to take the form of a seed-syllable, like the sun or the moon rising in the sky. That is the third samadhi, the samadhi of the seed-syllable.

That third samadhi is termed 'seed' because it is the source, the seed out of which the buddhafield, the palace, and the deities all unfold. By letting this seed-syllable in the middle of the sky emanate E YAM RAM LAM BAM and SUM, one syllable after the other, each transforms into the mandalas of space, water, fire, earth, and wind, and finally Mt. Sumeru. On the top of Mt. Sumeru appears the celestial palace and so forth. This is the sequence.

In other words, you evolve the development stage within the structure of the three samadhis. Never visualize the yidam as being in your own room, in your little house, in your own country, or even within your concept of this world. Even this is still too narrow, because in actuality there is not only this world. In Buddhist cosmology, one world-system is counted from the vajra hell up to the Summit of Existence, the highest god realm. In between there is Mt. Sumeru, the four continents, eight subcontinents and so forth. All this makes up one world-system, while one thousand of these are called a first-order world-system. If you take each thousand as a single unit and multiply it a thousand times, that is called a second-order world-system. Multiply these again a thousand times, so it becomes one billion, and that is the extent of the sphere of influence of one supreme nirmanakaya buddha. His spiritual reach is such that one billion simultaneous buddhas appear in all these worlds at the same time. Thus, there is no need in practicing development stage to narrow the scope down to being only in one's room or one's house.

The basis out of which development of a deity takes place is primordial purity. From this unfolds the manifest aspect, the spontaneous presence. This spontaneous presence is sometimes called magical compassion, as the luminous cognizance is identical with the compassion. There isn't a single buddha lacking compassion.

The essence is primordial purity beyond mental constructs, while the nature is a spontaneously present compassion. The indivisibility of these two, emptiness and experience, is the seed samadhi. Once again, the first, the essence, the empty, is the samadhi of suchness, dharmakaya. The second, the nature, the cognizance, is the samadhi of illumination. The third, the indivisibility of emptiness and cognizance, the compassion, the nirmanakaya, is the seed-syllable from which the celestial palace and the deity arise.

I am trying to give you a hint as to how the three kayas actually are. Dharmakaya is like space. You cannot say there is any limit in space in any direction. No matter how far you go, you never reach a point where space stops and that is the end of space. Space is infinite in all directions. So is dharmakaya. Dharmakaya is all-pervasive and totally infinite, beyond any confines or limitations. This is so for the dharmakaya of all buddhas. There is no individual dharmakaya for each buddha, as there is no individual space for each country. You cannot say there is more than one space, can you? It is all-pervasive and wide open. It's the same with the dharmakaya level of all buddhas. That is the dharmakaya sphere within which sambhogakaya manifests. No world anywhere in the universe takes form outside of the three kayas—it is simply not possible. The three kayas are the basic dimension within which all mundane worlds manifest and disappear.

This basis is also known as dharmadhatu. Out of this the sambhogakaya appears. The greater sambhogakaya is described as the Five-Fold Immense Ocean Buddhas. In the middle is Buddha Immense Ocean Vairochana. To the east is Immense Ocean Akshobhya. To the west is Immense Ocean Amitabha. To the south is Immense Ocean Ratnasambhava, and to the north Immense Ocean Amoghasiddhi.

The size of these greater sambhogakaya buddhas is described as the following. The buddha Immense Ocean Vairochana holds in his hands, in the gesture of equanimity, a begging bowl of pure lapis. Within this there is an immense ocean. Within it a lotus tree grows and puts forth twenty-five fully opened lotus flowers. The thirteenth of these blooms at the level of his heart, while the twenty-fifth is at the level of his forehead. We ourselves, our world, are somewhere in the thirteenth lotus at the level of the heart center. This lotus has thousands of petals and hundreds of thousands of small anthers. Within each atom in each of these anthers are one billion universes, each group being the sphere of one supreme nirmanakaya buddha.

According to the general Mahayana system, this is as far as the sphere of influence for each of the thousand buddhas of this aeon extends. Their influence is like only one of the particles within the thousands of places within one of these lotuses. Also, in each pore in the body of Buddha Immense Ocean Vairochana, there are one billion world-systems. And he is merely one of the five greater sambhogakaya buddhas: in the other four directions are Ratnasambhava, Akshobhya, Amitabha and Amoghasiddhi. Now you see the immense dimensions involved, as well as the difference between the sphere of a nirmanakaya buddha and a sambhogakaya buddha.

Padmasambhava once explained this to Yeshe Tsogyal, who begged him, "Please show me in actuality what it really looks like." He said "All right, I won't show you the whole thing, but I will show you one fraction." And he showed her the one billion world-systems that fall under the influence of Buddha Shakyamuni. Yeshe Tsogyal fainted from this vision—it was too much. Guru Rinpoche threw water on her and revived her. Then he said "If you can't even grasp the extent of the one billion universes of a nirmanakaya buddha, there is no way you can experience the extent of the greater sambhogakaya realm."

Within these Immense Ocean buddhas is an uncountable number of billionfold universes of nirmanakaya buddhas. In each of these, countless billions of nirmanakayas appear. Whenever there is the opportunity for anyone to be influenced, emanations manifest in whatever way or form is necessary. All these are within one sphere of a nirmanakaya realm, that is for one buddha. The other worlds don't necessarily exist in the same way. While one universe or world-system is being formed, another one might be dissolving, and a third is in the middle of existing. This is a small hint about the extent of the world-systems.

Again, one world-system begins with the eighteen hell realms at the bottom of the six classes of sentient beings. The gods are at different levels: first are the gods in the desire realms which have six abodes. Above that are the sixteen abodes of the realms of form, and above that again are the four spheres of the formless realms of infinite perception. All that taken as one is called one world-system. If you multiply that a thousand times, that is called the one thousandfold world-system or the first-order world-system. If you count these one thousand as a single unit and multiply them a thousand times, that is called a second-order world-system. If you take that resulting one million again as one and multiply it a thousand times, you have the third-order world-system, which is one billion. That is what is talked about when you say the third-order thousandfold universe or the billionfold universe. It is one billion world-systems counted as one. That is the extent of nirmanakaya buddhas like Shakyamuni or Padmasambhava. Their sphere of influence is one billion world-systems.

These buddhas do not have bodies of flesh and blood; they have bodies of rainbow light. Try to count exactly how many worlds there are altogether! The three kayas of the buddhas are amazing and their benefit inconceivable. When we practice development stage, starting with the samadhi of suchness, there is no need to narrow it down to our own little area of the world. If possible, at least take the dimension of one billion world-systems.

Actually, if you want the real truth, a supreme nirmanakaya buddha's sphere of influence is not just one billion! It is a hundred times a hundred billion, however many that is. Usually in the general Sutra system you only talk about the universe being one billionfold world-systems, but according to Vajrayana, it is a hundred times a hundred times billion in each pore of the body of a sambhogakaya buddha. The Vajrayana system views things straightforwardly, exactly as they are, without limiting their scope. There is a difference in depth between sutra and tantra. In tantra, nothing is held back. Buddha Vairochana has in his body a hundred times a hundred billion pores, each of which has a hundred times a hundred million universes. That is the kind of extent we are talking about.

We may wonder why the Dzogchen teachings are available in this particular world. It is because our world is situated at the heart level of Buddha Immense Ocean Vairochana. Our world-system is only one among the hundred times hundred billion, upon one of the thousand pistils in thousand-petaled lotus. In each of these universes or world-systems are one billion or more worlds with sentient beings. There is an unfathomable amount of sentient beings!

For sentient beings in general, there is no end to samsara. But for each sentient being individually, there is an end. Because when we recognize mind essence and become stable in that, the very root of further samsaric existence has been exhausted. For the individual sentient being, samsara does end. But for sentient beings as a whole, there is no end to samsara.

Dharmakaya is all-pervasive and infinite like space. Sambhogakaya is as vast and unfathomable as just mentioned. It is within all these bil-lionfold universes that the nirmanakaya buddhas appear, in order to ben-efit and guide sentient beings. It is possible for sentient beings to be en-lightened, because both samsara and nirvana are pervaded by the three kayas. All worlds and all beings dissolve and unfold within the sphere of the three kayas; nothing takes place outside of it. Therefore, everything is originally and still utterly pure. Yet, what help is this, if individual sentient beings do not recognize the fact that everything is utterly pure? If one is deluded and confused, it doesn't help much. Nevertheless, while being deluded and confused, one's nature is never separate from the three kayas. Even though we wander in samsara, the essence of our minds is the three kayas. By recognizing the essence, training in it and attaining stability in this, we can become enlightened. When thinking of this, there is a point in practicing the Dharma, isn't there?

It is said in one tantra that, "All beings are in fact buddhas, but they are covered by temporary obscurations. When these are removed, they are truly buddhas." What does it mean that all beings are buddhas? It means that within every single sentient being the enlightened essence, sugatagarbha, is present as their nature. It is not that there is some prin-cipal buddha nature that we have to somehow get back to and find. It is not like that. The buddha nature is present, at hand, within everyone already.

Buddha nature is empty in essence; it is also cognizant. There is some ability to know; we can perceive and experience. This is not something way above our heads; we can understand this. We can also understand that being empty and cognizant are indivisible, not two different entities. Isn't it clear by now that the three kayas are intrinsically present in ourselves?

Here's an example. Buddha nature is not the same as space, because obviously space doesn't know anything. Yet we have to use the example of space as a way to point at how buddha nature is. Here in the Kathmandu Valley are thousands of houses. In each house there is space. This space in itself doesn't really differ in quality from one house to another. Let's say that this space is lit up by the rising sun. When there is light, there is no darkness. In the same way, cognizant space is the nature in each sentient being, and yet they are separate, like individual houses with sunlit space in daytime. Still, there is space; the cognizance or clarity is like space suffused with sunlight. Can you separate space and sunlight in the daytime? Can you separate the dharmakaya, which is like space, from the cognizance, which is sambhogakaya? This is how the nature of each sentient being is already. Please understand the meaning of this analogy. It becomes quite obvious when you train in the recognition of mind essence. While being empty, everything is vividly and distinctly experienced, not by the senses, but by mind.

The scriptures of the Great Perfection clearly and exactly describe the basis or origin of samsara and the main essence of nirvana, exactly as it is. These scriptures also explain that which is all-pervasive throughout all states, whether samsara or nirvana. This is not taught in any of the other vehicles. In Dzogchen there is the outer Mind Section, the inner Space Section, the secret Instruction Section. Only in the fourth of the four parts of the Instruction Section, the Innermost Unexcelled Section, is this fully described.

The way to train in the unity of development and completion is without leaving behind the samadhi of suchness. Having been introduced to the nature of mind, the state of emptiness, there is a natural cognizance. This natural cognizance is the samadhi of illumination, sometimes called magical compassion. Allow this compassion indivisible from emptiness to manifest in the form of the seed-syllable that emanates the other letters — E YAM RAM LAM BAM. After this, Mt. Sumeru, the celestial palace and the mandala of the deities unfold. This is called practicing development stage within the completion stage, meaning without leaving the continuity of the completion stage. Without ever parting from the samadhi of suchness, allow all of the visualization to take place.

If we have not been introduced to the natural state of nondual awareness, we must create the visualization through thought. First we imagine emptiness, then the illuminating light, then the seed-syllable, and we try to picture the palace, the deities and so forth. This is not the authentic development stage; rather, it's an imitation of the real development stage. While it's definitely better than nothing at all, it's not the authentic way. The authentic way of practicing development stage is to allow the visualization to unfold as the natural expression of rigpa.

There is another way to unify development and completion: include the completion stage within the development state. While trying to imagine oneself as the deity, palace and so forth, at some point remember to recognize mind essence: "What is it that imagines this? What is it that thinks this?" In the moment of recognizing mind essence, development and completion stage are a unity, because the empty quality of that which visualizes is and always was dharmakaya.

Whichever particular way we choose to practice, we should always unify development and completion. It's only intelligent to do so. If one is deluded, one will sit and try to construct something with thoughts. The best case is when the development stage naturally unfolds from the completion stage — when the natural expression of awareness is the development stage. Let the natural expression dawn as knowledge, as *sherab*, so that it is liberated and the essence is not lost. The true development and completion stages are always interconnected. It is not particularly intelligent to try to solely practice development stage without the completion stage, since this leads neither to liberation nor to enlightenment.

I'm going to talk a little more about practicing the development stage as an imitation of the real thing, as a mere resemblance. At some point in a sadhana there is the mantra OM MAHA SHUNYATA JNANA VAJRA SVABHAVA ATMA KOH HANG. The syllable OM is the nature of all form, and it expresses that everything perceived is Buddha Vairochana, the emptiness of all form. MAHA SHUNYATA means great emptiness. JNANA means original wakefulness, emptiness and cognizance indivisible. In essence, when one recites the mantra one is saying, "I am of the nature of indestructible wakefulness in which everything perceived is a great emptiness."

Then, after a few seconds, one says, "From this state of emptiness, in one instant, I appear in the form of the deity." Imagining this is called the resemblance of the actual development stage. This moment of remembering emptiness is necessary, because to start and finish without emptiness is like the development stage having no head and no tail. Following this, within the state of emptiness, in one instant, the syllable e manifests the mandala of space. Then yam becomes wind, ram becomes fire, and so forth. sum becomes Mt. Sumeru, and bhrung the celestial palace on the summit of Mt. Sumeru.

Development stage is not something false; it is not self-deception, because primordial purity is naturally endowed with spontaneously present qualities. These are the qualities of rigpa, of nondual awareness. If our nature was merely empty, there would be no qualities at all. Instead, it is empty while being an original wakefulness, and the qualities of this wakefulness are inconceivable. This wakefulness aspect means that original knowing is never really lost, even though for us original emptiness may seem to be without such wakefulness.

Right now we are still ordinary sentient beings within the three realms, among the six classes, and life may be hard. We undergo a lot of trouble and experience a lot of misery. It is in our interest to aim in the direction of enlightenment. Enlightenment is what we actually need. Suffering is what we already have. We have already gone through the suffering of taking birth—we may not remember this now, but we have. We now know the suffering of getting older and of falling sick. Ahead of us is the suffering of dying, which we cannot avoid no matter what we do. People can try to soothe themselves by saying there is nothing after death, but that is an idea they have, an assumption. Total extinction is impossible, really, because mind is not something that *can* die. Remember, it is mind which experiences, not the body which is left behind after death. A corpse doesn't suffer; neither does it feel pleased. You can chop a dead body up into a hundred pieces and it won't feel a thing. You can stick all sorts of weapons into it or shoot it, and it doesn't react at all. You can burn it over and over again; it doesn't feel that either. Only mind feels. That which feels suffering is mind and mind only.

Unless this mind attains some stability in the recognition of its own natural state, its nature of original wakefulness, there will be no end to its suffering. What we should kill is dualistic mind, but there is no way to do that. You can kill its temporary dwelling place, but the present house guest which is mind is impossible to kill. Without attaining liberation or enlightenment there is absolutely no way to avoid experiencing further suffering. The mind cannot die—but it *can* recognize its own nature, which is the three kayas.

An important principle in Vajrayana is that the confused state of mind is its own best remedy. In other words, when being angry, attached or closed-minded, you need to recognize the nature of the disturbing emotion. At that moment, it vanishes completely. Nobody else can do it for you. You can ask someone to please take away your disturbing emotions, your three poisons, but there is nobody who can do that. The only solution is to recognize your own essence.

You could, of course, try another method and counsel yourself very sternly, saying, "You have been so bad in the past, chasing after the three poisons, getting involved again and again, roaming through the ocean of samsara. Now don't do it any more!" Will your mind listen? Or you could remind yourself, "I have been through so much, suffered so much, all caused by my disturbing emotions. I resolve that this is the end, I won't ever do it again." But will you truly listen to yourself?

Isn't it better to recognize the nature of mind? To see that there is no 'thing' to see, which is dharmakaya? That which sees the dharmakaya is the sambhogakaya quality. Its indivisibility of being empty and cognizant is the nirmanakaya. In the very moment of looking it is seen. In the moment of seeing, it is liberated, free. That is the best solution, isn't it, because that perpetually cuts through the three poisons. When the three poisons are absent, what is left over but the three kayas? Train in this, and you will capture the throne of the three kayas. You will take hold of your real heritage, your true legacy.

Ordinary human life means neglecting this most precious thing and roaming around chasing after what is utterly futile and pointless. We make ourselves the slave of good reputation, food and clothing. This is what most people pursue: a comfortable life. If we never died, it might be worthwhile to do that! We could go on trying to achieve and achieve, amassing more and more. What happens, though, is that while we may achieve these aims, there is no time to really enjoy them. Sooner or later, tomorrow or the day after, we die, and other people take our possessions away. Maybe our friends will enjoy them, maybe our enemies. After we die, others say, "He had no chance to enjoy everything he had—oh well, now we will!" And they will spend your money and have a good time. They will say, "He has no use for this because he is dead! Now we can use it. He took so much trouble to achieve this, but now we're enjoying it." How useless it is to spend a lifetime accumulating things!

Meanwhile, the spirit of the dead person perceives this whole situation from the bardo, and becomes furious. He thinks, "I took all this trouble so that my descendants could enjoy my wealth, but now other people are taking it. I'm so angry!" That wealth was difficult to gather and difficult to protect. First you had to work hard in order to make money and make it increase. Later, you had to be constantly careful that nobody took it away by theft or by force. After death, through clairvoyance, you can see very clearly exactly what happens. It would be better not to see anything! You would at least be free from stinginess and anger at that time.

The state of samsaric affairs is really sad. It would be better not to know anything. However, the spirit in the bardo has conditioned clairvoyance and pays attention to what happens to his possessions—who is taking it and what they do with it. This creates miserliness and resentment, and these two feelings are a direct cause for falling into the lower realms. If we knew this beforehand, and if we recognized mind essence, there would be no getting involved in stinginess and anger. In original wakefulness, those feelings cannot remain. The five poisons become the five wisdoms. But without recognizing, existence is only miserable. There is nothing but one painful state after another.

Please understand the necessity of recognizing mind essence when practicing development stage. To omit the samadhi of suchness is like having a body with no head. How much use is somebody without a head? How many people do you know without heads?

The most important point in Dharma practice is the samadhi of suchness, knowing mind essence. We can examine this entire world as scrupulously as sifting through a bag of flour, but we won't find anything more important. You have to identify the real starting point and the real starting point has to be *real*—that is the samadhi of suchness. Begin with the actuality of rigpa, because rigpa is not blank or vacant. It has a natural cognizance out of which the development stage can take place.

On the other hand, when your starting point is thought and you want to include the completion stage within that, that completion stage undermines the thought-constructed development stage by dissolving it. You could call this dissolution the "dismantling phase." After building up a lot of stuff, the whole setup vanishes the moment you recognize who thinks this. It's like a child building a sandcastle on the beach. A wave comes, whoosh, and everything is gone. The name for this is not development stage; it is dismantling stage! This approach is not pointless thought, of course; it is fine. But it is not the unity of development and completion. It is not training in rigpa as the samadhi of suchness.

Rigpa is not a state of being oblivious. In it is a vibrant, cognizant quality that can unfold as the development state. That is the way of letting the development stage unfold within the completion stage. There are four types of visualization practice, including the fivefold true perfection, the ritual of the four vajras, and the threefold visualization ritual.[3] The most profound is instantaneous recollection. Out of the samadhi of suchness, whatever should be brought forth is brought forth instantaneously, without having to think of it. That doesn't mean that the state of rigpa somehow gets lost—not at all. This is not the same as when you try to bring completion stage into development stage, which then destroys the development stage, like throwing a bucket of water on a sand castle.

While all four of these approaches are definitely beneficial, the one I discussed is the one to train in. Start with what is real: the samadhi of suchness. There is a reason why all sadhanas have a text. Simply chanting the lines is called 'using words to bring the meaning to mind.' Take a short sadhana of Padmasambhava, for example. There is one line for the samadhi of suchness, another for the samadhi of illumination, and a line for the samadhi of the seed-syllable. Without leaving the state of rigpa, continue the chanting. Each line helps unfold a part of the visualization. That is how to train. That doesn't make the previously mentioned way of recognizing the one who imagines useless at all. However, it is not the perfect development stage which is the luminosity of rigpa. If you start the sadhana with thought, you have by definition already lost the samadhi of suchness.

Let's use a clear, bright mirror as an example for the samadhi of suchness. Then the other two samadhis are like its brightness and the reflection appearing in the mirror. Does that reflection in any way influence or affect the mirror? Does it even change the mirror? If a white reflection appears, it is not that the mirror becomes white, is it? It's the same principle when truly training in development stage. A complete *tangka* can be instantly reflected in a mirror, can't it? The mirror doesn't have to reach out to reflect the tangka; nor does the tangka have to get up and more towards the mirror. The reflection appears instantaneously, fully and completely. The whole image appears, not just the faces and arms minus the legs.

This approach is different from conceptually trying to see a deity reflected in one's mind. When we do it like that, we think of one thing and forget another. Instead, everything is reflected all at once. This is possible because the brightness of rigpa is like a clear mirror. That is the completion stage, where all the things are reflected simultaneously. The development stage is like the tangka.

Right now, when we think of the legs, we forgot the head. When we think of the left hand, the right is forgotten. This is a process of destroying what you have made. The real development stage should unfold within the samadhi of suchness, like a reflection appearing in a bright mirror. Then the samadhi of illumination is like a reflection of a tangka appearing, and the mirror doesn't lose its brightness when the reflection occurs. In other words, don't leave the completion stage behind in order for the development stage to take place. Otherwise, development stage becomes construction work, like making something out of clay or wood. Can a tangka be reflected in a piece of wood?

When practicing the samadhi of suchness, you have to be somewhat familiar with the state of rigpa. When there is a steadiness in rigpa which is the completion stage, development stage is not a problem, because it can manifest as the display or expression of the completion state. In this context, the 'unity of development and completion' is the same as the 'unity of appearance and emptiness.' It's like a reflection in a mirror. A mirror doesn't have to chase after the object. The object is reflected into the mirror.

Please understand well this principle of development stage. Development stage which is initiated by conceptual thought is not the real development stage. It becomes a process of merely replacing one thing with another, because when you think of something new, the former instance is supplanted or replaced; it is destroyed. Better to be like a mirror, letting reflections occur in the state of rigpa without fixating on anything. That is the state of suchness. The quality of experience unfolds just as the tangka is reflected, naturally and easily, in the mirror. When you hold a tangka in front of a mirror, it is not that the mirror somehow chooses what part to reflect. Rather, everything is reflected. To reflect the pure development stage, first be a bright mirror. First understand, then experience, then realize. Try first of all to be a good mirror; a mind essence mirror, a rigpa mirror. A drawing of a mirror is like the mirror of dualistic mind. The real mirror is the rigpa mirror. We can draw a mirror. But can the drawing of a mirror reflect?

7

Capture the Life-Force of All Deities

✻

The different schools of Tibetan Buddhism vary in how they regard the practices of the yidam deity. In the New Schools, the *Sarma* schools, particularly the Sakya, one has to keep the link to the yidam alive through daily recitation of the mantra. Although the link is obtained through empowerment, you must maintain it by keeping up daily samaya practice; otherwise the link vanishes. While it's never said that one who misses daily practice will go to hell, the Sakya tradition insists on daily practice in order to keep the link to the yidam deity. That is why some Sakya lamas have a thick book of daily practices. It's not the same in the Kagyü and Nyingma system, where the emphasis is placed on 'condensing all into one.' In this approach, if you practice one deity, all the others are automatically included within that. If you realize one buddha, you automatically realize all other buddhas at the same time.

The statement, "Realize one buddha and you realize them all," means that all buddhas are one within the expanse of original wakefulness. It is like the immensity of space, the expanse of the sky: we cannot say there is one sky for one part of the world and another sky for another. The entire expanse is the same space. Likewise, the space-like enlightened mind of all buddhas is identical, although they show themselves in different forms. Still, the essence of what they really are does not consist of different entities.

The fact that all buddhas are one in the expanse of original wakefulness is not merely my invention. This is taught by the buddhas themselves. If you can feel confident in that, you will also understand that all the different forms of the buddhas are not like different people that you have to keep in close contact with. It is not as if there were thirty people and you had to maintain a good friendship with each and every one of them. Wisdom beings like buddhas don't have any thoughts, and they don't discriminate as to whether someone likes them or doesn't like them. They are not like normal people. All the many forms of the buddhas have the same identity. By practicing one of them, you automatically keep the link with all of them. Feel confident that that is how it is.

Although all the buddhas are in essence the same, they show themselves in a variety of different ways. In this respect it's the same with us; in essence, we all have buddha nature. With respect to our buddha nature there is no difference between us; we are all basically the unity of empty cognizance. But there are definitely differences between us in how this buddha nature expresses itself as thoughts. While I am happy, another person might feel sad; we don't feel the same. Still, in essence, we are the same.

Deities don't have thoughts, they don't discriminate, and in terms of identity they are like the single expanse of space. Imagine the space within each room in all the houses in Nepal. Although these houses are separate from each other, still the space in itself is not different from one house to another. In terms of basic essence, all buddhas are identical. Therefore, if you realize one you automatically realize all of them.

Whenever you visualize a deity in the development stage, please understand that the basis of that is completion stage. If you can visualize after recognizing mind essence, simply allow the form of the deity to manifest, to take place, within that state. Then there is basically no difference between which deity you practice, because you are simply allowing the form of the deity to be displayed while you are still in mind essence. If one doesn't practice like that—if one practices with ordinary dualistic thought—then all the deities are definitely different: the thought of one automatically excludes the thought of another.

When it comes to realizing a certain yidam, the most important points are: recognize emptiness, do the practice out of compassion for all sentient beings, and be free from hope and fear. If you practice in that way, you are certain to realize the deity; there is no doubt about that. But if you do the practice out of a materialistic motivation, that "I wish I could obtain such-and-such," this expectation postpones the accomplishment. You will never realize the deity through hope and fear. First of all recognize mind nature; next, engender compassion for all beings; then, give up hope and fear. By training in this way, you will definitely accomplish the deity.

You can begin to visualize a deity by looking at a tangka. It gives you a visual impression, a visible form, but the real deity is not exactly like that, because a tangka is tangible; you can take hold of it with your hand. The form of the deity you imagine is visible, but not tangible. It is empty and yet you can see it. It is like the reflection in the mirror, in that you can see it but you cannot take hold of it.

There are four major schools of Tibetan Buddhism: Kagyü, Sakya, Nyingma and Geluk. In all four of these traditions, when we practice development stage, we need to start with the samadhi of suchness. Suchness means the innate nature of your own mind. It is not some other suchness from some other place. That suchness is simply the completion stage. The *complete* in completion means what is completely present as your own nature, which is the dharmakaya nature of mind. To recognize that is called completion stage. While recognizing mind essence, while remaining in the samadhi of suchness, one allows the visualizations of the development stage to take place without leaving the natural state behind. Out of the expanse of the three kayas, the practice of sadhana takes place for the benefit of beings. Both samsara and nirvana always manifest out of the expanse of the three kayas.

The first of the three samadhis, the samadhi of suchness, means primordial emptiness. It is actually the essence of the kayas of all buddhas. The empty essence is the quality of enlightened body. The cognizant nature is the quality of enlightened speech. The unconfined capacity of awareness is the quality of enlightened mind.

The body, speech and mind of all buddhas are also expressed as follows: the unchanging quality is body, the unceasing quality is speech, and the unmistaken quality is mind. In the deluded state of being, a manifestation of these three qualities becomes the body, voice and mind of sentient beings.

Thus, in these three qualities you have both samsara and nirvana, the body, speech and mind of all buddhas, and the body, speech and mind of sentient beings. In this way the nature of the three kayas permeate both samsara and nirvana. It may sound like there are three separate things, like one is dharmakaya, another is sambhogakaya and the third is nirmanakaya, but actually it is one indivisible identity. That is the *svabhavikakaya*, the essence body, which is no other than the nature of your own mind. This pervades or is present throughout all of samsaric and nirvanic states.

The body, speech and mind of all sentient beings is nothing other than the expression or the manifestation of the body, speech and mind of all the buddhas. They don't come from anywhere else. If we fully recognize the identity of this, we become totally stable. That is called 'awakening to the enlightenment of the body, speech and mind of all buddhas.' But if we fail to recognize our own nature, we are bewildered and continue to roam about in samsaric existence, just as we are doing now.

To repeat the tantra, "All sentient beings are buddhas, but they are covered by temporary obscurations. When these are removed, they are truly buddhas enlightened." Although the very identity of all buddhas and beings is the same, when we don't recognize it we continue in samsara. It is a case of 'one identity with two aspects.' We can be enlightened and are able to attain buddhahood because we already have the very essence of enlightenment—buddha nature. Without that, there is no way that we could attain any enlightenment.

Of completion stage and development stage, completion stage is the most important. It's like the very life-force in that we already possess it; the innate three kayas are the nature of our mind. Completion stage is the three kayas of the awakened state. While we already have these and don't need to work to create them, we *can* develop their manifest quality. Development stage is what we imagine, what we allow to play in the field of our mind.

There is mind and mind essence. Mind is different from essence. That which thinks and imagines is dualistic mind, while in the essence there is nothing thought of or imagined. The three kayas are naturally present in the essence, and in one way they become manifest in form through the act of visualization. We do so in order to gain the accomplishments and to purify obscurations. The foremost way to do this is to allow all the different aspects of the development stage to take place while recognizing mind essence. That is first-class, the best way. However, even if one does not know mind nature and practices development stage, development and completion are still a unity, since mind essence is an unconfined empty cognizance. It is essential to understand the basic principles of yidam practice with regard to these points.

In order to outwardly manifest the qualities of the three kayas—the yidam's body, speech and mind—we go through a variety of different steps during sadhana practice: we make offerings, recite the mantra, imagine light rays being radiated out and absorbed back, make praises and apologies, request to turn the wheel of Dharma, beseech the buddhas not to pass away into nirvana, and dedicate the merit. All these steps are different ways of removing the clouds in the sky. Together, they constitute what is traditionally called purifying the obscurations, the gathering of the accumulations of merit and wisdom. They are the skillful and compassionate means of the buddhas, and as the expression of wisdom, are incredibly effective. Never regard development stage as meaningless, pointless or unimportant.

The most vital point in development stage is described as 'capturing the life-force of all buddhas.' In other words, if you realize the completion stage there is no way you can avoid realizing all buddhas and yidams. Without the completion stage, all the buddhas and yidams are only something we imagine. When you recognize well that mind essence is beyond achieving, the deity is automatically accomplished. Really, there is no other profound technique than this to realizing the deity.

The ultimate aim of yidam practice is to recognize the nature of the three kayas as indivisible from your own mind. The visible aspects that can manifest are automatically accomplished within recognition of our mind essence. Though they manifest outwardly, inwardly one is not creating anything whatsoever.

Completion stage is like having an electric light bulb in the center of your heart, while development stage is like painting an image of a light bulb on the wall. The painted light can never really be switched on, but will remind you that there actually is a real light, and you can thus recognize it more easily. This is the difference between the two.

We need both development and completion stages. While we are not yet stable in samadhi, in the completion stage, the visible aspects of the development stage help us to purify obscurations and gather the accumulations of merit and wisdom. This has a great and deep significance in that they remove the obscurations. Never think that the development stage is unnecessary. Often the phrase 'identifying the deity to be accomplished' is mentioned. It means we should identify that the ultimate deity is actually the completion stage, the very nature of our mind. That is what we should acknowledge as the deity to be accomplished.

The buddhas never teach that we can attain enlightenment only by means of the development stage. One attains enlightenment by the unity of development and completion. But the real, vital force in attaining enlightenment is the completion stage. It's possible to attain enlightenment only through the completion stage, but not only through the development stage. Still, the swiftest way to attain enlightenment is by unifying means and knowledge.

Means is the development stage and knowledge is the completion stage. You may have knowledge in the form of a person who can put an entire airplane together, but if you don't have the means, which is all the parts, you can keep that person as long as you like, but you'll never have an airplane. Conversely, you can have every single part of an airplane, all the means, but if there is not the know-how of a person who can assemble them, there is no way that those pieces will fly by themselves. It is only when you put the knowledge together with the means that it is possible to have an airplane that can actually fly.

The reason why the Secret Mantra, Vajrayana, is said to be a swift path to enlightenment is simply because of unifying means and knowledge, development stage and completion stage. Vajrayana practice involves combining the visualization of a deity together with the recognition of mind essence; that's why it's a swift path.

Here's another example for 'realizing one deity, you realize all of them.' Let's say that you have one thousand electric bulbs. You wire them, but you haven't switched on the electricity. What good are those thousand bulbs going to do in terms of illuminating anything? But if you turn on the electric switch, the one thousand bulbs will light up at the same time. Even though they are individual and distinct, the light that shines through them is the same in identity. In essence it is the same light. No matter where in the world you have electric light, that light shines and illuminates in exactly the same way, although it may vary according to the condition of the bulb. The main force, like the electricity that lights the bulbs, is what we call original wakefulness, *yeshe*. And that is the most important thing. If you realize that, you've realized the light in every single one of the bulbs, not just one of them.

Or maybe the bulbs are different colors, so that when the light shines through them, one bulb is yellow, the others blue, green or red. This is an example for the lights of the five wisdoms. While the colors or the specific qualities of each emanation may differ, the light that shines through them is the same original wakefulness. Please understand this.

If this wasn't so, we would be able to argue whether development or completion stage was best. It would be like development stage and completion stage getting into a fight. Please understand that the means is development stage and the knowledge is completion stage, and that they are both important. It is the union of the two that is most vital.

Don't think that there are no real deities; that they are nothing but our imagination. There are deities intrinsic to our buddha nature, which are wisdom deities. In the same way, no matter what color the bulb is, whether blue, red, white, or green, the light that shines is exactly the same. You may have ten thousand or a hundred thousand bulbs, but without electricity to shine through them, they're useless. In the same way, we need completion stage together with development stage.

You may succeed in visualizing ten thousand or even a hundred thousand different yidams as clearly and distinctly as if they were present in person; but your practice still needs to combined with the completion stage. If not, it's like having all the parts of an airplane but lacking the knowledge of how to put them together.

Without knowing mind essence, one is forced to practice Vajrayana as an imitation of how it really is. That is a second-rate development stage. One needs first to say a mantra, such as OM SVABHAVA SHUDDHO SARVA DHARMA SVABHAVA SHUDDHOH HANG, and imagine that everything becomes emptiness. Out of this state of created emptiness the seed-syllables for space, wind, earth, water, fire, and the celestial palace gradually appear, followed by the deity, and so forth. These are all something that one imagines. Honestly, saying that the mantra makes all things become emptiness is not really true, because all things were *already* emptiness. It is not that they all of a sudden become emptiness because you think it. If one hasn't recognized mind essence, one doesn't see that. The thinking of one thing after the other then becomes an imitation of the true development stage because of not really knowing the completion stage.

On the other hand, you may have been introduced to the nature of mind and recognized the samadhi of suchness. Suchness means how it really is, not merely how one imagines it to be. While not departing from this state of suchness—while recognizing mind essence—one can then allow the different aspects of development stage to be played out or displayed, without leaving the state of suchness behind. That is the real unity of development and completion. There is a real way and a simulated way, and without recognizing mind essence there is no chance that one can practice the real way.

The real way of practicing the unity of development and completion means that you have been introduced to the view of Trekchö, cutting through, the real samadhi of suchness. It is like the example I gave of a blank mirror. Anything can be reflected, and when reflected, the reflection has no substance or materiality whatsoever. And yet, it is clearly visible.

The seed samadhi, the third of the three samadhis, is like the reflection appearing, while the brightness and the mirror itself is like the first two samadhis, which are emptiness and cognizance. The samadhi of suchness is emptiness and the samadhi of illumination is the cognizant or bright quality. These two are indivisible, and out of this indivisible unity of emptiness and cognizance, also called emptiness and compassion, any reflection can take place; any form of development stage can take place freely. Whatever unfolds as development stage indivisible from completion stage is experienced, but it has no material nature. This is only because of recognizing completion stage. Without that, development stage is like the building work going on outside my room. It becomes construction work, which means that something is visible, but also tangible.

Let's say that you've received all the empowerments for the *Rinchen Terdzö*, the *Treasury of Precious Termas*, a cycle of teachings with many, many deities. It takes four months to receive all the empowerments. If your style of practice is according to the New Schools, you would have a huge stack of daily practices, all of which you have to chant. You'd have to be chanting continuously from morning to evening in order to get through these and say the mantras. At the end, you'd think, "Whew, today I made it, I got through this; I still have the sacred bond to all the deities, they haven't left me." Then perhaps one day you forget one of them or you are not able to do the practice. You think, "Oh no! Now I broke off the sacred link to this yidam, I've broken my samaya, and for sure I will go to hell." Then you're really in trouble. The trouble comes because there are so many different forms of yidams that it becomes very difficult to keep the bond to each of them individually.

You can also take the approach that every yidam and every buddha is identical in the expanse of original wakefulness. Then you can keep the bond to all of them very simply, for example, by chanting the three syllables for the body, speech and mind of all the buddhas, om, ah, hung. om is the essence of Vairochana, the Manifester of Forms, the enlightened body of all the buddhas. ah is the essence of Amitabha, Boundless Light, which is the speech of all buddhas. hung is the essence of Akshobhya, the Unshakable, which is the nature of mind free of conceptual thinking. The hung syllable is the essence of the mind of all buddhas. Actually it would be perfectly fine to chant om, ah, hung ... om, ah, hung while recognizing mind essence. You are then keeping the samaya with every possible aspect of the yidams and buddhas, because all of them are included within enlightened body, speech and mind.

Now think of all the teachings given by the buddhas. In this world, the *Tripitaka,* the *Kangyur* and *Tengyur*—the Words of the Buddha and the treatises that are the commentaries upon them—fill hundreds and hundreds of volumes in incredible detail. Then there are all the tantras. However, the very essence of all these teachings is development and completion stage. When seeking to perfect comprehension you can go into great detail, but when it comes to applying this comprehension to your experience, you should condense everything and simplify it. In other words, these three syllables, om, ah, hung, contain the body, speech and mind of all buddhas, all teachings and all samadhis.

Similarly, the body, speech and mind of the victorious ones are contained in a single instant of recognizing mind essence. om the essence of Vairochana, which means 'manifest in form.' The form of the deity is something visible, something manifest in form. For example, in the bardo state we meet the sounds, colors and lights, the major and minor spheres of light, the peaceful and wrathful deities, and so forth. Everything we meet here is something perceptible, which is manifest in form, and that is the body aspect of all buddhas. Next is ah for speech. Speech is Amitabha, boundless light, which is all the unending infinite teachings all contained within one syllable. The hung for mind is Akshobhya, which means unperturbed or unshakable—the state of nondual awareness, free of any conceptual thinking whatsoever. In this way, the three syllables om, ah, hung embody or include the body, speech and mind of any buddha form in any way whatsoever. You can go into all of this in great detail when trying to comprehend, but when applying it in your own experience, condense everything into the essential.

The essence of the body, speech and mind of all the buddhas is called deity, mantra and samadhi. The way to condense that into the essential is that deity is something you visualize, rather than something you make by hand. It's not a big construction. It is the recollection that "I am such-

and-such deity." At that moment you have imagined yourself as being a certain deity, so that is very simple. With your speech, which is mantra, say om, ah, hung. With your mind, which is the samadhi aspect, recognize mind essence. Everything is included within this simple approach.

Unless we train in the three principles of deity, mantra and samadhi, as sentient beings our minds are always carried away by the three or five poisons. For example, look at this cup. You think this is a nice cup—well, that is desire. When you look at this used handkerchief you don't like it. That is anger or aversion. This unused toothpick is neither good nor bad, right? When you look at that you don't feel attracted to it, you don't get angry at it, you just feel neutral. Any thought that we think is like one of those three. There is no state of dualistic mind which is not mixed with the three poisons. When we see something nice, we like it. If we see something ugly, we dislike it. Something in-between, we feel indifferent, right? Also, when we hear something nice, when we smell something sweet, when we taste delicious food, we like it. If it tastes foul, we dislike it. We all have the three poisons. When something appears in our mind which is pleasant, we like it; if it's painful, we dislike it. We do have pleasure and pain, don't we? But anything in between we don't care much about, we dismiss. Whatever appears to our six senses, we always react to with the three poisons.

Development stage is simply changing this pattern into white thoughts, by imagining the celestial palace, the form of the deity, the offerings. When we imagine Mt. Sumeru after the five syllables, the celestial palace on top of the vajra-cross, the deity and offerings, all this purifies our habitual thinking. We chant the invocation, and the wisdom deities appear in the sky and dissolve into ourselves. "I myself am a deity; I emanate rays of light turning into offering goddesses who turn around and present boundless offerings and praises to myself as a deity." All this is something we imagine, and it changes our thought pattern into white thoughts. That was about the deity, for the body aspect.

Next we imagine the three *sattvas*: samaya sattva, jnana sattva, samadhi sattva, which are the triple beings called the samaya being, wisdom being and samadhi being. The samadhi being is a seed-syllable in the center of our heart encircled by the garland of the mantra, which spins and shines out rays of light. There are a lot of different activities and functions related to the recitation of mantra that belong to the speech aspect. When it comes to the samadhi or mind aspect, you simply recognize what is it that imagines all this. Experience the state of indivisible, empty cognizance.

The development and completion stages are taught by the buddhas out of skillful means and great compassion. These teachings are extremely precious and effective. The whole purpose of the development stage is, first, to transform black thoughts into white thoughts. The purpose of the completion stage is to let the white thoughts dissolve tracelessly. When you recognize mind essence and see the state of indivisible empty cognizance, that dissolves even the whitest of thoughts, so that no trace is left behind.

People sometimes say, "I want a vision of the deity." They expect that after reciting a certain number of mantras the deity will arrive in front of them and they will see it. Actually, that attitude externalizes the deity. The real deity is the unity of emptiness and cognizance, the nature of your own mind. Instead of ringing the bell and beating the drum, expecting the deity to appear up there in the sky before you, you should simply recognize what it is that imagines all this. At that time you see the state in which emptiness and cognizance are indivisible. That is being face to face with the real deity. Isn't that much easier than hoping a deity will appear from the outside? The real vision of the deity is to recognize the nature of your mind.

Even if you look for a billion years into the nature of your mind, you will never see that it is any concrete 'thing' other than being empty. That is the dharmakaya deity, and when you look, you see it. No matter how you investigate, analyze and scrutinize this nature of mind, you will never find it to have any sort of concrete, material substance. That's why it's called unconstructed emptiness. To recognize this is to be face to face with or have a vision of the dharmakaya buddha. What is it that sees that mind is empty? There is some cognizant, aware quality that can see that it is empty. This is unlike space; space doesn't see itself. Mind, on the other hand is cognizant as well as empty. The empty quality is dharmakaya, the cognizant quality is sambhogakaya, and their unity is nirmanakaya.

This is the easiest way to have a vision of the deity, as well as the real way. The superficial way is to expect a deity to appear as coming from outside, after ringing the bell and beating the drum. Actually, though, the easiest way is to have a vision of the deity as the completion stage. That is also the true way. If you only practice the development stage by feeling, "I wish the deity would come, I wish the deity would come," that is training in hope and fear. It only pushes the true deity farther away.

Recognizing mind essence captures the life-force of thousands of buddhas. When you take hold of the life-force they cannot escape you. Through the power of the genuine state of samadhi you capture the life-force of all the deities, without having to conjure them up as being somewhere over there in the distance.

There is another way as well, in which one tries to please a deity in a solid, rigid sort of way, thinking that the deity really exists somewhere up there. This kind of attitude thinks, "I must put offerings out, otherwise he will get angry. If I put nice offerings he will be pleased. If I chant the mantra I make him happy, and if I forget, he will be upset. If I break the bond with him, it will make him feel very bad." That attitude is also called training in hope and fear, and it is not the genuine way.

It is much simpler to practice like this: first, remind yourself with the thought of being the deity, for example, "I am Vajra Kilaya." Then, recite the mantra, om benza kili kilaya, or simply om, ah, hung. Next, recognize what is it that imagines the deity and what is it that chants the mantra as being nothing other than your own mind.

Without this mind, there would be no visualizing the form of the deity. Without mind, there would be no chanting the mantra. When you look into what it is that imagines or recites, recognizing your own mind, you see that it is an indivisible empty cognizance, and not in some round-about way. For example, if you want to touch space with your finger, how far do you need to move your finger in order to touch space? Doesn't it touch it the moment you first stretch your finger out? In the same way, the moment you recognize, you come in contact with the completion stage—the empty and cognizant nature of mind. It is recognized immediately. Thus, while seeing the nature of mind, you can carry on chanting the mantra.

When beginning your practice session, don't neglect to imagine the form of the deity. Without looking in the mirror, the face is not seen. Visualizing the deity means the mind mirror is allowed to think, "I am Vajra Kilaya." It is all right to remind yourself that you are the deity, because your five aggregates and five elements from the very beginning are the mandala of buddhas.

In this way, by using the single thought, "I am the deity," visualization takes no more than an instant. This instantaneous recollection, bringing the deity vividly to mind in an instant, is the highest and best form of visualization. With your voice, chant the mantra, and with your mind, recognize. If you can decide that this type of practice is sufficient and all-inclusive, that is perfectly all right. It's not like we have to please the wisdom deity, which has no thoughts anyway. Wisdom deities don't get pleased or displeased, so it is really more a matter of making up your own mind and practicing in this simple, all-inclusive way. This is my opinion. Maybe I'm being too simple here. On the other hand, maybe it is true.

The wisdom deity represents what is called *rangjung yeshe* in Tibetan, or *swayambhu jnana* in Sanskrit: self-existing wakefulness. In this way, the wisdom deity is indivisible from the nature of our own mind. The wisdom deity has no thoughts, and thus doesn't discriminate and is not pleased or displeased by our actions. However, a text cites, "Although the wisdom deity holds no thoughts, still, its oath-bound retinue sees the faults of people." While the wisdom deity itself is not made happy by offerings or is not displeased if one forgets. Its total realization acts like a magnet to attract all sorts of mundane spirits. These mundane spirits do have shortcomings, they do have thoughts, and they do see the faults of people. They can either help or harm. The retinue of wisdom deities include the *mamos*, the *tsen*, the *dü*, and all the different earth, fire and water gods. Whether you make offerings or not does make a difference to them. But for wisdom deities themselves, it makes no difference, because they have no thoughts.

To reiterate, carry out whatever yidam practice you are involved in while practicing it within the structure of the three samadhis and while recognizing mind essence. If you practice like that, I can guarantee that within this one lifetime you can accomplish both the common siddhis and the supreme siddhi of complete enlightenment.

Let me tell you a story to illustrate this. Sakya Pandita was not only an extremely learned master, but he was accomplished as well. He had developed clairvoyance based on sound. Traveling through a place along the Tibetan border, he listened to a stream running down the mountain. Through the water he heard the mantra of Vajra Kilaya mispronounced OM BENZA CHILI CHILAYA SARVA BIGHANAN BAM HUNG PHAT. He thought, "Someone must be saying the wrong mantra up in the mountains; I'd better go up and correct him." He went up there and found this insignificant little meditation hut with a lama sitting inside. Sakya Pandita asked his name and what he was doing, and the lama replied, "My yidam is Vajra Kilaya and that is what I'm doing." Sakya Pandita asked, "What mantra are you using?" and the lama said "OM BENZA CHILI CHILAYA SARVA BIGHANAN BAM HUNG PHAT." Sakya Pandita said: "Oh, no! That's the wrong mantra; it's supposed to begin with OM BENZA KILI KILAYA. That's where the real meaning lies, in the words: 'Vajra Kilaya with consort, the Ten Sons and all the Eaters and Slayers.' They are contained within the sounds of the mantra." The meditator replied: "No, no, the words are not as important as the state of mind. Pure mind is more important than pure sound. I said CHILI CHILAYA in the past and that's what I will continue to say in the future. No doubt about that! You, on the other hand, will need my phurba." And the meditator gave Sakya Pandita his kilaya dagger, saying, "You take this with you." So he did.

Some time later, in Kyirong, which is on the Tibet-Nepal border, Sakya Pandita met with Shangkara, a Hindu master who wanted to convert the Tibetans. The two had a big debate, with the winner of each round getting one parasol or umbrella as a symbol of his victory. Each had won nine, and there was one left. At that point Shangkara flew up into the sky, as a magical display of his siddhis. While he was levitating there, Sakya Pandita took his dagger and chanted "OM BENZA CHILA CHILAYA. . . ." Shangkara fell straight to the ground, and Sakya Pandita won the tenth parasol. It's said that Buddhism in Tibet survived because of that.

An old saying has it that, "Tibetans ruin it for themselves by having too many deities." They think they have to practice one, then they have to practice another, then a third and a fourth. It goes on and on, and they end up not accomplishing anything, whereas in India a meditator would practice a single deity for his entire life and he would reach supreme accomplishment. It would be good if we were to take this attitude. If we practice Vajrasattva, it is perfectly complete to simply practice that single yidam. One doesn't have to be constantly shifting to different deities afraid one will miss something, because there is absolutely nothing missing in the single yidam one practices.

A line from one tantra says, "I apologize for accepting and rejecting the yidam deity." Sometimes one feels tired with a particular practice, like "It's enough, practicing this one yidam!" Then you give up that one and try practicing another one, then after a while, another. Try not to do this.

As I said earlier, if you accomplish one buddha, then you accomplish all buddhas. If you attain the realization of one yidam, automatically you attain realization of all yidams at the same time. Of course, there is nothing wrong with practicing more than one. The point is to not skip around between them.

Practice whichever yidam you like best. You will naturally feel more inclined towards one yidam than another, and this feeling is a very good indication of which yidam you are connected to. The basic guideline is to choose whoever you feel most inspired by. Once you choose one, practice it continuously.

There are no essential differences between the yidams. You cannot say that there are good or bad yidams, in that all yidam forms are included within the five buddha families. It is not that one buddha family is better or worse than any of the other ones—not at all. People's individual feelings do make a difference, in that some people want to practice Padmasambhava as their yidam, while some want to practice Avalokiteshvara or Buddha Shakyamuni or Tara. The preference varies from person to person due to karmic inclination. It is not that there is any distinction in quality between yidams. If you take the one hundred peaceful and wrathful deities as your yidam, you have everyone included.

Once you reach accomplishment, you have simultaneously accomplished all enlightened qualities, regardless of which yidam you practice. It doesn't make any difference. For example, when the sun rises, its warmth and light are simultaneously present. If you accomplish one buddha form, you simultaneously accomplish all buddha forms. The reason is that all yidams are essentially the same; they differ only in form, not essence. The fundamental reason one attains accomplishment is because of recognizing mind essence while doing the yidam practice. The real practice is recognizing rigpa, and you use the yidam as the external form of the practice. Even though every yidam manifests various aspects of different qualities, in essence they are all the same.

You can describe the rising sun in all sorts of different ways: some people will say that when the sun rises, it's no longer cold, or that there's no more darkness, or that it becomes light and you can see. It's the same with describing the different qualities of the enlightened state, in which all the qualities such as wisdom, compassion and capability are spontaneously present.

Try to see yidam practice as a gift which the buddhas have given to us because we have requested it. When we take refuge we are asking for protection, to be safeguarded, and the real protection lies in the teachings on how to remove the obscurations and how to attain realization. The real protection is the yidam practice. Through it we can remove what needs to be removed and realize what needs to be realized, and thereby attain accomplishment.

Although we have this enlightened essence, it is like a butter lamp that is not yet lit, not enlightened yet. We need to connect with, to touch it with a lit butter lamp in order to light our own. Imagine two butter lamps together here: one is not lit, the other is already enlightened. The one that is as yet unlit has to bow to the other in order to get the light.

In the same way, we already have the buddha nature, but we haven't caught on to it yet. We haven't recognized, trained in it, and attained stability. There is great benefit in connecting with those other "lamps" because they *have* already recognized their buddha nature, trained in it, and obtained stability. Our butter lamp is ready to be kindled, to catch the flame, but it hasn't recognized itself, it hasn't trained, and it hasn't yet attained stability.

There is benefit in yidam practice. Mipham Rinpoche had a vision of Manjushri, his supreme deity, and through that became a great pandita, an extremely learned scholar. Many of the Indian *mahasiddhas* practiced Tara sadhana. They combined recognizing mind essence with the yidam practice and attained accomplishment. All the life stories of those who became great masters tell of yidam practice. You never hear of anyone saying, "I achieved accomplishment and didn't use any deity. I didn't need to say any mantra." The yidam deity practice is like adding oil to the fire of practice; it blazes up even higher and hotter.

8

Overcoming Obstacles and Demons

※

There are definitely obstacles, and generally speaking there are three kinds: outer or external, inner, and innermost. External obstacles are imbalances in the outer elements, which manifest as natural disasters like earthquakes, floods, fires, and hurricanes. These create a lot of obvious difficulties for sentient beings.

Inner obstacles are imbalances in the nadis, pranas and bindus—the channels, energies and essences, also called the structuring channels, the moving winds and the arrayed essences. These can be disturbed in various ways. The channels can be constricted, the winds or energies can be reversed and move in the wrong way, or the essences can be deranged. 'Essence' here means mainly the white and red elements obtained from the father and mother. These three serve as the blue-print, the basic structure, for the human body. When they suffer from imbalances, we feel that our illusory physical body is sick. Of course, there are certain remedies we can use to cure such imbalances.

Most considerable, though, are the innermost obstacles, which involve fixating on perceiver and perceived. Basically this refers to our habit of dualistic experience, which is caused by lack of stability in the original basic state of empty cognizance. When this empty cognizance is not stable in itself, its expression is to reach out and fixate on the five objects of experience—the five sense objects. They are the perceived. The perceiver is the mind that fixates upon them.

Although this basic original state of self-existing wakefulness has no duality whatsoever, because of fixating upon the experience as being something other, seeming duality takes place. This seeming duality is then continued. This perpetuation of dualistic experience is exactly what characterizes the minds of all sentient beings. The minds of sentient beings are caught up in fixating on perceiver and perceived. This is the very core of samsaric existence, and this is in itself our innermost obstacle.

No one is beyond obstacles. We are all hurt and injured again and again by these three levels of obstacles. External obstacles, the calamities of the four elements, can be dealt with by either moving to some other place or performing certain practices to appease or pacify the elemental forces.

The inner obstacle of imbalances in the vajra body, in the channels, energies, and essences, shows itself in physical sickness as well as various other ways. You can take medicine to treat these, as well as perform yogic exercises to control, manipulate and master the movement of the energies in the channels and the placement of the essences. Such practices belong mainly to Mahayoga and Anu Yoga, but there are some aspects concerning this within Ati Yoga as well.

The most important point, though, is how to overcome the innermost obstacle of dualistic experience, the habit of holding on to perceiver and perceived. The only way to conquer that duality is to not let the expression stray into being dualistic mind, which apprehends duality where no duality exists. It is said, "Until duality dissolves into oneness, there is no enlightenment." We therefore need to acknowledge the nondual state of *rangjung yeshe*, the self-existing wakefulness that is our original state. After acknowledging it, we need to train in that and become stable. It is only through such stability that we can become totally victorious over all obstacles.

There is another way of describing obstacles: the four *maras*. Regardless of what they are called, the only way to dispel all obstacles is through mastering self-existing wakefulness. If we do this, we can't be harmed by any obstacles, be they outer, inner, or innermost. First we need to recognize; next, train in that recognition; and finally, attain stability. There is no better method than that.

The major obstacles for samadhi are called dullness and agitation. Our original state has two aspects, emptiness and cognizance, which are basically indivisible. When there is slightly more focus on the empty quality, dullness can set in. When there is too much emphasis on the cognizant aspect, agitation sets in. But when there is stability in self-existing wakefulness, one does not fall prey to either dullness or agitation. They have no sort of hold whatsoever over that state of mind. Becoming stable in self-existing wakefulness is how to deal with dullness and agitation.

About the four maras: everyone who is not enlightened is in the grip of the four maras. They are the mara of the lord of death, the mara of disturbing emotions, the mara of the aggregates, which actually means our physical body, and the mara of the son of the gods. The mara of the lord of death means that everyone is subject to death, which of course interrupts their practice. The mara of the aggregates refers to the physical body. As soon as you are born you are encased in this material thing called the human body and subject to its changes; that is a mara. The mara of disturbing emotions is to be caught up in disturbing emotions, as all sentient beings are.

The most subtle, and the most difficult, is the mara of the son of the gods, who is the demon of seduction. It is the little voice that whispers to oneself and gives the wrong advice: "There is something more interesting than practicing. Why not do it later, like next month or next year—then you can really get into intensive practice. Right now, there is something more important." That is the voice of the mara of the son of the gods. It is by far the most difficult to notice, the most difficult to overcome.

When attaining rainbow body, as did Padmasambhava and the great siddha Vimalamitra, you overcome the mara of the aggregates. By being stable in mind essence, you overcome the mara of disturbing emotions. It is only by attaining total stability through recognizing and training in mind essence that one can totally be said to have vanquished the four maras. Otherwise, sentient beings are not free. They get overcome again and again; they are definitely under the power of the four maras.

Rangjung yeshe can be illustrated by using the image of the sky and sunshine, which are indivisible in the daytime. They are often used as metaphors for basic space and original wakefulness. All buddhas and bodhisattvas are stable in this unity, and thus are not subject to any of the levels of obstacles. Our problems as sentient beings began because of not knowing our own true nature. It's as when the sun temporarily sets, and it becomes pitch-dark; we can't see anything, we don't know anything. This is the picture of our own ignorance, of not knowing our own nature. Such ignorance is the first link in the chain of the twelve links of dependent origination. Ignorance is what creates samsara. If we recognize self-existing wakefulness, we cut the root of the twelve links of dependent origination and samsara, and there is no ignorance. In the case of the buddhas and bodhisattvas, ignorance was cleared up in the ground. What happened with us is that we didn't recognize, and the twelve links of dependent origination and samsara came about.

The basic difference between samsara and nirvana lies between knowing and not knowing. Knowing is awareness wisdom; not knowing is wandering in endless samsara. There are two choices: either knowing what this nature is, awareness wisdom, or not-knowing, ignorance. It's not that there are two different basic natures.

Unknowing or ignorance forms the first of the twelve links of dependent origination, upon which the following rest and are supported. Because of ignorance, there is formation. Due to formation, there is dualistic consciousness, which is the cooperating cause for taking rebirth into a womb, forming the six sense-bases and the aggregates of 'name-and-form.' Taking birth propels one into involvement in grasping, craving, and becoming, not to mention a new rebirth, old age, sickness and death. It goes on and on. The hub of this wheel is ignorance itself. If you want to blame one big demon for all of samsara, then blame ignorance, the lack of knowing.

The only way to clear up the problem of samsaric existence is to dissolve ignorance into the primordial ground. This is done through simply recognizing the natural state of mind and not perpetuating the habit of dualistic fixation; by simply letting be in naturalness, without accepting or rejecting. That is what overcomes all obstacles. Recognizing this precious self-existing wakefulness is like the sun that vanquishes all darkness. It is something very close; like the dividing line between light and shadow, which are really not that far from each other. That which overcomes all obstacles is recognizing self-existing wakefulness.

Sustaining the continuity of nondual awareness clears up basic ignorance. There is no ignorance at that moment, and therefore no formation, no dualistic consciousness, no name-and-form, no six sense-bases, no grasping, craving, becoming, sickness, old age and death, and so forth. This is thanks to recognizing the essence of our mind, rigpa, the self-existing wakefulness that is pointed out by your guru. It is the three kayas intrinsic to our mind. The nature of our mind is empty in essence and cognizant by nature, and these two are indivisible. Seeing that and sustaining its continuity is what clears up the basic ignorance.

We should recognize this and sustain the natural face of this recognition. This doesn't mean that one is deliberately keeping a state that is the natural state. 'Sustaining the natural face' means allowing its continuity without something being sustained or someone to sustain it. It's not the same as thinking, "Oh, now I've got it; this is what I should keep, and this is what I should avoid. I won't do this, but I will do that." Alternating between accepting and rejecting as a meditation practice is not the way to clear up samsaric existence. On the contrary, it is the link of formation, the second link among the twelve links of dependent origination. Each concept forms the basis for the dualistic state of mind, and that creates further samsara. Clearing up basic ignorance is nothing other than simply recognizing and letting be—seeing the empty cognizance which is an indivisible unity. That is called dissolving ignorance into basic space, and is the way to go beyond all obstacles.

Another way to look at this concerns obstructing forces, the obstacle-makers for the practitioner. Please understand first that obstructing forces are really nothing other than our own thoughts, arising out of our own mind. The term 'obstructing forces' describes that which will not relinquish control over the site of the mandala, and which can steal the accomplishments, sneaking away with the offerings and interfering in all sorts of different ways. In reality, though, the obstructing forces are nothing other than conceptual thinking. The obstructing forces arise out of your own mind. When the five outer mental objects are grasped at by the inner fixating mind, coupled with attachment to the five sense perceptions—this is conceptual thought. It is the act of conceptualizing objects, apprehending an object as 'that' and forming ideas about it as being attractive, repulsive, or neutral. These obstructers or thought movements which obscure the state of perfect enlightenment originate from ourselves, not from anywhere else.

The negative attitudes of the three poisons manifest as the three basic evil spirits: the male *gyalpo*, or anger, the female *dremo*, attachment, and the neuter *maning*, or closed-mindedness. Their entourage of followers total 84,000 kinds of obstructing forces, demons, and evil spirits who make all kinds of troubles, creating havoc and disasters in many different ways. As manifestations of our own mind, these can be condensed into the three poisons. In short, conceptualizing subject and object as duality is the basic hindrance or obstructer. The word 'obstructer' means that which creates a hindrance for realization of the enlightened state.

In accordance with the compassionate teachings of Secret Mantra, one gives this obstructer the gift of a *torma*. (Rinpoche laughs). In order to get a handle on these different kinds of obstructing forces, the sadhana practice first gently offers them a gift, a torma. This torma is given to the obstructer, to our own conceptual thinking. One visualizes a very beautiful torma emanating sweet music and a lovely fragrance, having delicious flavor and a perfect texture and so forth, arising out of emptiness. From the state of emptiness, one imagines the torma appearing as fully endowed with the potency, power, color, smell, taste, and texture that gives rise to all the five kinds of sense pleasures. One consecrates the torma with ram, yam kham and om ah hung. Next, one summons the obstructing forces by means of a certain mantra, presents the torma, and requests them to leave.

A second way involves a commanding approach with a chant, the essential meaning of which is, "Take this torma and get out, or you will feel the heat of the herukas." A third, more wrathful method, involves

one wrathfully expelling the obstructers by emanating many tiny herukas. While chanting a particular mantra, you imagine emanating a mul-
titude of herukas like a terrific hurricane, blowing away all obstructing
forces as though they were a pile of ashes scattered by a strong gust of
wind. Powerless, they fly away to the ends of the universe.

Remember, the real demon is our conceptual thinking. Falling into
conceptualization is the demon. By recognizing our mind essence, all
demons are defeated; the four maras are vanquished and all obstacles
are removed. The main point is to train in that recognition. The most vital point in all of samara and nirvana is to meet mind essence. Mind has
fallen into thought, and yet the essence of thought is wisdom, original
wakefulness. There is nothing more important to know than this. Know
what is the closest.

To repeat what I have said innumerable times, the difference between sentient beings and buddhas is knowing and not knowing. We
are introduced to rigpa by our master. When looking and seeing no
thing, that is the essence of mind. At this point the 84,000 types of
thoughts are cut.

STUDENT: What about hope? I understand the issue of fear, but it seems
that there is still sort of subtle hope of awakening. Is that necessarily a
problem?

RINPOCHE: In the moment of recognizing self-existing wakefulness,
what is there to focus on — is there something else? You need to let both
hope and fear collapse. Hope by definition implies something you need
to accept and adopt, while fear implies something to avoid or be free
from. The view, however, is to be free from both something to attain
and something to avoid. The basic space of our nature is originally an
indivisible empty cognizance, which is already the dharmakaya buddha
Samantabhadra with consort. Why should one hope for some other buddha than that? The moment of knowing, of rigpa, is enough. When it is
said that the ultimate view means to be free from accepting and rejecting, it means there is no extra deity to be achieved in the moment of
knowing one's nature. There is no extra awakened state to be attained.

At that moment, there is no force to cause further rebirth within the six realms of samsara.

STUDENT: Could you explain more why the demon of the son of the gods is the most difficult?

RINPOCHE: What fools or seduces us, is our own thinking. Almost everybody is taken away by that mara. Of course we are also under the power of the mara of the aggregate, unless we don't have a body.

It may be difficult to deal with these maras, but then again maybe it's not so difficult. Simply don't do anything to this present wakefulness. Then the mara won't pop his head out of that wakefulness, because it's not possible. Sustain present wakefulness in a vivid, wide-awake fashion, and allow it to be *as it is*. That is enough. There is nothing extra to find from within that. If we think there is something other than that to achieve in our waking state, such anticipation is only a fetter that ties us down.

We usually get tied up in the web of past thought, future thought, thought of the present. Let go of those three. This is the vivid present wakefulness. 'Vivid' here means transparent, wide-open, unobscured — like crystal. To yearn for some extra superior state than this present wakefulness is simply fooling yourself. This uncorrected or unfabricated present wakefulness is the true Buddha Samantabhadra, which has never been apart from yourself for a single instant. While recognizing, rest naturally. If you recognize it, you are buddha; if not, you are a sentient being. It's very simple, very clear, like the dividing line between light and shadow. You cannot separate a lit area and a shaded area from each other, they are so close. It is like the front and back of your own hand. Buddhas and sentient beings are only that far from each other. (Rinpoche shows his hand). This is what it is in actuality: this is the front, this is the back. They may seem to be apart from each other, but actually they are very close.

The way to be sure in this is to recognize. There is no thing to see whatsoever, is there? Recognizing mind essence is not to see anything other than that. Once you get to where you are not distracted from that throughout day and night, you have earned the name Buddha. If you can remain undistracted for one hour, you are already an arhat. If you are stable in that state there is nothing to fear about dying, because the bardo is only a continuity of this state.

The old Kagyü masters said: "Death is not really death; for a yogi, death is a small enlightenment." It means that mind itself is no thing that dies. Death is merely the falling-away of the temporary guest house of the body. A normal person falls unconscious at the moment of death, but a practitioner who recognizes the state of rigpa does not fall unconscious. If in the bardo state a recognition of rigpa occurs, it is as I said before: within the duration of time it takes to wave a Tibetan long sleeve three times, you recognize, are fully trained and attain stability. That is not possible while we are alive because of being in a material body. It's like a bird tied down with a chain; it cannot fly.

We need to train in this nondual awareness right now. Nothing else can stop our thinking, and if thinking doesn't stop, neither does samsara — it just goes on. Samsara needs our thinking in order to perpetuate itself, because only our own thoughts can keep samsara alive. There is nothing else.

Once you recognize this nature you can lean back in a comfortable seat or bed and just totally relax. The three worlds of samsara can be turned upside down and the hells open up below you, and not even a hair on your body will move in fright. Until that point, there is no real confidence while in samsaric existence. Everything perishes moment by moment. Everything changes — the seasons, the body — nothing lasts. Our body is changing like the hand on a clock, second by second. The world outside and the beings within it change all the time, moment by moment. Nothing ever remains the same. Our essence, however, does not change; it is the unchanging natural face of awareness. All buddhas see the pain of this subtle change, called the 'all-pervasive suffering of being conditioned.' Sentient beings, however, don't really notice the pain of subtle impermanence. You could say that yogis or buddhas are sensitized to this pain, just as we wince when we have an eyelash caught in our eye. For ordinary beings, on the other hand, the pain is imperceptible, like a single eyelash held on the palm of the hand. They don't know that this being conditioned is actually painful, so they don't notice the pain that arises from the fact that from this moment until we draw our last breath, we change continuously.

STUDENT: Why do we get carried away so easily?

RINPOCHE: Because we are unstable in awareness, we start to wander off in a train of thought. All sentient beings do this. Not being stable in our own essence is an incredibly strong habit developed through countless past lives. Distraction involves the awareness wisdom being overtaken by ignorance, the knowing by unknowing. This unknowing has two aspects: innate and conceptual. If these two were purified, we would be buddhas. But as long as the innate and conceptual aspects of ignorance are not purified, we are sentient beings.

Innate ignorance is simply to forget. Conceptual ignorance comes in the moment after forgetting, when we start to think, forming thought after thought. As one thought follows after another, a long train of thought can develop. These innate and conceptual ignorances form the original borderline between buddhas and sentient beings. They are what make the difference between confusion and nonconfusion. The Tibetan term for enlightenment translates as 'purified perfection,' or 'cleared up and perfected.' It's the ignorance that needs to be cleared up. The qualities of wisdom don't need to be perfected; they are already perfected. The ignorance, however, is like clouds covering the sky. We need to let the clouds of confusion naturally disperse into basic space.

Since we have not yet attained enlightenment, why shouldn't samsara be difficult? This is a difficulty that everybody shares. We need to practice slowly and steadily, not merely for a few months. If this task was easy, all sentient beings would have attained enlightenment long ago. It is difficult; this ignorance is the thing that is actually giving sentient beings a hard time. All sentient beings are governed by these two ignorances.

Here's a very important statement: "The more you try, the more your natural face is covered. The more you let go, the more your natural face is cleared." Any mental effort is dualistic mind. Dualistic mind is what we need to let go of. What is left over is unobstructed nondual aware-ness. Non-fixating awareness is already present the moment you recog-nize rigpa; it is there for everyone. Unfortunately, sentient beings don't know how to look—and they don't trust it even if they do see.

9

Expression of Awareness

✻

I would like to explain in more detail two important principles: essence and expression, *ngowo* and *tsal*. The relationship between these two is like the relationship between the sun and sunlight: you cannot have sunlight without the sun shining. It's the same with the expression of mind essence and the essence itself. The essence doesn't increase or decrease, is neither improved or worsened. Whether it is recognized or not recognized, in the essence itself, there is no difference whatsoever. The only possibility of recognition lies in the expression. The expression of this essence can either know itself or not know itself, that is the whole importance of knowledge—in Sanskrit, *prajna*, in Tibetan, *sherab*.

It is said that when the expression dawns as sherab, as knowledge—when the expression knows its own nature—it is liberated, there is freedom. When the expression moves as thought, as thinking, it is bewildered—there is delusion. In this distinction lies the whole difference. In other words, whether the expression is liberated as knowledge or confused as thinking is determined by the practitioner knowing or not knowing his own nature. In the essence itself, there is no difference; it's not improved by recognizing or made worse by not recognizing. "When the expression moves as knowledge, it is liberated. When the expression moves as thought, it is deluded." This is what makes the whole difference. To be a normal sentient being is to never recognize the nature of this expression. It is like an idiot who never sees the sun shining in the sky, and who thinks that the sun is the light that illuminates everything.

This expression is your own expression. It doesn't come from anybody other than yourself, just as the light of the sun doesn't come from any other place than the sun itself. The ability to distinguish between essence and expression marks the difference between buddhas and sentient beings.

It is like one identity with two aspects. The identity itself, the essence, is like the original sun that is naturally radiant and unmade. The expression, your own expression which you don't recognize, then takes the form of perceiver and perceived. The perceived is seen as external, while the perceiver is here. When the essence in the expression is not recognized, the expression takes the form of thinking. The recognition of mind essence is like an intelligent person who understands, "There must be a source for this sunlight that shines everywhere." When a master points out your nature, he's saying the equivalent of, "All this light is the expression of the sun; now look up into the sky. Do you see that there is one sun that shines over the whole world?" And the intelligent person replies, "Yes! That is the sun itself, and its expression is the light everywhere." This is how one should understand.

What is the point of knowledge? When recognizing the essence of the expression of thought, the expression immediately dawns as knowledge. It is like seeing the sun itself. If not, we don't notice where the expression comes from, and we end up looking everywhere for the sun. That is called 'the expression moves as thoughts'—how it becomes thought patterns. The expression gets caught up in the thoughts of the five perceived objects of the senses—visible forms, audible sounds, tastes, smells, and textures. Thoughts move after mental objects like pleasure and pain as well.

An intelligent person can figure out that there is actually a real sun shining. Longchenpa's *Dharmadhatu Kosha* says:[4]

The original essence is like the radiant sun,
Naturally luminous and primordially unformed.

Sentient beings do not recognize the nature of their expression, and get caught up in it. These two stages are described as the primary and secondary expressions. Primary expression is simply the lack of knowing what the essence is. That takes the form of the five poisons, which is the secondary expression. The five poisons can turn into the eight innate thought states, or even more, the eighty-four thousand disturbing emotions. This is the creation of samsara. However, when the expression dawns as knowledge, it is like an intelligent person thinking, "There must be a sun itself. Where is it?" He looks towards the sun and realizes, "There it is!" It is like seeing the sun itself. Immediately, the essence is seen as an unconfined empty cognizance.

Usually we regard mind as being either empty or conscious. Please understand that mind essence is an *unconfined empty cognizance*. The empty aspect is the dharmakaya, cognizance is sambhogakaya, and the unconfined quality is nirmanakaya. Recognizing this in actuality is like being face to face with the three kayas as one, the essence body, svabhavikakaya. Isn't that moment empty of perceiver and perceived? In the Mahamudra system, this is exactly what is meant by one taste. Not two tastes, you never hear two tastes. Two tastes means subject and object are held in mind. One taste means nothing is held, there is no act of fixating. When there is no fixation, it is impossible to have two tastes. It is only one taste. This oneness is objectless, traceless. If some kind of oneness is still believed to be, it is only a fixation. We may pretend that we have let go of dualistic fixation, but we still believe in the concept of a state of nonduality. In order to be truly objectless, that should also be let go of.

RINPOCHE: Are you recognizing mind essence?

STUDENT: It's difficult; it is very short.

RINPOCHE: What's the trouble you're experiencing? What is the difficulty, exactly? If it's very short, what is the problem in repeating it many times? Is this short moment something you create by meditating?

STUDENT: No.

RINPOCHE: Then it's not really difficult, is it? If you want the moment to last a long time, and you want to immediately become an arhat, then you can say it is very difficult. From beginningless lifetimes until now we have been deluded. To accomplish great achievements in the span of five or six years is difficult, because we have such a deeply ingrown habit of fixation and delusion. Now we need to attain a new habit—not by meditating on an *it*, but by growing accustomed to this recognition. If you had not strayed into this bad habitual pattern to begin with, it would be easy. If you were already an enlightened bodhisattva, if the natural stability of the essence had not slipped away, you would be unconfined empty cognizance suffused with knowing. But that is what all sentient beings have lost. It's not quite right to say that it's lost; rather, it's slipped out of sight by being preoccupied, by the power of our minds being caught up in thought. That is our deeply ingrown habit.

Since beginningless time the essence body, the awakened state of the indivisible three kayas, has always been unceasing; it was never cut off, never lost. Because mind fools itself, it creates this negative habit; and fails to actualize the innate stability of its essence. Right now this recognition of mind essence is like a small infant, whereas the deluded thinking is like a strong person, a grown-up who takes this infant on its back and runs around everywhere. The small infant appears to be powerless. Our rigpa right now is like infant rigpa. It is born, but it's not developed. The powerful grown-up running around is dualistic thinking, the expression we are caught up in right now. The infant rigpa is carried off by the grown-up trickster who runs around and does all kinds of scams, day and night.

STUDENT: How does the expression arise as the development stage?

RINPOCHE: For development stage to arise as the expression of rigpa is of course only possible after one has fully recognized rigpa. This approach of rigpa's expression is like allowing images to appear unobstructedly in a clear mirror. Before that, development stage is a training in creating 'white thoughts'—not samsaric thoughts, which are black thoughts, but devotion, compassion, pure perception, and so forth.

As long as your expression moves as thinking, which is delusion, this deluded thinking can be either white or black. If you are caught up in black thoughts, you are caught up in the three poisons. Whatever comes out of that is black, like the eighty-four thousand types of disturbing emotions. When caught up in that, one will definitely go to the three lower realms. White thoughts, on the other hand, are devotion and pure appreciation towards enlightened beings, compassion for unenlightened beings, and a strong sense of honesty. Whatever comes out of these is automatically goodness or virtue, which is why they're called 'white.' Creating a virtuous frame of mind is thus not something impossible.

What is the use of training in this? Recognize your essence in the moment of strong devotion, which is an emotion so powerful that tears come to our eyes and the hairs on the body stand on end. As the third Karmapa said, "In the moment of love, the empty essence dawns nakedly." In that same instant, uncontrived self-existing awareness is totally devoid of any error or fault. Your empty essence has been laid totally bare, and has dawned nakedly.

The same can be experienced through intense compassion. Think of all sentient beings who for so long, through such misery, roam about in samsara. They circle endlessly and yet they never seem to get enough. What a pity! Once again our eyes are filled with tears; the hairs on our body stand on end, we feel overwhelmed. When you recognize mind essence at such a moment, again there is no error. This is how 'white' thoughts, virtuous thoughts, can be beneficial. In the moment of devotion towards enlightened beings, or compassion towards unenlightened beings, your state of mind is not mixed with the three poisons. Isn't it true that devotion and compassion are unmixed with desire, anger or stupidity? Neither are they mixed with dishonesty or deceit. Devotion is sincere, honest, and straightforward, and so is compassion. Through the path of honesty, one attains an honest state. This is why all buddhas are called *rishis*, which means an upright, totally straightforward person, whereas sentient beings practice a sly path and attain the state of trickster. 'Tricky' here means kind of dishonest. This is why it is said that white, virtuous states of mind lead towards a pure path.

Devotion and compassion are not the same as merely paying lip-service to the buddhas and sentient beings, saying, "Buddhas think of me," or "Poor sentient beings," without putting any heart in that. To be truly authentic, the feeling of devotion and compassion should be almost overwhelming. To avoid being sidetracked from the view, there is no method superior to devotion and compassion. These two are universal panaceas, the basis for being able to journey along the white path and attain the ten bhumis. Without these two, it is impossible to progress. It is said, "With a good heart, all paths and levels are good; with a evil heart, all paths and levels are evil." Everything depends on whether one's heart is good or evil. To reach enlightenment we must pass through the paths and bhumis. That progress depends on pure attitude and good heart. Without this pure attitude, all paths lead in a perverted direction. This is why everything depends on a pure heart.

First, recognize your own nature. Then keep devotion upwardly, compassion downwardly, and be diligent in between. Diligence means a sense of constancy. It's like the proper tension of a bowstring: if the bow itself is taut, the string doesn't change, becoming looser sometimes, tighter sometimes. Rather, it is constant. 'Diligent' here means some sense of being undistracted, a gentle nondistraction. These three qualities of devotion, compassion and diligence make you progress through the paths and bhumis. In addition, the application of purifying obscurations and gathering the accumulations, the ngöndro, is extremely important.

It's not so necessary for a meditator to be involved in a lot of debate and analysis about whether something is or is not, proving and refuting and affirming and denying. You can get so caught up in this kind of debate that sweat appears on your forehead, your hands shake and your lips quiver, because you so badly want to prove your point and invalidate your opponent's. But the whole purpose of the Dharma is to be free from anger and competitiveness. If one cultivates fury and rivalry through the Dharma, it's like Gampopa's famous saying: "If the Dharma is not practiced as it should, it can become a cause for rebirth in the lower realms."

STUDENT: Recognizing mind nature during a meditation session doesn't seem to be so difficult. It's simply a matter of remembering. However, it seems difficult to mix this with daily life. Is this what is meant by diligence?

RINPOCHE: Diligence is like the example with the electric switch I used earlier. Unless you flip the switch, the light never comes on. When receiving pointing-out instruction, one is told how to recognize mind essence. Without that, there is no recognition of how this essence is. It doesn't happen by itself, just as the light never switches on by itself.

We have heard that we should not forget mind essence, that we shouldn't lose its continuity. But this is not like insistently looking, looking, and looking again, as if continuously pressing the switch to keep the light on. The moment of recognizing has a natural duration. It's like when you take a Tibetan bell: you ring it once, and the sound simply continues. It doesn't last forever, it wears off at a certain point, but that doesn't mean you have to sit and ring the bell continuously—ding, ding, ding. That's the analogy for sitting there thinking, "I should be undistracted, I should be undistracted, I should be undistracted." To do so would only create more thoughts; it is totally superfluous.

In the moment of recognizing, you already see it. It is not that there is something extra there that needs to be recognized on top of seeing mind essence. It is as I said: when you point towards space, you touch space from the first instant. You don't have to extend your finger further in order to touch space. As beginners, we do forget mind essence. The way to remember again is by noticing that you have forgotten, by noticing distraction. Then you can remember to be undistracted. The teacher has explained the difference between distraction and nondistraction, right? Our job now is to notice when we are distracted.

When noticing we are distracted, there is some slight sense of regret. A meditator doing this type of practice should actually experience some regret when mind essence is totally lost; when he or she becomes totally oblivious to the continuity of recognition. Yet we don't have to nurse the regret; we simply recognize what is it that feels sorry for having lost the recognition. Honestly, unless we cultivate that sense of noticing when being distracted, there is only distraction, nothing else. This is what we call the 'black diffusion of samsara,' where there is only ignorance, never any knowing of what the essence actually is. For a samsaric person this black diffusion is continuous.

What is necessary now is to recognize mind essence and then not do anything to it. There is no need to try to improve the already cognizant empty essence. You don't have to adjust it or correct it in any way. It's like a tree growing on a mountain; nobody needed to shape it that particular way, it just grew. Or, the continuity of mind essence is like the steady flow of a river. Wakefulness simply goes on by itself, like the water flowing along the riverbed. Nobody needs to pull the water down the river, nobody has to push it; it continues by itself. There is one phrase which is always repeated in all Mahamudra and Dzogchen instruction manuals: "Don't lose the continuity!" That is how you are to train.

The way to not lose the continuity is, in the moment of recognizing, not to do anything to it. If you attempt to alter or improve upon the recognition, you lose it entirely. When simply leaving it *as it is*, in what is called the 'natural flow,' it does continue, it is not lost—just like the natural flow of a river. The moment we try to do something to it, it's immediately interrupted. The moment we forget, it is also lost. At that point it is simply a matter of remembering or of noticing that one was carried away, and then recognizing mind essence again.

It is said, "Uncontrived ordinary mind is the highway of the victorious ones." To contrive means to correct or improve, to hope or fear, to affirm or deny, to accept or reject. Not getting involved in any of that is what is meant by being uncontrived. One may get the mistaken idea that this natural emptiness is not so effective or useful, that, "There is another emptiness, the real emptiness, which I somehow have to discover." If you begin to entertain that idea it gets really difficult, because it would then mean that there should be another mind than the mind you already have. You know what is meant by being naked, having no clothes on, don't you? Well, thinking, "I need the state of rigpa, it should be such-and-such; this is what I need," is just like putting more and more clothes on. Naked awareness, like a naked body, is without trying to improve or alter, accept or reject, affirm or deny—without hope or fear. By being just like that, your awareness is already naked.

"Uncontrived ordinary mind is the highway of the victorious ones."

This doesn't mean that this present mind should be thrown away and some new state should come down or materialize, like being possessed by another spirit. That simply won't happen. Self-existing wakefulness is the vital point. You can recognize the sun based on its light: you simply look to where the sunlight comes from. In the same way, if you recognize the nature of the thinker, you recognize rigpa. That's why it is said one should look, recognize.

You have to recognize because, as the tantras say, "The great wisdom dwells in the body." Once the body and mind separate at death, the great wisdom will no longer dwell in the body. Right now, in this city of an illusory body, in this city of the five aggregates, there is something very precious. It has not yet begun to flounder around in the bardo because it is still in this body, which ties it down in a way. This is quite nice. Being in a physical body is like a wild horse tied down to a stake: it can move around in a circle, but it can never run away. While this unruly mind is in a physical body it cannot suddenly take leave; so in this sense, the physical body is very useful. Once we die, though, it's like the wild horse's tether has broken. The horse will run wild over valleys and mountains, and we won't be able to catch it very easily.

While body and mind are together, we need to train in recognizing this essence. At present, when we recognize rigpa for a few seconds, it doesn't mean that we are liberated. But after death, when body and mind separate and we are free of the body, it is said recognizing and being liberated are simultaneous. The yogi breaking loose from the encasement of the body is said to be like a garuda bird hatching from the egg. But someone who doesn't train while alive in a body will not be able to recognize rigpa when body and mind separate. For such a person with no experience of recognizing, perfecting the strength and attaining stability, there is surely no liberation.

If you have trained sufficiently to reach the complete recognition of rigpa and have some degree of stability—say, for twenty or thirty consecutive minutes, you will be successful in the bardo. There is no doubt about this, even though you haven't attained the complete enlightenment of having fully exhausted delusion throughout day and night. Otherwise, the bardo is a place of awesome terror. You feel like you are being chased from behind by the four terrifying enemies, the four elements, while in front of you is the threefold immense abyss of attachment, aversion and dullness. Desire is like falling into a vast ocean. Aversion is like falling over the brink of a bottomless pit. Dullness is like being immersed in immense darkness. These are only one step ahead, while right behind you are the four terrifying enemies. The bardo is not a fun place to be in!

The element of earth is experienced as being like an avalanche just about to topple over you from behind. The water element feels like a flood of a huge ocean coming at you. Fire feels like an entire blazing mountain, while wind feels just like when you pump a bellows right at an ant, who is powerlessly blown away. Right now the body is made of the five elements, but in the bardo they arise as enemies. Or at least it seems like that. But if you can manage to recognize mind essence, the five aggregates are naturally seen as the five wisdoms, while the five elements appear as the five female buddhas. This is why the body is called the mandala of the victorious ones. If you don't recognize, they seem to be enemies, but if you recognize, they are helpers.

We have to know one thing only. It is often said, "If emptiness is all right, everything is all right. If emptiness is not all right, nothing is all right." What that means is if we recognize the state of emptiness everything is fine. All of you, please train in recognizing this empty nature of your minds. You don't have to hope to become a great scholar or a great siddha. Through this training, the twofold knowledge of knowing the nature as it is and seeing all that exists will naturally unfold from within. You cannot avoid being enlightened; you cannot help but benefit sentient beings. If you recognize this fully, no one can hold you back from being enlightened, and no one can prevent you from benefiting beings. The twofold knowledge will overflow from within. 'Overflowing from within' means spontaneously present, fully awakened. If he were to train in this, even a cow herder would be liberated, and we would all have to pay our respects and bow our heads to him. If he becomes a siddha, we would all fight with each other for the privilege of drinking his urine!

STUDENT: How do we recognize mind essence during the dream state? That is very difficult for me.

RINPOCHE: It's difficult because you haven't trained enough to become accustomed to it. A beginner experiences no obvious duration of recognizing mind essence, and therefore recognizing while falling asleep or in the state of deep sleep just doesn't seem possible. The possibility comes after having attained some degree of stability in the recognition of mind essence. Because of the strong habit of many lifetimes, we always get caught up in thoughts, regardless of whether it's day or night, whether we're awake or sleeping. It's not so easy to step out of that habit. Only when we grow really accustomed to recognition during our waking state is it possible to recognize during sleep as well. We are already caught up in the wheel of the twelve links of dependent origination, the root of which is ignorance, basic unknowing. The period of deep sleep is a subsidiary aspect of ignorance: the real ignorance is the unknowing of our basic nature. As long as this ignorance is perpetuated, the twelve links continue. That is why it's not so easy to recognize during deep sleep; we have to work with the daytime first. If you can recognize mind essence during the sleeping state, you'll certainly be able to cross the bardo. This doesn't require a continuous recognition of rigpa during the sleep state. A scripture says, "If you recognize the state of nondual awareness seven times during sleep, there is no doubt that you will be liberated in the bardo."

The ordinary state in which we have not recognized the state of rigpa is called delusion. The dream state is called double delusion. The big sleep of ignorance has continued since beginningless lifetimes until now. Nighttime is double-delusion, one delusion on top of another. Isn't it true that the duration of nondual awareness in actuality is very short and slips away almost immediately? During the rest of the time, which is the predominant amount of time during our waking state, we are caught up in one deluded thought after the other, all of them unaware of their own nature. This is the black diffusion of deluded mind, which goes on throughout day and night. After you train assiduously during the daytime in repeatedly recognizing the state of nondual awareness, it becomes possible to recognize during night time. The measure of guaranteed success in the bardo is to recognize seven times during the dream state.

Here is one method of how to begin. Visualize a four-petaled red lotus flower in your heart center. Imagine that your mind is in the form of the syllable ah in the center of this lotus flower. The syllable ah is brilliant and radiates light. While visualizing this, at the same time also recognize what visualizes. Recognize that which your own guru pointed out as being the state of rigpa, and simply leave it *as it is*, naturally, while allowing the visualization to continue. In that state, gently fall asleep. This is not something that happens overnight; we need to train in this every evening when falling asleep. Maintain the visualization while falling asleep, and while in the state of the naturalness of rigpa as well.

In this context, the light of the letter ah is called manifest luminosity, and the rigpa that is recognized is called the empty luminosity. In this way, appearance and emptiness are a unity. That is the luminosity of rigpa.

The light is brilliant, radiant white, just like when you switch on the electric light. The traditional image for this is a butter lamp inside a vase, because there was no electricity in Tibet. That is the image for manifest luminosity. The white light is manifest luminosity, whereas the empty luminosity is the primordial purity of empty mind essence. Recognize that. The object that is being held in mind to a certain extent is the radiant white syllable ah, while the awareness of it remains without any fixation. Simply fall asleep in that state.

The posture used in going to sleep is called 'the posture of a sleeping lion.' It's important to lie on the right side, because the channels through which disturbing emotions move are mainly on the right side. To suppress that flow of disturbing emotions, one lies on the right side. When pressing the channel through which the current of disturbing emotion flows, there will be less conceptual thought. It's like when you exhale the stale breath: don't you start by exhaling through the right nostril?

The physical body is said to be a city, the city of the illusory body. This body is a big city. There are so many channels, so many winds moving through them—thousands and thousands of channels, and twenty-one thousand six hundred movements of pranas or winds during a single day and night. There are eighty-four thousand different types of mental states or disturbing emotions. This enormous scale of movement is like that of a big city, isn't it? How many microbes are there within this one body? It is impossible to count. Each of these is sentient, so it really is like a big city. The illusory city of the physical body is like Kathmandu!

When mainly practicing the recognition of mind essence, the currents called the karmic wind, which means conceptual thinking, are naturally transformed into the wisdom wind. Impure channels are naturally transformed into the wisdom channel, and dualistic mind is naturally transformed into original wakefulness. Usually this is described as the winds dissolving into the central channel. The immense traffic of wind through the different channels all dissolves into the central channel.

(In response to a student's explanation of an experience Rinpoche says:)
I'm going to tease you a little. Mind essence is Buddha Samantabhadra, right? Buddha Samantabhadra has no front and no back. From whichever direction you see him, he is always excellent. When you look from the south, you see his face. You look from the west and you also see his face. You may be in any of the four cardinal or the four intermediate directions, or perhaps more than one at the same time, and you can still see his face in front of you. No matter which direction you are in, Samantabhadra has no front and no back. From whichever direction you look, he is always excellent. That is a play on the word Samantabhadra, which means the Ever-Excellent.

This analogy is actually referring to rigpa. Rigpa doesn't have a direction, does it? It is all-pervasive, a wide-open, expansive state. All-pervasive openness is the characteristic of rigpa. Confined narrowness is the characteristic of dualistic mind. This experience you talked about is a sign of the all-pervasive openness. It is a sign of rigpa, which is not confined, narrowed or limited in any direction whatsoever. Whatever is empty is not a concrete substance. Whatever is empty is not confined into any direction; it has no east, west, south or north. Rigpa is unlimited, unconfined, it has no finite dimension or specific size. Neither does it have a fixed direction—there isn't an east or west of rigpa.

Rigpa is like space—whichever direction you journey in, you can't ever reach the end of space. Space has no top or bottom. You can dig an enormous hole in the earth, and whatever you drop in it will always reach the bottom, won't it? Space is not like this. You can travel down through space for a million years and still never reach the bottom. This is towards the east (Rinpoche touches the eastern wall with his hand); I've reached the limit right there. But you can travel in this direction through space for a billion aeons, and you will never reach the limit towards the east, or towards the south or west or the north. There are no limits in the four cardinal directions, so of course there are no limits in the four intermediate directions either. There is no top or bottom. so, if there is no limit or end anywhere, how can space have a center?

Try to imagine space. Wherever there is space, there are sentient beings. Wherever there are sentient beings, there are disturbing emotions and karma. Wherever there are disturbing emotions and the creation of karma, there is buddha nature. This is an example for being unconfined and unlimited. Try and imagine how space is. The characteristic of *rangjung yeshe*, self-existing wakefulness, is unconfined and wide-open. That is the characteristic of rigpa. Confined narrowness is the characteristic of dualistic mind. Isn't there a huge difference between the two?

This unconfined openness is not an object held in mind; it is not something we can conceive of. It lies beyond the domain of thought. You hear about the celestial mansion that the sambhogakaya deities reside in. The literal term is 'immeasurable palace,' something so vast it's beyond measure. That the deity's palace is measureless or immeasurable means there is no size, no dimension to it. It is beyond dimension. You never heard about the palace of fixed measure; the word is never used. Rather, it lies totally beyond dimensions. Buddha mind or rigpa is likewise beyond limit and category. You cannot find a set parameter for how big or how vast rigpa is. And it has no category, meaning it isn't in one place and not another. Like space, it is beyond that.

Rigpa is also free of meditator and meditation object. Meditation object means something that we focus on, and meditator, that which focuses. It is totally devoid of subject and object. Self-existing wakefulness is free of reference point and the fixation on attributes. This state is also called transcendent knowledge, *prajnaparamita*. It means knowledge that has passed to the other side of dualistic concepts. The usual understanding is always on this side; it hasn't gone beyond yet. Transcendent means transcending both thinker and what is thought of. This is how the nature of mind actually is.

This nature of self-existing wakefulness is something from which we have never been apart for even one instant. Recognize it, train in the strength of that recognition, and attain stability, and you are a buddha. Your mind and self-existing wakefulness have never, ever been apart. They are inseparable. Sentient beings just do not know how to look. Though from time to time they see that there is no thing, they don't realize that this is their self-existing wakefulness. To recognize your own nature, your natural face which is self-existing wakefulness, you need to see that it is an unconfined empty cognizance. If buddha nature was only empty it would be impossible for it to recognize itself, just as space cannot see itself. We are empty cognizance, and this cognizance is what can recognize.

You can recognize who you are, right? If you look some other place, how will you ever know who you are? It's like a crazy man, an idiot, losing himself in the bazaar in Kathmandu. He runs around in the bazaar trying to find himself, until someone points at him, and says, "You are right here, you are you." Noticing himself, he finally says, "Oh, yeah!"

That is the same job the master takes on when pointing out a disciple's mind essence. He says your mind is empty cognizance; recognize yourself and you will see it. What does it look like? It is seeing that there is no thing to see. It is called empty. The knowing of that is the cognizance. And these are not two separate things, they are indivisible. Do you agree that it isn't a thing to be seen? This is the fact of looking and seeing that mind is no thing to be seen. Seeing that is called the great sight. If you talk about this a hundred times, a thousand times, mind essence is exactly the same:

> *Empty cognizance of one taste, suffused with knowing,* ⁊
> *Is your unmistaken nature, the uncontrived original state.* ⁊
> *When not altering what is, allow it to be as it is,* ⁊
> *And the awakened state is right now spontaneously present.* ⁊

Understand those words! They are Padmasambhava's words from the *Lamrim Yeshe Nyingpo* and they show the true meaning.⁵ The sight of the unmistaken nature is extremely rare. Sentient beings don't see, and even if they happen to see, they don't believe. Yet this is the most eminent sight of all, and it's not something you need to look for elsewhere. If you know how to recognize your mind and you do it, isn't it vividly seen in the same moment, without you needing to imagine it?

Is there anything superior to this, or anything easier, anything simpler? What is wrong is that it is *too* easy—so easy that it's hard to trust. Sentient beings have a hard time believing it. If mind essence were some thing that would stare back at you and wave when you recognized; if, when you said, "Oh, there it is," it would reply, "Yes, my son. You got it!"—then you would believe, wouldn't you?

The recognition of mind essence is itself great peace. In that moment there is no subject and object. What is the need for anything to find on top of that? What we really need to discover is the absence of some concrete thing. No matter how much we search and seek and strive, we never realize mind essence as a concrete thing. It has not even as much as a single atom of concreteness. This essence, when fully realized, is often described as 'the all-pervading lord of samsara and nirvana,' the lord of all that appears and exists. This 'lord' is simply empty cognizance, which is totally inconcrete.

The more stable you become in this essence, the more thoughts dissolve. Then it is possible to be like the mahasiddhas of the past, and fly through the sky like a bird, move through water like a fish and pass through solid matter. That is the ultimate proof of the unreality of appearances. It is not that yogis are very strong and physically powerful beings who can force their way through real, concrete things. Their actions are merely revealing the fact that all appearances are unreal. Material appearances are in fact identical with the appearances in your dreams.

10

Various Applications

※

The main emphasis in Dzogchen practices is to recognize mind essence. That is the primary intent. As a support for that there are the different sadhanas. As an example I will use the *Kunzang Tuktig*, which involves the one hundred peaceful and wrathful buddhas.[6] This sadhana is a very precious and profound support because the mandala of peaceful and wrathful deities includes the Three Jewels, the Three Roots, and all the deities of the three kayas. The deities are no different than the inner core of our basic nature; often they're described as the deities who naturally dwell in the mandala of our vajra body. Thus, training in such a sadhana allows us to realize the different aspects of our basic nature.

A practice like *Kunzang Tuktig* is not limited to being in a retreat situation nor to a certain stretch of time. It is a sufficient path for one's entire life. It is not a practice that one is ever finished with. Nor is it only to be used when sitting down on one's meditation seat. Yidam practice is something that can be brought into one's life at any situation, at any moment. You bring along this practice whether you sit or whether you walk, whatever you are involved in. Don't have the idea that you should stop after a set number of recitations. This kind of practice is to continue your entire life. The reason why a sadhana is such a profound support is because it contains all the different aspects of Vajrayana practice.

The perspective of Ati Yoga is contained within the sadhana text, and the sadhana text is embodied in one's personal application. To use a sadhana text in one's personal practice accumulates immense merit and purifies a vast amount of obscurations. That is a great fortune. The sadhana embodies the tantras of Mahayoga, the scriptures of Anu Yoga and the instructions of Ati Yoga. A sadhana usually has three basic parts: preparation, main part and conclusion.

Preparation includes the preparatory stages such as taking refuge and forming the bodhichitta resolve towards complete enlightenment. Then comes the dispelling of obstructing forces. Obstructing forces are like bandits who steal the blessings. They can steal away the radiance of the butter lamps and the resplendence of the offerings, as I mentioned earlier. To avoid this, you give them a torma and say, "Take this and leave." Those who don't leave are expelled with wrathful means. After expelling the obstructing forces, you imagine the protection circle. After that is the showering down of the resplendence into whatever appears and exists, the whole world and beings. At the end of this preparatory section is the consecration of the offerings, in which whatever you actually have is multiplied, transformed and increased in all different ways. Everything up to that point is the preparation.

The main part of a sadhana includes an aspect for body, speech and mind. The part for body involves what is usually called development stage, which includes the visualization of the mandala of the deity or the circle of deities. This takes place out of the three samadhis. The mandala of the deities is visualized out of the expanse of the three kayas. The first is the samadhi of suchness, the dharmakaya. The samadhi of illumination is the state of sambhogakaya. The last is the samadhi of the seed-syllable, the nirmanakaya. This visualization of the mandala and the deities is called the samaya being. Into that you invoke the wisdom beings from the unmanifest state of dharmadhatu. You implore them to arrive in multitudes from the buddhafield of dharmadhatu and melt into your visualization, becoming indivisible with it. Through the invocation, you request them to take seat and remain; after which you make offerings and praises.

Next comes the part for realizing the speech of the deities, the recitation phase, in which one recites the essence mantra. One should pay attention to something called the 'recitation intent' while reciting the mantra. It has four aspects, which together are called the 'fourfold recitation intent of approach, full approach, accomplishment, and great accomplishment.' The first, approach, is described with the analogy of the 'moon with a garland of stars,' the second, full approach, with a 'revolving fire brand.' Accomplishment is described as the 'emissaries of the king,' while great accomplishment is the 'beehive breaking open.' Another aspect involves the application of activities for pacifying, increasing, magnetizing and subjugating. All these are particular aspects of the visualization while reciting the mantras.

Having recited the mantra a certain number of times, if one wants to gather an immense amount of merit, one can perform a *ganachakra*, also called a feast offering. The word *gana* means the 'gathering' of merit, feast articles, practitioners and wisdom deities. It is also a thanksgiving, which is like saying 'thank you very much' to all the deities for remaining as this presence and for bestowing the accomplishments. In a ganachakra one usually repeats the offerings and praises. There is traditionally a receiving of accomplishment in combination with the mantra, as well as an apology for any faults or shortcomings that have been committed, followed by the hundred-syllable mantra.

If one doesn't do a feast offering, next in the sadhana structure comes its own version of the completion stage. This has two aspects, dissolving and re-emerging. Dissolving means that the mandala with the deities manifested out of primordial purity as spontaneous presence dissolves back into primordial purity. Whatever spontaneous present qualities are manifest dissolve back into the state of primordial purity they originally arose out of. One doesn't remain there in an unmanifest state, however. Again one emerges in form, this time as the single form of the chief figure of the mandala.

While maintaining the vivid presence of being the deity, whatever is perceived is divine form. Whatever is heard is the sound of mantra. Whatever occurs in the mental field is the play of original wakefulness. That is the continual practice to maintain after completing the sadhana. While maintaining that, one dedicates the merit, makes aspirations, and chants the lines of auspiciousness. This dissolving and emerging together is meant to eliminate the two extreme views of permanence and nothingness, eternalism and nihilism.

This way of practicing, this sequence, is incredibly profound. A sadhana embodies all the intents of the three inner tantras within one's application. It is also an exercise in seeing things as they really are — a method for calling to mind the mandala of the basic purity of all that appears and exists. This is why Vajrayana is called the ultimate short path.

The buddhas teach in various ways according to the needs of different types of recipients. When the recipients are of the shravaka or pratyekabuddha types of mentality, it is not possible for the buddhas to teach the three principles of deity, mantra and samadhi. These three principles are taught to some extent to the Mahayana type of people, but not in completeness. The full, complete teachings are found only in the profound Vajrayana.

Vajrayana has two main aspects, known as the outer and inner tantras. The outer tantras, called Kriya, Upa, and Yoga, do not give the complete teaching either. While divine principles are introduced, in Kriya Yoga the deities always appear as superior to oneself and one is an inferior ordinary being. The deity is like a king while one is the subject. The emphasis here is on the purity of the deity. In Upa, the perspective changes slightly, so that the deity is perceived as being like an older brother rather than a king. In Yoga Tantra the relationship is like that between equals, but still there is a duality.

The perspective of the inner tantras is radically different. Everything from the very onset is accepted as all-encompassing purity. In other words, this body in itself is a mandala of the victorious ones, in the sense that the five aggregates in their pure nature are the five male buddhas. The five elements are the five female buddhas. The sense-bases, the consciousnesses and their objects, are the male and female bodhisattvas. Also included in this is the nirmanakaya quality of acknowledging the pure nature of disturbing emotions as the buddhas of the six different realms. Buddha Shakyamuni is one of thousands of nirmanakaya buddhas of this aeon, and he abides in only one of the six realms. In the mandala of the forty-two peaceful deities, all the buddhas of the six realms are represented.

This mandala of forty-two deities is present within our own heart right now, even without practicing a sadhana. And the wrathful forms of these deities are present within the so-called 'bone mansion,' inside our skull. In our throat is the mandala of the pure vidyadharas with consorts. At our navel chakra is Vajra Yogini. In the secret chakra is Vajra Kilaya, not as a single deity but surrounded by his entire mandala circle of seventy-four, including the Eaters and the Slayers, the Sons and the Dancers.

The presence of all these deities is like rays of light emanating from the sun. From the radiance of dharmakaya the sambhogakaya manifests. From the light of sambhogakaya, nirmanakaya arises to benefit beings. The mandala of the human body is the basically present mandala of the victorious ones. By this method of practicing a single sadhana, an incredible amount of evil deeds and obscurations are purified. This is the extraordinary quality of Vajrayana.

Vajrayana is characterized as having plenty of methods with only minor hardships, and as being suited to people of sharper faculties. This is why Vajrayana is extraordinary. When condensing all the extensive and profound principles into the very basics, all mandalas of all deities are included within the single indivisible unity of emptiness and cognizance. Training in that as the main principle will allow you to accomplish the state that is common to all buddhas.

Our ordinary experience is comprised of two basic aspects, mind and objects. Mind and phenomena. Mind, the *doer*, is in essence the male buddha Samantabhadra. Objects, the *deed*, are in essence the female buddha, Samantabhadri. These two—doer and deed—represent the nonduality of experience and emptiness. That nonduality itself is the primary source or root of all tantric deities.

Everything perceived, all sights, are of divine nature; 'all appearances are the deity.' Whatever is heard, all sounds, have the nature of mantra. All activities of mind have the nature of the awakened state, samadhi. To bring this to mind, to use a sadhana to remind yourself of this fact, is to acknowledge things to being as they really are. That is the main principle of Vajrayana.

This way of regarding sights, sounds and mental activity as being deity, mantra and samadhi involves relating to things in an external way. Internally we focus on the main training of recognizing the undivided empty cognizance, which is the three kayas of the awakened state. Finally, we do not maintain any separation between inside and outside in the training of development and completion, between deity, mantra and samadhi on the one side and the recognition of mind essence as the three kayas on the other side. That is another special quality of Vajrayana.

Vajrayana is also represented as the 'four great gates': mudras, offerings, recitation, and samadhi. They are traditionally described like this:

> *The verbal gate of utterance is to remind of the ultimate.*
> *The secret gate of mantra is to invoke the samayas.*
> *The mental gate of samadhi is to keep one-pointed focus.*
> *The playful gate of mudra is to link gesture with meaning.*

These are extremely important. Watching a person who knows these four gates and can manifest or apply them, it might look like a lot of childish play. Moving the hands, shifting objects around in the air, chanting different tunes and recitations, wearing costumes and so on—all this can look completely contrived. Some people find it to be extremely superficial and beside the point. They may complain by saying, "The real thing, the real Buddhist practice, is only to recognize mind essence." Those who say this lack a true understanding of Vajrayana, because all four gates are incredibly significant and important and are never to be regarded as pointless. It is said that if the three yogas, meaning the three inner tantras, are disconnected from melodious tunes, the tradition of Vajrayana will fade away and eventually vanish.

One may wonder what is the use of practicing a sadhana—what is the benefit? The words one says aloud are reminders of the great, naturally existing mandala of deity, mantra and samadhi. In short, sadhana application is an incredibly practical and simple way to embody the intent of the inner tantras.

STUDENT: Is there an uncomplicated way to practice a single deity?

RINPOCHE: All deities are embodied within Vajrasattva. All mantras are embodied within the Vajrasattva mantra. And leaving the mind un-contrived as it naturally is embodies all types of samadhi. It is said that the essence of all deities is Vajrasattva, and that the principle of Vajra-sattva encompasses all the infinite numbers of peaceful and wrathful buddhas. It's like the analogy of a single moon in the sky that can be reflected simultaneously upon the surfaces of a hundred thousand bod-ies of water. All the reflections appear from the same basis of emana-tion. When the different pools of water vanish from the different vessels, the reflection isn't left behind—it is reabsorbed by its source. It doesn't remain anywhere else. In the same way, all the other deities, when dis-solved, are subsumed within the principle of Vajrasattva.

The relationship between emanations and their base is like this. From dharmakaya, sambhogakaya manifests as the five buddha families, as well as all the countless forms of peaceful, wrathful and semi-wrathful deities. There are all different kinds—there is no fixed amount but an untold number of different ways in which the buddhas manifest. The buddhas attain dharmakaya for 'themselves' and display various *rupaka-ya*—the form-bodies of sambhogakaya and nirmanakaya—solely for the benefit of others. They manifest only in order to help sentient beings who fail to recognize their own nature and who continuously stray into samsaric existence. Out of skillful means, the buddhas and bodhisattvas appear in whatever appropriate form is needed in order to influence deluded sentient beings. The state of enlightenment means that all of their personal aims have been totally accomplished. There is nothing more to achieve or attain, and so any activity they perform is solely for the welfare of others.

It is not that these deities of unified emptiness and compassion have left samsara behind in order to attain a personal state of happiness. It is not that they are happy in their houses and merely slam the door. Nor is it that a particular incarnation appears in the world for his or her own sake, in order to carry out a task which he or she had left undone. All personal aims have been completely accomplished. The only activity that buddhas and bodhisattvas engage in is for the sake of others. There is no selfish aim left at all. Out of compassion for the countless beings wandering in samsara, all the infinite emanations and re-emanations appear out of skillful means. We should never think that the buddhas and bodhisattvas are restless and therefore need to go out for a hike, manifesting all different forms for their own pleasure and entertainment.

All of us sentient beings possess buddha nature as the nature of our minds, and that nature is identical with the emanation base of Buddha Samantabhadra. The basis for emanation is dharmakaya. The emanations themselves are sambhogakaya and nirmanakaya. Sambhogakaya is made of rainbow light. Normal people cannot perceive the manifest sambhogakaya, but they can perceive the nirmanakayas. A human nirmanakaya is described as the 'vajra body comprised of the six elements.' In other words, it is a material body that can be encountered by anyone, regardless of whether that person has pure or impure perception. For example, when Buddha Shakyamuni appeared in this world, he was visible to everyone—pigs and dogs as well as humans. He was not like a sambhogakaya form that can be seen only by high-level bodhisattvas. The emanation base is like space, while that which is emanated is like the rainbow in the sky.

The dharmakaya state is our own essence, but still we think of the dharmakaya buddha Samantabhadra as being 'up there' and descending 'down here' to give teachings. However, the nature of our own mind, our buddha nature itself, is the dharmakaya buddha. Because we fail to acknowledge this fact, the dharmakaya has to manifest in visible forms for us to be able to understand what our own nature actually is. Therefore, the dharmakaya appears in a form like Buddha Shakyamuni, who demonstrates to us, "Recognize your mind! This is what your nature really is!" And he explains how the buddha nature is. Out of incredible compassion and skillful means the buddhas appear to put us on the right track. To reiterate, deities and masters in incalculable numbers are manifested in order to teach us that our own nature, the buddha nature and the dharmakaya buddha Samantabhadra are not different. The true meaning is revealed to us by the Buddha, in the form of an eminent human being possessing the major and minor marks of excellence.

Since we are not able to know by ourselves, a buddha is emanated and teaches us how to recognize our nature. The nature of all beings is Samantabhadra. One can simply repeat that one is Samantabhadra, but such blabbing doesn't really help if one really hasn't realized it. Through skillful means and compassion the buddhas teach that in fact "I *am* Samantabhadra." Since we are unable to realize this by ourselves, the buddhas taught Dzogchen and Mahamudra. When the buddha nature that is present in everyone appears as being outside of ourselves in the form of a blue buddha, our buddha nature is named Samantabhadra, the dharmakaya buddha. When it is described as being present in everyone, it is simply called buddha nature.

Since we couldn't all meet the manifest Samantabhadra, the sambhogakaya appeared, and then in this great aeon Buddha Shakyamuni appeared and taught. Because I didn't know that "I am Samantabhadra," he has to come as a teacher to introduce me to that. The teacher says, in effect, "You are me. I pervade everything, all space, all worlds, and all beings. In order for you to know you are me I will teach the view, meditation and conduct."

Buddha nature, the dharmakaya, pervades everywhere. Even so, we still need to know this state of dharmakaya, and without taking the support of the teacher there isn't any other way. Teachers are emanated because sentient beings don't see their own natural face—because they don't recognize their own nature. If sentient beings had truly recognized this fact, then everything would be dharmakaya! So, to sum up, the buddhas have to appear in order to teach beings the state of dharmakaya. These teachings include the extraordinary Vajrayana, and it is for that reason we visualize ourselves as the deity and our speech as mantra, and let our minds rest in samadhi.

When we imagine, "I am a deity," it is the mind thinking this; it is only an idea. Creating a visualization doesn't necessarily mean that we know our buddha nature. Fabrication doesn't make buddha nature—isn't it already in oneself? It can't be made; it is spontaneously present.

If you could make the dharmakaya you would also be able to create space. In the context of sadhana, we should just allow our nature to be *as it is*, what it actually is, which is no different from the nature of all the buddhas. Just read the sadhana's lines while leaving your mind in its natural state and the three samadhis naturally occur. Simply think "I am the deity Vajrasattva, my speech is the Vajrasattva mantra and my mind is inseparable from Vajrasattva." Remain like that in uncontrived naturalness.

The famous statement, "Vajrasattva is vast space," refers to dharmakaya, to the fact that our buddha nature is the samadhi of suchness. The tantra continues, "As ungraspable as the moon in water," which is the example for the sambhogakaya state which is the samadhi of illumination, the second of the three samadhis. The deity Vajrasattva arises "from the display of Samantabhadra." He appears without possessing a self-nature. If Vajrasattva had flesh and blood or was like stone and earth, we could grasp him. Appearing without a self-nature, though, is like the moon appearing in water—can you grasp an image reflected in water? Vajrasattva holds a vajra and bell to show that appearance and emptiness are indivisible—we cannot separate the two. Finally, at the end of the sadhana, when we dissolve the deity and emerge again in the form of the deity, we do so to eliminate the wrong views of permanence and nihilism.

Understand these two principles: the emanation basis, which is dharmakaya, and the emanation, which is sambhogakaya and nirmanakaya. Vajrasattva comes from the dharmakaya Samantabhadra. All the different forms that are taken, such as different gurus, yidams, dakinis, dakas, Dharma protectors, wealth gods, treasure lords, and so on, are all displays of Samantabhadra. He represents the dharmakaya state, which appears in different ways for the benefit of beings. We should acknowledge and appreciate this display of immense kindness. Actually, whatever we encounter in terms of the various forms and ways in which the state of buddhahood is manifested, is a demonstration of great kindness toward us, the perceivers. They manifest to guide us because we are deluded and do not recognize our own nature. It is all simply for our own benefit. We should acknowledge and appreciate this tremendous kindness.

We are taught that we can achieve enlightenment by practicing Dharma, engaging in virtue and avoiding nonvirtue. The whole reason for this is because we have the potential—because our nature is potentially the state of enlightenment. A gold lodestone has the potential to yield gold when it is smelted, but a piece of wood does not have this potential because it doesn't have the nature of gold. We have the capacity for enlightenment because our nature is enlightened in essence. In order to awaken us to this fact, the dharmakaya appears in different forms to help us recognize our own nature. The state of enlightenment appears in an inconceivable variety of forms to influence beings. We should acknowledge that anything that appears before us in our field of experience and turns our mind towards recognizing our own nature—whether it be a spiritual friend, an image or whatever—is an emanation of the dharmakaya buddha. It is showing us tremendous kindness.

STUDENT: How do we practice the Dharma throughout the day?

RINPOCHE: My uncle Samten Gyatso was also my root guru. He practiced in the following way, which I feel is a very convenient method for structuring a day. He divided his day into four sessions. First is the dawn session, and at the end of it there is breakfast. After breakfast until around eleven o'clock is called the morning session. When that session is finished again there is a break for a meal, up until one or two in the afternoon. The afternoon session is from two until the late afternoon. Once more there is a meal. The evening session begins at dusk, and continues up until the point of going to sleep.

Upon waking up in the early morning, Samten Gyatso did the 'awaking from the sleep of ignorance,' a short chant and visualization which you can find in the *Barchey Künsel*.[7] For the daybreak or dawn session Samten Gyatso got up at four and did the ngöndro, the preliminary practices, in completeness. He did the preliminaries for both his main practices, *Chetsün Nyingtik* and *Kunzang Tuktig*. He knew them both by heart, so it wasn't a problem.[8]

It's necessary to do the ngöndro in completeness before focusing on the yidam as the main practice. That doesn't mean that after completing the ngöndro that one doesn't do it anymore. One always does the preliminaries completely during the first morning session. Do it once from beginning to end. Many great lamas in Tibet would do the ngöndro once every morning throughout their entire life. It is not that somehow they graduated beyond ngöndro; they didn't have that attitude. Similarly, when doing the ngöndro practice, it's not the case that one is not allowed to or shouldn't do yidam practice.

For the morning session Samten Gyatso would do the sadhana practice according to *Kunzang Tuktig*. He also knew that by heart. He would chant it all the way down to the recitation and spend the major time on reciting the mantra. Right before ending that session he repeated the offerings and praises, did the dissolution and re-emergence, and chanted the dedication and verse of auspiciousness. For the afternoon and evening sessions, he would again practice the sadhana. Since it is very short, it wasn't a burdensome task.

Samten Gyatso said there were other practices to add in between which are excellent to do. He practiced chö in the evening. Chö practice is best done at dusk, when all the ghosts, gods and demons are out traveling. They don't move much at all in the daytime. There is a short one page *chö* practice from the *Barchey Künsel* which is extremely concise and also immensely effective.

In the morning time he did the sang smoke offering. There is an extremely nice sang in the Barchey Künsel, starting with "nonarising primordial purity ...." Samten Gyatso also did a torma offering, another practice from *Barchey Künsel*. The torma offering to unfortunate spirits and hungry ghosts is a way for them to get some benefit and sustenance. One can do that before breakfast; it is very short also. You have a little torma, you pour some water, there are a few mantras and a four-line verse.

At the end of the afternoon session he did a *mending-and-apology* ritual. You can do whatever prayers of suitable length you prefer. Combine with that the gift to the Dharma protectors, like the *Maza Damsum* or whichever one you are usually doing.[9] That should be done in late afternoon. After the end of the last session, when falling asleep, he practiced the luminosity of deep sleep.

One should try to apply the instructions on luminosity, literally, 'seizing hold of the luminosity of deep sleep.' This may sound like something that is totally beyond ordinary people, but it isn't. It is simply a matter of training. Whoever trains in this will be able to recognize the luminosity of deep sleep. By following the pith instruction on how to fall asleep in the state of rigpa, you will slowly grow more and more accustomed to recognizing the state of rigpa during sleep. One falls asleep with the motivation to become enlightened for the benefit of all beings. One combines this with a visualization and rests in rigpa. As you train more and more in this, virtuous signs that appear ensure that any doubt you have about such a practice will dwindle away. You feel more and more confident from within. It is very important.

In between, of course, throughout all situations, Samten Gyatso practiced Trekchö, which is not to be ignored. This is the most essential at any moment, regardless of whether you are in a session or not. He practiced Tögal mainly in the morning and evening, at dawn and dusk. My uncle used all periods during the day to include and incorporate all the various aspects of practice.

STUDENT: How to actually structure the practice from morning to evening if you have to work?

RINPOCHE: There is one way of structuring that I feel is very practical. In the morning you begin a sadhana and practice up until the recitation. You recite as much as you feel like at that point. Immediately, without leaving the sadhana behind, go and start doing your daily work. At the end of the day, sit down again and recite the vowels and consonants, repeat the offerings, praises and the purification mantra. After that, bring the sadhana to a conclusion. In this way, your entire day is part of the sadhana. This is extremely important. One shouldn't think that the practice is only when sitting down at the puja table, but rather view practice as being as often as one can remind oneself. That is what really counts.

Practice is not only the mantra and visualization; it is the recognizing of mind essence. You shouldn't think that recognizing mind essence is only limited to sitting down on a meditation seat. It can take place while walking, while talking, while eating, while working, and so on. Whether these activities become practice or not depends on whether you remind yourself to recognize mind essence. That is what you should put effort into, because that is what really counts. Try as much as you can to recognize the state of rigpa during the daytime, from the time you wake up in the morning and continuing throughout the day. In between, during free moments, you can recite the mantra. If there is no chance to do so, if something has to be done, then take care of it. However, while doing it, again and again remind yourself to recognize and simply allow the natural state to be sustained repeatedly. This is what is really necessary. I encourage you to practice in that way.

11

All-Encompassing Purity

✳

Although their aim is the same, Vajrayana is far superior to Mahayana in its profundity because it offers so many methods. These include the different procedures for visualizing the peaceful and wrathful deities, making offerings and praises, reciting mantras, emanating and absorbing rays of light and so forth. Vajrayana has few hardships and it is meant for people of higher faculties. That's why Vajrayana is especially exalted.

We should understand that Vajrayana is not some clever system of invented techniques. The nature of the peaceful and wrathful deities is present as our own physical and mental make-up, as the basic nature of the aggregates, elements and sense-bases. These deities are also called the *three seats of completeness*. These three seats are of male and female tathagatas as the aggregates and elements, of male and female bodhi-sattvas as the sense-bases, and of the male and female gate-keepers as the times and beliefs. They are what is mentioned when saying, "the hosts of the empowerment deities of the three seats of completeness, vajra samaya!" That is referred to in the practices of Mahayoga when making the invocation, but the actual meaning is the pure aspects of our current state.

The first seat is that the aggregates and elements are the five male and female buddhas. The natural purity of the aggregate of consciousnesses is Akshobhya. For the aggregate of forms it is Vairochana, for the aggregate of sensations it is Ratnasambhava, for the aggregate of perceptions it is Amitabha, and for the aggregate of formations it is Amoghasiddhi.

Earth is Buddha Lochana, water is Mamaki, fire is Pandara Vasini, wind is Samaya Tara, and space is Dhatvishvari. The second seat is that the sense-bases are the eight male bodhisattvas and their corresponding objects the female bodhisattvas.

The third seat involves the actions and senses, sometimes described as the completeness of the male and female wrathful gatekeepers, sometimes as the natural purity of the four beliefs and four times. The four male gatekeepers are Amrita Kundali, Hayagriva, Achala and Vijaya. The four beliefs are the notions of permanence, nothingness, self and conceptions. The notion of nothingness means 'there is nothing at all.' The notion of self means thinking 'I.' The notion of conceptions means 'earth is earth; water is water,' and so on. The four female gatekeepers are the past, present, future and the unfixed time. These are the power of action and the four times the power of karma.

There are other interpretations of this third seat of completeness. These deities can be combined in different ways, as the intent of the tantras is vast. You can find all the details of this in the *Guhyagarbha Tantra* and its commentaries, which are very extensive. However, in general it is as I have mentioned.

Here is how this applies to us: At some point our body dies and the 'thatness wisdom,' our true nature, manifests outwardly. There is a definite benefit in realizing the deities of our body through practice because when we die, these forms of the deities will manifest at the time of the bardo. Moreover, when practicing Tögal and progressing through the 'four visions,' it is these very same deities that manifest.

Some people think that deities are someone's invention and don't really exist anywhere. On the contrary, we cannot claim that deities like the peaceful and wrathful deities do not exist, because to quote one tantra, "rigpa lives in the mansion of light." Rigpa refers to primordial purity, which is indivisible from its own 'mansion of light' of spontaneous presence. This is the dharmakaya that manifests as rupakayas—the form kayas comprised of sambhogakaya and nirmanakaya. Dharmakaya is primordial purity beyond constructs, and rupakaya refers to the spontaneous presence—the forms of deities, which are indivisible from primordial purity. It is not that there aren't any deities. The deities are the unity of primordial purity and spontaneous presence.

So, the awakened state of rigpa lives in the mansion of light, and from here the deities manifest. Although they manifest from within our own nature, we still visualize them as being outside. This is one of the skillful methods of Vajrayana, the swift path for those of the higher capacity. Our basic state is not like physical space—a complete nothingness from which there is nothing to accomplish. The deities can be realized because they are our own light. The purpose of completion stage is to realize primordial purity, while for development stage it is to realize spontaneous presence. Development stage and completion stage in Vajrayana are what makes the difference between an ordinary person and a Vajrayana practitioner. An ordinary person has no development or completion stage practice. In this regard, he is not much different from an ox. Someone who familiarizes himself or herself with the two profound stages of Vajrayana will have a great advantage when meeting death.

Let me repeat this important point: development stage is spontaneous presence and completion stage is primordial purity. The crucial point here is that primordial purity and spontaneous presence are indivisible. Our body is the buddha mandala. That is why the person of sharpest faculty can develop and realize the deities. The way to combine these profound teachings is to practice a sadhana. Understand that the Mahayoga tantras are contained within the Anu Yoga scriptures. They again are contained within Ati Yoga, while Ati Yoga is contained within sadhana practice. The sadhana itself is contained within your application. This is why you can quickly perfect the accumulations and purify the obscurations through sadhana practice. Even a small sadhana text embodies all the key points of the incredibly profound Vajrayana system in a way we can connect with and practice. A sadhana of even a few pages contains something extremely important and profound.

The Body, Speech and Mind of the buddhas as well as the body, speech and mind of sentient beings can all be experienced in actuality. The three kayas of buddhahood—the three vajras as the essence, nature and capacity—are intrinsic aspects of our buddha nature itself. This is the basis for their undeniable connection with the body, speech and mind of all sentient beings. Without these three, without the buddha mandala, without the Body, Speech and Mind, there would be nothing. However, they are complete within the aggregates, elements and sense-bases.

A practitioner could also focus on some nihilistic void and assert that nothing whatsoever exists, but that would be untrue and useless. It's very important to understand this principle. If our basic nature was a nihilistic void, nothing would take place: we would be like empty space, experiencing nothing—which is definitely not the case. Once again, this way of acknowledging reality *as it is*, is the skillful means of the profound and swift path of Vajrayana. We apply the methods to realize just this. It is extremely important.

Everything is all-encompassing purity; that is the Vajrayana perspective. This approach is not imagination, making up something or thinking that what isn't, is. Vajrayana is totally unlike that. All that appears and exists actually *is* all-encompassing purity. We really should understand that everything, all world-systems and all beings—whatever appears and exists, meaning the 'perceived' and the 'perceiver'—all takes place out of the sphere of the three kayas. Everything originates from the three kayas, takes place within the sphere of the three kayas, and dissolves back again into the sphere of the three kayas. That is what meant by all-encompassing purity. It is not the act of believing something that isn't true. It is not like thinking that wood is gold. To regard gold as gold, that is knowing what is to be *as it is*.

Once we have entered the path of Vajrayana, training in all-encompassing purity is training in the path of *what is*. The Buddha from the beginning clearly knew the development and completion stages, the intent of Vajrayana. All-encompassing purity is not mentioned in Sutra system only because it wouldn't fit into that type of individual's perspective. That is the only reason why the Buddha did not teach it, not because some teachings are better than others.

If one doesn't know things as they are, as all-encompassing purity, one thinks that earth is just earth, fire is just fire and water is just water.

From the beginning the door is blocked by preconceptions. In accordance with the all-encompassing purity everything originates, remains and dissolves within the expanse of the three kayas.

If you have to imagine the development stage you now practice, it is a still a resemblance. The way of imitation thinks, "This is the samadhi of suchness, the nature of mind, and it corresponds to dharmakaya. Out of dharmakaya unfolds sambhogakaya, the all-illuminating samadhi, the naturally cognizant aspect. The indivisibility of these two is the seed samadhi, the compassionate nirmanakaya. Out of the unity of emptiness and compassion, nirmanakaya takes place."

Whether one is carrying out the actual or the resembling development stage, at the beginning of the practice, we need to 'unfold the structure of the three samadhis.' Then we unfold the 'support and the supported,' the palace and the deity. Gradually we become more and more accustomed to this. At the end of a sadhana there is a reversal of what was initially unfolded. The nirmanakaya aspect dissolves into the sambhogakaya, and that dissolves back into the unconstructed sphere of dharmakaya. Yet, even though everything has dissolved, there is a re-emergence. These two phases, dissolution and re-emergence, are to destroy the wrong views of nihilism and permanence. They eliminate the tendency toward eternalism, the belief in the permanence of all things, as well as the tendency toward nihilism, the idea that nothing exists.

The Vajrayana perspective is very important to have. Literally translated, the term Vajrayana means 'vajra vehicle,' with vajra meaning 'unchanging,' 'indestructible.' For ordinary practitioners, development stage is like a resemblance, a mask or portrait of the real thing. It is like the painting of Padmasambhava here on my wall. It's not really Padmasambhava in person, because he actually resides in his pure land, the Glorious Copper-Colored Mountain. But it is his likeness, isn't it? In the same way, the ordinary development stage is a likeness or imitation of the real thing. Although it's a resemblance and not the real thing, it's not exactly false, because development stage is a valid exercise in seeing things as they actually are, rather than as something other. Completion stage is the true thing, the view, the natural state.

To practice these two stages as indivisible has incredible depth of meaning. Sentient beings are constantly experiencing impure phenomena. To change that into the experience of pure phenomena, we train in development stage. The basis for development stage is completion stage, the realization of dharmakaya, the view. The fruition is when the rupakayas again dissolve into dharmakaya. The place where the rupakayas abide is dharmadhatu. That is the profound meaning in the unity of development and completion stage.

While reciting the lines of the sadhana, we come to the seed samadhi. From the seed samadhi the mandala of the deity unfolds; this is also the way everything really is. In the case of our practice, the seed samadhi is being created by mind, but the reason we mentally create it is that, from the very beginning, all that appears and exists is the buddha mandala. Vajrayana training is the means to realize it *as it is,* that all that appears and exists is the buddha mandala. That is why we train in sadhana practice.

The New Schools have the same basic intent; there is no difference whatsoever. In the Nyingma School there are the three inner tantras of Maha, Anu and Ati, while in the Sarma Schools there are the mother tantras, father tantras and nondual tantras, as well as their quintessential and innermost essence tantras. These levels include the tantras and deities of Kalachakra, Hevajra, Guhyasamaja, Chakrasamvara, and Mahamaya. The deities may have different names, but there is no difference in the basic principle.

All sadhanas have a main structure that resembles the way that everything evolves, remains and vanishes. All of reality unfolds from the three kayas. Dharmakaya is free of constructs, sambhogakaya possesses the major and minor marks and is like a rainbow, and nirmanakaya appears in the form of the vajra body endowed with the six elements. Each of these unfolds from the previous one, while dissolution occurs in the reverse order.

Completion stage is the origin. The path of development stage is a training in knowing things to be as they are. From the very beginning, we need to be in harmony with this. First, there is the unfolding of the buddhafield within the sphere of emptiness. In the center of the buddhafield is the celestial palace. Within the celestial palace we visualize the deities, the main figure and its entourage of the peaceful and wrathful deities. They are like the sun and the rays of light emanating from it.

After visualizing the details of the deities, who are the *samaya sattvas*, they are sealed with the three vajras of the Body, Speech and Mind of all enlightened beings, marked with OM AH HUNG. Then they are empowered by being crowned with the five buddha families, usually while saying OM HUNG TRAM HRIH AH. Next, one invites the *jnana sattvas*, the wisdom beings, from the realm of Akanishtha, the buddhafield of dharmadhatu. It is said, "The deities are oneself and oneself is the deities." It is the same meaning; they dissolve indivisibly within oneself. There is a mantra for this, whereby we request them to arrive and be seated. The meaning is, "Please remain indivisibly, by means of the four immeasurables." It is accompanied by a mantra such as JAH HUNG BAM HO, KAYA VAKA . . . etc.

We then mentally create offerings. Since there is no duality in this type of mandala, the ones who make the offerings are emanations of oneself who turn around and make offerings to oneself. It is exactly like this in some of the god-realms. For example, in the god-realm called Mastery Over Others' Creations lives Garab Wangchuk, who is the chief of the maras. The gods there mentally conjure up their own sense-pleasures and enjoy them. Then they dissolve these, and again manifest. In this fashion, one emanates countless offering goddesses carrying all different kinds of sense-pleasures. After that are praises. This corresponds to purifying the mundane tendencies to invite an important person, to cater to him, to flatter him and finally to ask him for what you want. All this was for the accomplishment of body.

Next is the accomplishment of speech by means of the recitation. Recitation traditionally has four aspects: approach, full approach, accomplishment, and great accomplishment. Through this fourfold intent of approach and accomplishment, everything is accomplished.

After the mantra, the feast-offering section can be added to mend breaches of samaya, meaning to re-link or make up with the deities. Tormas are also presented to the protectors, and evil forces are suppressed by means of special requests to the Dharma protectors. An elaborate sadhana also includes the 'threefold neigh of Hayagriva,' meaning the 'horse-dance' at the end of the feast-offering. The threefold neighing proclaims that the ultimate state of awakened mind, described as the three doors of emancipation, is totally beyond the constructs of past, present and future. This ultimately will suppress all evil forces that might otherwise backfire or create hindrances for this realization.

At the end of the sadhana come the phases of dissolution and re-emergence. Just as everything evolved out of the sphere of three kayas, the entire mandala again dissolves back into the sphere of the three kayas. The mandala gradually dissolves into the palace, the palace into the deities, the retinue into the central figure, and the central figure into the seed-syllable in the heart center. It also dissolves and you remain as unconstructed emptiness. Then, once again you manifest as the single form of the deity and carry out your daily activities. Before closing the session, recite the verses of dedication, aspirations and auspiciousness.

Taken together, these main sections of sadhana practice are extremely profound. We engage in them in order to purify habitual tendencies and delusion. The real nature of things is all-encompassing purity. All things in samsara and nirvana and the path are pervaded by the Body, Speech and Mind of the victorious ones. It is only temporarily that sentient beings do not know this. They have conceptualized and labeled the pure as being impure. The true nature of things is primordial purity, pure from the beginning, primordially enlightened.

Primordially pure, with nothing impure at all; that is all-encompassing purity. What happened is that we made the mistake of not recognizing mind nature. It is only temporarily that sentient beings do not recognize. Once the sun begins to shine in a dark place, the darkness doesn't remain. All of samsara and nirvana—all of existence and peace—is the great purity. That is why Vajrayana is so profound.

There is no difference whatsoever in what a deity really is between the Old and New Schools. There is not a single deity that isn't included in the five buddha families of Vajra, Ratna, Padma, Karma, and Buddha.

Only one's own individual tradition differs. The fundamental aim is to accomplish the deity. One is taught this by means of training in the development and completion stages.

If one doesn't know mind essence, development stage is essentially blocked. It is very important to understand the basic principles of Vajrayana. In order to accomplish a deity, one must know the nature of the deity one is trying to accomplish. This is called 'identifying the deity to be accomplished.' The names, colors and attributes may differ, but a deity is actually the unity of primordial purity and spontaneous presence. In this way, development and completion are contained within Trekchö and Tögal.

Without recognizing mind essence, development stage practice is like laying bricks. It becomes a lot of hard work! This is most important. An incredible amount of evil deeds and obscurations are purified by this practice, if you know what is to be *as it is*. It is the path of pure perception. Know the origin. All of the worlds and beings unfold from the expanse of the three kayas. The three kayas are not over there. They pervade everything. If one doesn't know this, it is like doing masonry, laying down one brick at a time. Or else it's a flight of fantasy, merely an act of imagination. What we really need to do is to begin with unfolding the samadhi of suchness. The real suchness samadhi is mind essence.

Unless you understand all-encompassing purity, the development stage becomes very simplistic. You sit and imagine that there is nothing whatsoever; everything is emptiness. Then you try to imagine that now there is a place for the mandala, and you try to build the mandala up, step by step, through your imagination. Such a practice is conducted with a materialistic sense of constructing a mansion and inviting over a group of beautiful rich people. The deities all have arms and legs and faces, and wear special silk garments. In order to please them, you dish out exotic offerings, flatter them, and make them happy; then they give you something in return. That is some people's understanding of development stage.

We need a deeper understanding than that. Honestly speaking, there is no way around understanding all-encompassing purity. The five great elements are the female buddhas. The aggregates are the male buddhas. That is why I have repeatedly stated that the all-encompassing purity is the main principle to understand. I go on and on about this point because the principle of primordial purity is so vital to understand. *Everything* is of the nature of primordial purity. This is not something that is achieved through practice. It is an uncovering of how things actually are to begin with; that the minds of all sentient beings are, at this every moment, the unity of experience and emptiness. This is nothing other than Buddha Samantabhadra in union with his consort, the female buddha Samantabhadri.

The name Vairochana means 'manifest form' and refers to all experience of perceivable form. Forms experienced among the five aggregates are indivisible from emptiness itself. That is the nature called Buddha Vairochana. Speech is Buddha Amitabha, meaning that the semi-manifest, such as sound and communication, is indivisible from emptiness. Mind is Akshobhya, the unshakable. The nature of cognition, the consciousness aggregate, is indivisible from emptiness. Similarly, all qualities are Ratnasambhava, and all activities and interactions are of the nature of Amoghasiddhi.

Although *aggregate* means a group or a conglomeration composed of many parts, the five different aggregates all have the same nature, which is the five buddhas. It is the same with the five elements. Everything in the world is made out of elements; therefore, everything is of the nature of the five female buddhas. In this way, we cannot find anything that is not already the mandala of the five male and female buddhas. This is what is meant by the phrase 'all-encompassing purity.' We need to pay close attention to this and try to understand it, because there is not anything that isn't all-encompassing purity. That is the true meaning of development stage.

The simplistic views of the palace, the ornaments, the offerings of delicious food and so on is totally interconnected with the normal habitual tendencies of mundane people. It is not that deities of rainbow light have any concepts of near and far, or that they are pleased by being praised. It is only for one's own benefit that this is done, in order to gather the accumulations and to purify bad karma and habitual tendencies. We should clearly understand the profound intent of the Vajrayana.

Please gain full comprehension of the principle of this practice! The materialistic way to practicing the development stage is not that effective. It becomes like the guy who visualized himself as Yamantaka and couldn't get out the entrance of his cave because his horns were too big. His guru called for him to come, and he sent back a message, "Sorry! I can't come out! My horns get stuck in the doorway."

To reiterate, a sadhana may have several sections. In the main section, one erects the basic framework of the three samadhis. The samadhi of suchness is the intent of primordial purity. The samadhi of illumination is the intent of spontaneous presence. The samadhi of the seed-syllable is the nirmanakaya aspect, the indivisibility of primordial purity and spontaneous presence. This is how to start out the sadhana practice. Next, visualize the support, which is the mandala of the celestial palace, and the supported, the mandala of the deities. Bring to mind the details of all the deities and seal them with the syllables of Body, Speech and Mind. Crown them with the five syllables of the five buddha families, empowering the deities with deities. After that, consecrate the *samaya sattva*, which has been visualized until now, with the *jnana sattva* invited from the buddhafield of dharmadhatu. They arrive and dissolve into yourself indivisibly, like water dissolving into water.

Next are the outer, inner, and secret offerings. The outer offering is the offering-cloud exemplified by the bodhisattva Universal Excellence, the inner-offerings are the sense-pleasures represented by *amrita, rakta* and *torma,* and the secret offering is the unity of bliss and emptiness. The ultimate thatness offering is the offering of dharmadhatu indivisible from nondual awareness. Then, one makes praises. Both offerings and praises are performed by the offering goddesses who are emanated from oneself. They carry the offerings in their hands. At the time of making praises, they dance and perform mudras and sing the lines of praise, praising the Body, Speech, Mind, Qualities and Activities of both the peaceful and wrathful deities. At the conclusion, the offering goddesses again dissolve into oneself.

Up to this point, we have completed what is known as the body aspect of the development stage. Next comes the speech aspect, which is the recitation. The recitation intent is nothing other than deity, mantra and samadhi. Through the mantra, we acknowledge whatever is seen is the body of the peaceful and wrathful deities; whatever is heard is their voices, the sound of mantra; and that the nature of mind of all sentient beings is the state of nonconceptual, thoughtfree awareness which is by nature an unconfined empty cognizance. Although the deities appear in inconceivably different ways, they are in essence, identical in being the unity of basic space and original wakefulness. While keeping this in mind, one recites the mantra. This completes the speech aspect.

As I have repeatedly said concerning development stage, all phenomena, all deities, whatever appears and exists within samsara and nirvana, arise out of the sphere of the three kayas, remain within the sphere of the three kayas and finally dissolve into the sphere of the three kayas. Nothing takes place outside of the three kayas. In order to train in accordance with this principle, at the beginning of the sadhana let everything unfold out of the three kayas by means of three samadhis. Then let everything dissolve back.

Among the concluding sections of a sadhana, the first is dissolution. The empty forms, empty sounds, and empty awareness dissolve back into basic space. After that is the re-emergence. Whatever appears is the body of the peaceful and wrathful ones, whatever is heard is their voices, whatever takes place as natural awareness is the mind of the peaceful and wrathful ones. Following that is the dedication of merit and the making of aspirations. Finally there are the four lines for auspiciousness of dharmakaya, sambhogakaya and nirmanakaya. This conclusion again reminds us of the sphere of the three kayas.

12

Indivisibility

※

As I mentioned before, the way to train in the unity of development and completion is to begin any visualization with the samadhi of suchness. This means to recognize your own nature and remain in that. In that very moment, you are actually in the state of the primordially pure essence. The samadhi of illumination then occurs as the natural expression of rigpa. Mind essence is the unity of being empty and cognizant. The empty aspect is the samadhi of suchness, the primordial purity, dharmakaya. From this the spontaneously present phenomena manifest, and this is the second, the samadhi of illumination. The unobstructed cognizant aspect is the samadhi of illumination, the sambhogakaya. It means that there is a compassionate flavor to emptiness, that the expression of the primordially pure essence, the unconstructed nature, is naturally compassionate. These two—emptiness and compassion—are indivisible. That is the vital point.

To repeat, the empty quality is primordial purity. The manifest is a spontaneous compassionate presence. This unity of emptiness and compassion is the basis of all Dharma practice, and it is this unity that takes the form of the seed-syllable. That is the third samadhi, the samadhi of the seed-syllable, which is the nirmanakaya. The unity of being empty and compassionate appears as the seed-syllable that is the deity's spiritual life-force. For example, if one is practicing Guru Rinpoche, his spiritual life-force is hrih.

Once the seed-syllable appears, it sends out E, which is the seed-syllable of space. YAM is for wind, RAM for fire, KHAM for water, LAM for earth, SUM for Mt. Sumeru, finally BHRUM for the celestial palace at the top of Mt. Sumeru. Next, the syllable HRIH descends like a shooting star, lands on the throne within the celestial palace, and transforms into the deity. All this takes place without having to leave behind the state of mind essence. Without leaving the empty suchness samadhi of rigpa behind, the compassionate illumination of spontaneous presence unfolds unobstructedly from the primordially pure essence. The development stage can take place while recognizing mind essence, since its expression is unobstructed. If the essence was obstructed the development stage could not arise, but it isn't so. The development stage is allowed to develop, to manifest, without harming the primordial purity one bit. Without moving away from unchanging primordial purity, the spontaneous presence, the expression of awareness, takes place. This is the indivisibility of primordial purity and spontaneous presence.

This is also why development and completion are basically a unity. The *developed* in development stage refers to what is formed as an expression of unobstructed awareness. Thought, on the other hand, can obstruct rigpa. When the expression moves as thought, there is delusion. Ordinary thinking is to form one thought, then to think of something else, and so on, incessantly. The new thought interrupts the previous one, and the next thought interrupts that one. True development stage is not like that at all. The key point lies in this unobstructed quality of rigpa; the samadhi of illumination does not cut off the samadhi of suchness. The seed-syllable manifesting in the middle of space doesn't obstruct the compassionate emptiness. In fact, it is the *expression* of compassionate emptiness. Thus, you are not only allowed to let visualization unfold out of compassionate emptiness; it is the real way to practice.

This type of development stage takes place without having to leave behind the state of mind essence. There is no need to avoid recognizing mind essence in order to think of these things; let them naturally unfold. Simply allow the visualization to unfold out of compassionate emptiness, the unity of empty cognizance. This is called 'letting development stage unfold out of the completion stage.' In this way, there is no real separation between them. Otherwise, a common misunderstanding is that the development stage steals the completion stage, and that later you have to kick out the development stage to give the completion stage a chance. It's just like when one starts to think of one thing, the previous thought disappears. That is called visualizing with dualistic mind.

This is how it may seem in the beginning when one is being taught, but really, it isn't like that at all. The reason is that primordial purity and spontaneous presence are a natural unity; they cannot really be divided. If not, you would have only primordial purity, a void state where nothing can take place, or a spontaneous presence that was the same as dualistic mind. There would be a battle between dharmakaya and sambhogakaya. In actuality there is no conflict, because spontaneous presence is indivisible from primordial purity. You are not only definitely allowed to, but also it is perfectly all right and permissible to let the development stage unfold from within the completion stage. There is no conflict between the two. A famous saying goes, "Some say development stage is right. Others say completion stage is right. They pitch development against completion."

The unity of emptiness and cognizance has an unobstructed capacity. If it were obstructed, we wouldn't be able know anything. It would be a total blank. If cognizance and emptiness were not a unity, one would occur when thinking and the other when not thinking. Conceptual thought blocks, obstructs, confines; this is how development and completion can be obstructed. However, the expression of awareness is unimpeded. If this were not so, rigpa would not have any capacity. But the essence does have a capacity. The dharmakaya and sambhogakaya do manifest.

Dharmakaya is a totally unconstructed state and sambhogakaya is the great enjoyment, meaning an abundance of perfect qualities. From the empty essence of primordial purity, the spontaneously present nature manifests unobstructedly. Likewise, we are allowed to practice the development stage unobstructedly. Otherwise, without the samadhi of suchness, development stage would be an imitation. We might even think the wrathful deities were literally angry!

A very good way to understand this is that when a rainbow appears in the sky, it doesn't damage the empty sky at all, and yet the rainbow is totally visible. It doesn't change the sky, doesn't hurt it in the slightest. It's exactly the same when recognizing the essence of mind that has been pointed out as being utterly empty. That is the samadhi of suchness. That recognition doesn't have to be left behind in order for cognizance, the samadhi of illumination, to be present; it is spontaneously present by nature. That is true compassion. The sky is the samadhi of suchness, while the rainbow is the samadhi of illumination, the development stage. There is no fight between space and a rainbow, is there? It's exactly like that. First of all you need to know the samadhi of suchness. Having recognized that, the expression of awareness arises from the essence as the development stage. It is not like construction work. Like the rainbow appearing in the sky, the expression of awareness is the perfect unity of development and completion stage.

This approach is not always possible for every practitioner. The next best way is when one thinks of one detail at a time, like the head of the deity, the arms, the legs and the body and the attributes and so forth. Every once in a while one recognizes who it is, what it is, that visualizes, and again one arrives at the state of original empty wakefulness. Then again think of some visualized details, and again recognize, alternating back and forth between the two. That is called the next best, the medium way of practicing. The least or minimum requirement is to first think that everything becomes empty. One recites the mantra om maha shunyata... and after that one says, "From the state of emptiness such-and-such appears." In this way one thinks of one thing at a time, and at the end of the sadhana again dissolves the whole thing into emptiness. These are three ways in which one could practice development and completion together.

However, while again and again recognizing your buddha nature, it is possible to allow the visualization to take place unobstructedly. There is no law that one has to think of one thing after another. The expression of awareness is unobstructed. It is not like brick-laying, where one puts things on top of each other in a very concrete way. Whatever unfolds out of the samadhi of suchness is like a rainbow. The celestial palace, the deities, are all like rainbows. This rainbow manifestation doesn't have to somehow block off the space in which it unfolds. It is not necessary at all. The first two samadhis are the unity of primordial purity and spontaneous presence. In the seed samadhi, the word 'seed' means that it is the source or origin of the whole mandala and all the deities. The seed-syllable is also called the 'life essence of the mind,' the deity's 'mental life-force.' As mentioned before, for Guru Rinpoche that is the syllable HRIH. That is the beginning of the visualization. But remember, this HRIH and whatever comes after is not something tangible or material.

The authentic way of practicing is to let visualizations of the development state unfold out of the samadhi of suchness. That is the best, foremost way. The samadhi of suchness is the dharmakaya state. The samadhi of illumination is the sambhogakaya state, and the seed samadhi is the nirmanakaya state. In actuality, all of samsara and nirvana unfold from the expanse of the three kayas. This is the example for the unity of development and completion stages.

Here is another way to understand development stage. All things take place from within the space of the five mothers, meaning the five female buddhas. The five elements are empty. What knows is the cognizant quality. This perceiving quality is the male buddha Samantabhadra, the *yab*, while the empty quality is the female buddha Samantabhadri, the *yum*. The outer objects, the five elements, are not the perceiving; they are the empty aspect. The five elements are in actuality the five female buddhas; what is perceived in the impure state as being earth, fire, water, wind and space is in fact the properties of the five female buddhas. In this way, everything in this world is already the mandala of the five female buddhas. Within this type of celestial palace is the pure nature of the five aggregates, the five male buddhas. We are not inventing anything here; this is our basic state as it is. Mind and phenomena, the experiencer and the experienced, is Samantabhadra and consort. In the development stage we don't perpetuate ordinary impure perception in any way whatsoever. Everything is regarded as the pure wisdom deities, the unity of experience and emptiness.

All phenomena are already by nature the unity of experience and emptiness. Every experience, all things in this world and in your life, is already the unity of experience and emptiness. There is nothing that is not empty. The essence of development is the experiencing aspect. The essence of completion is the empty aspect. These two are primordially a unity. There is nothing impure whatsoever. This is how everything already is. Therefore, everything takes place already as the unity of development stage and completion stage. When practicing development and completion stage you are training yourself in seeing things as they actually are, seeing it *as it is*, not as pure fantasy that has no basis whatsoever.

In Dzogchen there are two quintessential principles: primordial purity and spontaneous presence. Primordial purity is the empty; spontaneous presence is the experiencing aspect. These are an original unity. When training in development stage and completion stage, we train in manifesting as a pure form, which is already the case. This is the basic situation of everything, how it really *is*. Reality is already the unity of male and female buddhas in the sense of the indivisibility of primordial purity and spontaneous presence. The whole mandala with the deity is a display of primordial purity indivisible from spontaneous presence.

It is also this indivisible unity that appears as the deities in the bardo. Likewise, it is the unity of primordial purity and spontaneous presence which are the deities in Tögal practice. These are two instances in which the mandala of the deities of one's own body arise or manifest, like rainbows in the sky. These deities are five-colored lights, as a sign of the indivisibility of primordial purity and spontaneous presence. In both cases these are things as they are; you don't need to think that what isn't, is. Your own deities appear to yourself.

From the perspective of manifest aspect of buddha nature, the deities can be said to abide in our body. These deities of the development stage *do* appear to us in the bardo and in Tögal practice. One's own deities manifest to oneself. In terms of the essence of our mind, nonexistence is primordial purity; existence is spontaneous presence. Our essence is the unity of existence and nonexistence. The deities are the experienced aspect; this is how things are. This is the preciousness of development stage; it is not an unimportant point.

If in the state of primordial purity there was not the experienced aspect of spontaneous presence, nothing would happen. However, this is not the case, because these two, primordial purity and spontaneous presence, are a unity. Primordial purity means the absence, no concrete thing, the empty quality, whereas spontaneous presence means the presence. It is not only absence or only presence; they are indivisible. The primordial indivisibility of absence and presence is a very good example. Experience and emptiness are a unity. The experiencing aspect is development, the empty is completion. The rainbow in the sky is not tangible, but still visible. There is no thing, and yet there is something. That is a very good example. Also, rainbows only appear in the sky. You don't have rainbows in wood or in stone and so on.

All phenomena are the unity of existence and nonexistence. Primordial purity and spontaneous presence are a unity. The kayas and wisdoms are a unity. There is a quote that goes, "All the scriptures say that everything is empty, but the fact that our nature is not empty of the kayas and wisdoms, that is the real tradition of the Buddha." This is how it really is. In the second turning of the wheel of Dharma, the Buddha said that everything, from the aggregate of forms all the way up to and including omniscient enlightenment, is empty and devoid of self-entity. Of course that is correct, but it is not the full truth; that statement emphasizes the empty quality. Liberation is only possible through realizing the basic unity of emptiness and experience. Like space, the empty aspect cannot get liberated.

All phenomena are the unity of experience and emptiness. Without the experience aspect, the kayas and wisdoms would be hidden, and would never manifest. Kayas and wisdoms are very important principles. It is said "If the kayas and wisdoms are empty, there is no fruition." If the state of fruition is empty, it is just like space, which is called nothing whatsoever. 'Just like space' means nothing to understand, nothing there. Think about this. Everything is of course empty, but not empty of the kayas and wisdoms, in the sense that they are nonexistent or absent.

If the kayas and wisdoms were absent, there would be no twenty-five attributes of fruition. If they were absent, how could there be five kayas, five types of speech, five wisdoms, five qualities and five activities? The twenty-five attributes of fruition are not some kind of concrete material substance. There is ground, path and fruition; not only ground and path. If everything was empty there wouldn't be the two kayas of dharmakaya and rupakaya. The dharmakaya free from constructs like space is defined as, 'dissolved yet unobscured.' 'Dissolved' here means totally free of all disturbing emotions. At the same time, wisdom, meaning original wakefulness, is unobscured. That is the meaning of 'dissolved yet unobscured.' This is also called the dharmakaya of basic brilliance. Dharmakaya is not empty or devoid of a cognizant quality.

Furthermore, in terms of experience, dharmakaya is primordially the unity of experience and emptiness. Primordial purity is the empty aspect, while spontaneous presence is the experience aspect. These two are a unity. That is why we say that the kayas and wisdoms are a unity. Dharmakaya is a body of space, free from constructs. Sambhogakaya is a body like a rainbow. The five buddhas of the five families are called the bodies of the wisdoms of distinguished characteristics—white, red, yellow, green, blue, the five lights.

Once again: first are two kayas, dharmakaya and rupakaya. The rupakaya consists of two types: the sambhogakaya, which is of rainbow light, and the nirmanakaya, which is a material body of flesh and blood possessing the six elements.

If we claim everything is empty, then who would there to be to know that? There wouldn't be anything. There would be no wisdom, no original wakefulness. The wakefulness knowing of the original nature is a type of knowing that does not depend on an object. Thought, on the other hand, cannot stir without depending upon an object. When you say original wakefulness, *yeshe* or wisdom, it by definition means a knowing for which there is no object. When you say thought, or *namshey*, it means a knowing with the structure of subject and object. *Yeshe* is a knowing that doesn't fixate in a dualistic way, whereas our ordinary knowing is dualistic fixation. Dualistic fixation should be destroyed. That is the whole reason why we strive so diligently in meditation and recognize mind essence. *Yeshe* is primordial knowing. We get used to primordial knowing by recognizing our essence as primordial purity. Nondualistic wakefulness destroys dualistic fixation. When dualistic fixation is destroyed, deluded experience falls apart, and all conceptual activity collapses. This is what we should resolve upon and become completely clear about.

Ultimately, the vital point is the difference between consciousness and wakefulness, *namshey* and *yeshe*. Consciousness means knowing in which there is subject and object, and in which the subject gets involved in the object. The state of realization of all the buddhas, on the other hand, is a primordial knowing that is independent from an object. Trekchö training reveals this state of realization. If we, on the other hand, believe that our basic state is only empty, a blank empty state, this emptiness wouldn't possess any qualities. But the qualities are primordially present. This original wakefulness, *yeshe*, is inconceivable. The Dzogchen teachings describe it either as the unity of being empty and cognizant or as the unity of being aware and empty. Of course the dualistic consciousness is also empty and cognizant, but it is suffused with ignorance, with unknowing. Ignorance means not knowing rigpa. Yeshe is empty cognizance suffused with knowing.

In actuality, all that appears and exists, all world and beings, are the mandala of the five male and female buddhas, the mandala of the victorious ones. This is simply how it already is, and that is how we train ourselves in seeing things by means of development stage. To recognize rigpa is the true way to acknowledge what is to be *as it is*. At that moment, experience in itself is already the mandala of the male and female buddhas, without us having to think it is. When there is no recognition of rigpa, then it isn't, even though it is essentially. When one merely thinks it is, that is only a pretense, even though based on this pretense, called ordinary development stage, it becomes possible to realize in actuality. This is because whatever appears and exists is already the mandala of the victorious ones.

Development stage is a training in what really is. The perceiving quality is the *yab* and the empty quality is the *yum*. These two are an indivisible unity. This is the fundamental mandala of all the victorious ones, of all buddhas. This unity of experience and emptiness is also the source of the ordinary body, speech and mind of sentient beings. Sentient beings are, however, not simply ordinary body, speech and mind. We possess the enlightened Body, Speech and Mind as well. It is only that we don't recognize this; but it is not enough to pretend that this is so. We can pretend to be a buddha, but still we will not be enlightened by thinking, "I am a buddha." There has to be some authentic acknowledgment of what *actually* is. Even though our world is a nirmanakaya buddhafield, we need to also know it.

There are the six Munis, one for each of the six realms of samsara. There is Dharmaraja for the hell-beings, Khala Mebar for the hungry ghosts, Senge Rabten for the animals, Shakyamuni for the humans, Taksangri for the demigods, and Shakra for the gods. Each of the six realms of samsara is in fact a nirmanakaya buddhafield. Even though this is so, beings don't know it. What we need to know is that our nature is an unconfined empty cognizance. Knowing this to be *as it is*, is the mandala of the victorious ones — just as the buddhas know it to be. However, we have fallen under the power of wrong views and distorted concepts, and are wandering about in the confused states of samsara.

The four lines for ultimate bodhichitta in the preliminary practices of *Kunzang Tuktig* say:

> Namo༔
> I and the six classes of beings, all living things,༔
> Are buddhas from the very beginning.༔
> By the nature of knowing this to be as it is,༔
> I form the resolve towards supreme enlightenment.༔

"By the nature of knowing this to be as it is" means seeing reality *as it is*. It means that whatever appears and exists is already all-encompassing purity, the mandala of the victorious ones. It is not only something that we pretend it to be. However, it only becomes true when recognizing the natural state. Otherwise, one doesn't see it as it really is. The ignorance of the unknowing, the grasping at duality, the getting involved in the three poisons, obscures the all-encompassing purity of what appears and exists. The difference lies entirely between knowing and not knowing. When someone has recognized his or her nature through it being pointed out by a master, that is knowing what is to be *as it is*. This is what one then trains in—in the state of original wakefulness unspoiled by dualistic fixation.

To recognize self-existing wakefulness is to see things as they are. This is unlike taking a white conch shell to be yellow; there is no way that this is so. When you have jaundice, you see a conch as being yellow. The conch definitely isn't yellow, it never was, but because of the gall in the body making your eye yellow, you see white as yellow even though it isn't. That is the example for the confusion, the mistakenness of sentient beings. They don't see things as they really are

Since I and all other sentient beings are buddhas from the very beginning, I resolve to attain supreme enlightenment by the power of recognizing this to be *as it is*, by the ultimate bodhichitta. This is the way of acknowledging the all-encompassing purity of all that appears and exists. All-encompassing purity abides in yourself.

According to the Dzogchen teachings, the state of primordial enlightenment has never been confused. The basic state of buddhas is like pure gold that is not covered by any dirt. Dirt is the example for the confused thinking that temporarily takes place. If the gold always remains pure, there is no cleaning to be done and there is no achievement of purity, because it already is like that from the beginning. That is the analogy for the state of primordial enlightenment of self-existing wakefulness that was never confused. If, first of all, there is no being confused then how can you use the phrase 'being liberated'? It is impossible, because liberation is totally dependent upon having been confused. Since the awakened state of the buddhas are not confused, you cannot really say that buddhas become liberated either. It is only because of being mistaken that confusion can be cleared up. Unless there is confusion it is not possible to be liberated.

We sentient beings have the same self-existing wakefulness as the buddhas. There is no difference whatsoever in our natures. However, the self-existing wakefulness of the buddhas, all the infinite qualities, never became confused, like the gold that never became tainted. Even though we possess the same gold, ours fell in the dirt. Not knowing this dirty gold to be intrinsically pure, we fell under the power of confused thinking. This is what obscured us: our thinking. The gold of the buddhas was known to be what it was. Buddhas do not have discursive thinking. It won't help sentient beings to act as if they are primordially pure gold if they have already become confused and are now unaware of their own nature. It doesn't become true. The practice we have, of first recognizing the view, training in the meditation, acting out of that as the conduct and realizing it fully as fruition—that is like the special chemicals that clean away dirt from gold. In other words, view, meditation and conduct remove the confusion.

In recognizing our nature the confusion is liberated. For buddhas neither the words confusion nor liberation apply. The word confusion connotes bewilderment, being mistaken, deluded. Confusion is nothing other than the expression of rigpa, which moves in a mistaken way. As long as you are confusing yourself by your awareness being extroverted, there is nobody else *ever* who can solve that. There is only yourself, right? Otherwise, confusion goes on and on. That is exactly what samsara is, confusion going on and on. Even though we sentient beings are buddhas, we are like the dirt-encrusted gold; we don't recognize the gold for what it is. This is due to deluded thinking. In our basic essence there is no thinking; the essence is wakefulness that is pure from the beginning. By recognizing your buddha nature, the three kayas become an actuality.

The empty essence is dharmakaya and the cognizant nature is sambhogakaya. There is awareness and the expression of awareness. What is necessary is to allow the expression of awareness, of *rigpa*, to be liberated. It is said that nirmanakaya recognizes sambhogakaya, which in turn recognizes dharmakaya. In awareness itself there is neither the word liberation nor confusion. It is the expression that fell into conceptualizing. If the expression of rigpa recognizes itself, it dawns as knowledge, *sherab*. This is not the ordinary knowledge that is the outcome of learning, reflecting and meditating. It is the real *prajnaparamita*, transcendent knowledge, which means the expression of awareness recognizing itself. In that moment, the expression of awareness dissolves back into awareness and there is only the state of rigpa, which is identical with the state of primordial enlightenment of all buddhas, the state which never strayed out from itself.

A famous and important quotation describes this: "When the expression moves as thinking, it is confused. When the expression dawns as knowledge, it is liberated." That doesn't mean that in the state of the essence, meaning rigpa, there was ever any difference. The state of rigpa, buddha nature itself, is never confused and never liberated. The confusion and liberation can only take place in the expression.

The state of original enlightenment is the essence itself, where there is no confusion and no liberation. The state of sentient beings is to be constantly absorbed in confused thinking. It is the expression, the thinking, that can be liberated again. Yet the essence all the time was never different from that of any other buddha. That is the important point, recognize your own essence. That is also the key point in the first samadhi of suchness. There is no real development stage practice possible without the samadhi of suchness, and this suchness is not recognized without first having the nature of mind pointed out.

13

Two Demons

❋

Often the life-stories of past practitioners tell of demons conjuring up some magic to fool them or trick them. As a matter of fact, all appearances are a magical display, experienced only by mind. It is possible for this mind, in each individual sentient being, to become stable in itself without ever being fooled again. No matter which individual person's mind we are talking about, in essence it is the same as that of all buddhas.

Take the example I often use of the rooms of different houses here in Nepal. Each room has some empty space in it, and in essence the space is identical. The walls are different, the exterior containers are different, but the basic substance of space doesn't differ in the slightest from one room to another. Similarly, the essence in all sentient beings is an unconfined empty cognizance which is present as our nature of mind. Right now we may have the feeling that each person's mind is different and separate, but in the moment of realizing the state of dharmakaya, it is as if all the walls fall away. There is only the oneness of dharmakaya, like one space, the sky.

All the buddhas are like a thousand butter lamps in a room: the flames are distinct and separate, but their light is one. When realizing the state of dharmakaya, there is only one identity, like the identity of the light of a thousand butter lamps. Each flame is distinct, but their light extending everywhere in the room is indivisible. The expanse of realization is of one taste, like the indivisible light from the individual flames. That light is the analogy for dharmakaya.

Like the analogy of the individual flames, sambhogakaya is distinct and separate forms made of rainbow light. As for nirmanakaya, *nirmana* means magical apparition, something created magically to be perceived by ordinary beings. For instance, there is the vajra body comprised of six elements, as in the case of Buddha Shakyamuni who appeared as a physical human being. Dharmakaya is like space, one essence. Sambhogakaya is distinct and separate, like rainbows in the sky. Nirmanakayas act to influence beings in all necessary ways, as with the one thousand buddhas which are to appear in this aeon. To be perceived by ordinary beings—in other words, to 'appear within their personal experience'—a buddha has to come as a human being, in which case even animals can perceive him. One thousand of that kind will appear in this aeon. At the same time, simultaneously, there are six buddhas, one for each of the six realms of sentient beings. Their re-emanations and magical apparitions are countless. These are called the external three kayas.

To repeat once more, the inner three kayas are dharmakaya, which is the empty essence, sambhogakaya, which is cognizant nature, and nirmanakaya, which is the indivisible unity of emptiness and cognizance. These three kayas are present as the nature of mind of each and every sentient being. Sentient beings roam about in samsara because of not recognizing this nature, and therefore are caught up in their emotions of like, dislike and indifference. To recognize mind essence means to be face to face with the three kayas in oneself. The three kayas are not an outcome of meditation practice. Being face to face with them occurs the moment you recognize your mind essence and see that it is no 'thing.' That is the unconstructed dharmakaya of the awakened state.

At the same time, there is a cognizance which sees that there is no thing to see. This recognition does not require two entities, one empty and another cognizing that fact. The emptiness and the cognizance are an originally indivisible unity. To illustrate this, right now in this room there is some space, which is an area with no thing in it. That is the example for empty essence. Cognizant nature is, for example, like the daylight: the sun has arisen and it simply shines. Right now there is sunlight in the room. Can you separate the daylight from the space in the room?

That is the analogy for unity. If you can separate them, they are not a unity. There is space in the room, and at the same time there is daylight, so everything can be seen distinctly. This brightness and the space are indivisible. That is the symbol of unity, the example for it. Space and sunlight are a unity during the daytime. There is no place other than within space that the sun can go. For us there is day and night, but does the sun actually go somewhere else other than being within space?

Space, sunlight and their indivisibility are analogies for essence, nature and capacity, the three kayas. The empty sky is the example for the empty essence. Sunlight is the example for cognizant nature, while space and sunlight indivisible are the example for unity. The very moment you gently recognize your mind essence, isn't there some kind of brightness of knowing how it is? 'Gently' means that you are not staring at it as if your essence was some other thing. There are not two entities, are there? Actually there never were two. It only seems to oneself as if there are two entities, a duality, due to not allowing the natural oneness to just be oneness. It seems as if there is a watcher and something observed. This duality is a construct set up by the thinking in the mind of the individual. Therefore, the instruction is: in the moment of looking, let be. That does not allow the duality to be kept up or perpetuated. It is phrased like this:

> When looking, no thing is seen; it is inconcrete.
> In this absence, rest loosely.

When the indivisible nature is not an actuality for oneself, one keeps up the mistaken idea that there is something observed separate from the observer. Actually, though, the indivisible three kayas which are our own nature is an incessant presence, not something that occurs sometimes, vanishes, and then comes back. What seems to interrupt this continuity is, first of all, the lack of knowing how to recognize, and second, being caught up in thoughts about that over there—the perceived. The three poisons take over almost ceaselessly. That is how sentient beings' minds work. If the three poisons are incessant, samsara is endless. There is only one way to bring samsara to a halt, and that is to recognize the indivisible three kayas.

When we are enlightened, it means that our thinking is interrupted, dissolved, vanished. It is not possible to be enlightened and still have deluded thinking. To claim that is absurd. Isn't it true that in this world we find no other method or technique to bring thoughts really to exhaustion? Even if you blow up a nuclear bomb, will that stop thinking? You can destroy countries or cities, for sure, but unfortunately it won't stop minds from thinking. The only way to do so is the seeing of our own essence, which is the indivisible three kayas of all the awakened ones. It is said that when seeing the three kayas, the three poisons disappear. Here the three kayas means the indivisible empty cognizance. While seeing this indivisible empty cognizance, the three poisons are lost—gone for good.

Only when the recognition of this indivisible empty cognizance remains unbroken are the three poisons lost forever. We need to grow used to the recognition of mind essence by training. In the moment of seeing, whichever of the three poisons was present dissolves instantaneously. That doesn't mean that there won't be another of the three poisons coming back later. There is only one way to be perpetually free of the three poisons, to have brought an eternal end to samsara. That is to grow fully trained in the recognition of mind essence, so that there is no more break in the seeing of the indivisible empty cognizance—so it is unbroken throughout day and night. Otherwise we are not able to vanquish the three poisons because we already have the habit of them since beginningless lifetimes.

When you strike a match, there is a moment of flame, heat and fire. If that match is put to a heap of straw at the foot of a huge mountain, you can burn down the entire mountain. The difference lies in to what extent the fire catches. In the same way, one instant of recognizing mind essence creates a 'spark' of mind essence that is just like striking the match. This flame burns away any of the three poisons that were present at that moment. How much is burnt away depends on how much you have trained and grown accustomed to it, and how long it takes before mind nature is forgotten again — how soon the flame of recognition dwindles. If the recognition remains totally unbroken, all negative karma and past obscurations are totally obliterated. At the same time, the continuing creation of new obscurations and negative karma is interrupted, just like a whole mountain catching fire.

Each moment of wakefulness is the same: what makes the difference is how long the stretch is, how great the stability is. Since we have been deluded from beginningless time, karma and negative deeds lie latent. That is the reason why we make mending-and-apology rituals. When there is complete stability, when the mountain has totally burned away, then all past karma and evil deeds are purified and there is no more falling into the pattern of delusion. That state is equal to complete enlightenment, the dharmakaya of all the buddhas.

It is not possible to be enlightened while still having obscurations and negative karma. They need to be interrupted and purified, and that is why one does the purification practices and apologizes for the negative deeds one has done. There is a way to thoroughly and perpetually bring an end to negative karma and obscuration. The recognition of mind essence totally interrupts the karma and obscurations *for that moment*. It purifies the negative karma which has been continued from the past, and it interrupts any creation henceforth. As long as this recognition lasts, karma and obscurations are thoroughly and completely ended. Complete stability in the recognition of empty cognizance involves the total elimination of all obscurations and negative karma. That is like the single match that ignites the flame. The flame is fire. It has the same identity as an entire mountain ablaze. When the whole mountain has caught fire, it is possible to burn away everything, all trees and greenery, so that nothing whatsoever is left behind.

The nature of mind is primordially pure and free, but it is also temporarily obscured, moment by moment. The obscuration is not intrinsic, not an indivisible part of the nature itself, because then it would be impossible to be enlightened. If the obscuration was part of the nature of mind itself and not merely a temporary event, it could not possibly be eliminated. Obscuration is only temporary, like a room which is temporarily in pitch-black darkness. Although the temporary darkness can last for a long time—say, ten thousand years—the moment you switch on the light, the darkness is instantaneously gone.

Enlightenment is only possible because the mind is primordially free and pure; this is what all buddhas are stable in, primordial freedom. It is like the water from the source of a mountain river, which gets dirty as it flows down through the valley. At the source itself, it is pure. The dirt is something that mixes in along the way. Similarly, the minds of sentient beings have the nature of the three kayas. Impurity comes about when failing to recognize what our nature really is, then the temporary obscuration sets in. That is what can again be purified.

Buddhas have from the beginning recognized their nature, and thus are primordially enlightened. For us sentient beings, confusion is a temporary condition. Through recognizing, due to being introduced to our nature through the pointing-out instruction of our master and engaging in that practice, we can be re-enlightened. What we were at first, our original essence, became soiled along the way, but this dirt is temporary. It can be cleaned. The state of buddhahood is within us. The essence is primordially enlightened, but temporarily obscured. A quote from the tantras says:

> All beings are indeed buddhas,
> But they are covered by temporary obscuration.
> When this is removed, they are really buddhas.

I would like to quote another important text, the *Lamrim Yeshe Nyingpo*:

> The ground to be understood is the all-pervasive sugata essence. ⁜
> Unformed, luminous and empty, it is the natural state of
>   awareness. ⁜
> Beyond confusion and liberation, it is completely quiescent like
>   space. ⁜
> Although it abides without separation in samsara or joining in
>   nirvana, ⁜

Due to the great demons of coemergent and conceptual
 ignorance, ⁑
From the solidified habitual patterns of grasping and fixation, ⁑
And the different perceptions of worlds and inhabitants, ⁑
The six classes of beings appeared as a dream. ⁑

Although this is so, you have never moved and will never move ⁑
From the original condition of the essence. ⁑
Endeavor, therefore, in purifying the temporary stains. ⁑

How do we exert ourselves in clearing away these temporary obscurations? The long path involves training in the ten virtuous actions. The shorter route is the Vajrayana training in deity, mantra and samadhi. The fastest route is to exert yourself in realizing the wish-fulfilling jewel of the nature of mind, and recognizing mind essence itself. Because what obscures buddha nature is something temporary, exert yourself in removing this obscuration.

The kayas and wisdoms are an intrinsic part of buddha nature, always present in all sentient beings. Like the sky itself, buddha nature is unchanging, but the obscurations are temporary, like clouds. Clouds are temporary, space is not. The sun shines, warm and brilliant. It makes water evaporate, which condenses in the sky, forming clouds which then obscure the sun itself. The sky and the sun don't change through that: they are originally just so, just like space and original wakefulness, the kayas and wisdoms. You can say they are permanent, incessant, but the appearance of clouds creates a seeming discontinuity. The moment you abandon the cloud and just leave it to itself, *as it is*, it disperses. It is not able to linger forever. That is how to deal with confusion.

The essence itself is unidentifiable. What we need to recognize, to identify, is that our essence *is* unidentifiable; that there is no thing being recognized. We see that immediately the moment of looking in the correct way. That's not enough, though. We get distracted and forget, then we start to think, isn't that right? There are two types of ignorance: coemergent ignorance and conceptual ignorance. In the moment after seeing our essence, it almost immediately slips away. We get distracted and then we start to think of something. Forgetting and thinking—that is the twofold ignorance, coemergent ignorance and conceptual ignorance.

We do get carried away; that is how it is for any sentient being. If sentient beings are taught how to recognize, they will see their nature, no question. Yet immediately it slips away. After forgetting we start to think; first forgetting, then thinking. Our nature is always present, and yet we don't see it. This twofold ignorance, the coemergent and conceptual ignorance, comprise the root of samsaric existence. That is what we need to do away with. Even though we see our own essence, we still get distracted. Distracted, we start getting involved in thought, and then trouble starts. We need to train gradually so that this twofold ignorance becomes weaker and weaker, until it finally vanishes. This twofold ignorance is what ties down or fetters the buddha nature in sentient beings. Although the state of rigpa, of nondual awareness, is utterly tranquil, beyond being confused and liberated, unchanging like space, still there are the two demons of ignorance. Don't forget that!

In short, recognize mind nature. Don't project, don't focus, don't keep a state. Don't think of anything. For a few seconds there is no thing to describe. You can call it being empty and awake. That is mind essence. This is not an act of meditating, because it is already naturally present. If we start to imagine, think, plan, it is already forgotten. What we need is to 'capture the stronghold of nonmeditation.' It is never said we should capture the stronghold of meditation, in the sense of a meditation state which is created or produced.

Capture the dharmakaya throne of nonmeditation. This is not something which is imagined even as much as a hair-tip; it is naturally and spontaneously present. In that moment of nonmeditation, the objects of experience are not blocked off in any way. They are vividly present. That is how it should be, unobstructed. Do not get involved in fixating and labeling each distinctive feature; allow your eyes to see, allow your ears to hear. Otherwise you will fall into *inert shamatha*, where you don't hear or see anything. Rather, be wide awake, vividly clear, not holding onto anything. Let go of this holding. Be like a child in a temple hall who sees everything that is. The child gazing in wonder doesn't label or fixate on anything. Train in being like that.

When you feel doubt, remember that doubt is merely another thought. Recognize the essence of the doubter, and the doubt dissolves. You don't need to think, "Is this really it? What is it, actually? The three kayas must be something other, something totally special, some sort of impressive, enormous spectacle. Maybe it will slowly come into my experience, and then this state of mind I have right now will definitely be left behind." As a matter of fact, our basic state is already the buddha mind, so what is necessary is to let go of the present thought and not create or fabricate anything. If this present wakefulness is not here, we would be a corpse. You can hear sound, right? It is mind that hears, not the ears. Corpses have ears, yet a corpse doesn't hear sound, does it? Your present mind right now is what experiences; not the mind of yesterday, not the mind of tomorrow or the day after. When recognizing, don't do anything to this mind, make not even as much as a hair-tip of effort. Don't correct it. Leave it wide-open and natural, like space. Natural means *as it is*. That is the true Samantabhadra, which is never apart from your own mind. This buddha mind has never forsaken you for even an instant.

Recognize rigpa, your mind essence! This is what sentient beings don't do. They don't know how to look. Even if they do see, they don't know what it is. They immediately start thinking of something else, one thing after the other, adding endless new links to the chain of samsara. In this nowness, past thought has vanished, and future thought hasn't come yet. Don't correct your present wakefulness; simply acknowledge it. While recognizing, don't reconnect it with thoughts. This present wakefulness doesn't last very long; because of all our past lives of being distracted, you need to grow more used to it. Again we fall under the power of the two demons of ignorance. We forget, we start to think.

A real yogi is a practitioner who again and again recognizes, and for whom the moments of recognition thus slowly start to last longer and longer. Involvement in thought automatically becomes weaker and weaker, while the gap between thoughts grows longer and longer. When the present wakefulness is unbroken throughout day and night with no delusion, no distraction, that is truly having captured the stronghold of dharmakaya. It is also known as the 'exhaustion of phenomena and concepts.'

'Concept' here means the mind which conceptualizes, while 'phenomena' means the objects conceptualized. Before that, whenever a visual form presents itself, you tend to be startled: "What's that?" There's a sound—"What's that sound?" You touch something—"Hey, what's that?" Immediately, bewilderment happens.

A meditator may sometimes think, "Yesterday there were not so many thoughts, that was a good practice session! But today there are a lot of thoughts. My meditation is lousy!" Those projections are simply two other thoughts. How can the essence itself, which is like space, be either good or bad? Since this training is not an act of meditating, why worry about whether our meditation was good or not good? This is a training in not meditating, a training in naturalness, in letting be. Quite interesting, isn't it?

When your practice is a training in great openness free from aiming at pleasure or rejecting pain, you don't need to hold onto whether it is pleasant or painful. If you don't let go of pleasure, you won't leave the realms of desire behind. The word 'great bliss' doesn't mean some grand state of conditioned pleasure, but rather unconditioned bliss totally free of pain. Sentient beings expect enlightenment to be something which is not painful, but still really pleasant. That is called conditioned pleasure; once attained, it wears off, and again you suffer.

This training is not an act of meditating, but a 'growing used to.' If you try to improve upon or correct this state even as much as a hair-tip, it is already spoiled. The thought thinks, "This is not good enough," and the present wakefulness is already spoiled. Thought means thinking, and unenlightened sentient beings do think. Let go of the thoughts of the three times, but not by throwing them away—that is only more thinking—but by letting go. In the moment of seeing the essence, the thoughts of the three times are automatically dissolved, disbanded. In suspicion, there is already a thought. By recognizing what feels suspicious, the suspicion also vanishes. Ironically, seeing or not seeing the essence is not a big deal; it is always present, incessantly.

I don't want to sound presumptuous here, but perhaps this training is actually something incredibly easy. You don't have to meditate. You don't have to think of something. You don't have to do anything at all. There is no pushing, no striving. You don't need anything at all, except to train in that. Because it is *too* easy, because it is simply too easy, most people don't believe it. They don't trust it because there is nothing that *I* do. They think, "To totally disconnect, what is the use of that? If this essence is no thing whatsoever, what is the big deal about that? How could that be worthwhile? It would be much better to imagine some really magnificent-looking deity, and to recite a powerful mantra!"

Train in letting be in naturalness, without meditating. In order to do that, you need to genuinely recognize rigpa. Without recognizing, it's like the light that doesn't come on unless you flick the switch. Once you flick the switch, the light is on and there is no need to do anything. No need to look here or there, just let be—with the light on.

14

Involved

✿

Imagine a completely clean and nicely polished mirror that has the capacity to reflect whatever is present; nothing is held back. If you have it with you up here at my hermitage, the whole Kathmandu Valley in its entirety is reflected on its surface. It has that capacity. That doesn't mean that the mirror has to go out and chase after those images for them to appear there. The reflection happens on the mirror's bright surface, not in some other place. Rigpa is said to be like a mirror, in the sense that it doesn't have to move out towards and then apprehend objects in order to understand. That is the function of conceptual mind, *sem*. *Sem* reaches out, forms labels based on characteristics, and then gets involved in the field of that experience. Rigpa does not reach out and apprehend; it simply allows the reflections to appear as if on the surface of a mirror. That is a huge difference.

Rigpa has a certain capacity. Capacity here means the basis, the venue or the medium for unobstructed arising, for unblocked experience. It is not the arising itself. When it becomes the arising itself, which is then apprehended, that is what is called thinking. Capacity is simply the medium or basis for experience to take place. That is not the same as when experience actually occurs and is labeled as 'such-and-such.' That is called conceptual mind or thinking. This metaphor of the mirror is a very important example. Rigpa doesn't reach out and apprehend; conceptual mind does. Rigpa is also said to be primordially free of any movement that reaches out. Longchenpa's *Dharmadhatu Kosha* says the following about rigpa:

> *Utterly uninvolved, and yet this naked state of dharmakaya is*
> *inconceivable.*
> *Utterly flawless, and yet it is the source from which all qualities*
> *unfold.*

Rigpa does not reach out after perceived objects; nor does it become covered by them. The objects are reflected within the state of rigpa. This is unlike conceptual mind, which is diffused or absorbed into the perceived objects. Rigpa is like mercury. If you pour mercury on a plate of dust it remains separate, it doesn't become mingled with the dust. If you pour mercury on earth or dust or sand, it sticks to itself and stays separate from everything else. That is how rigpa is. Conceptual mind, on the other hand, is like pouring water on top of the dirt. It turns into mud; or, to put it another way, one gets caught up in perceiver and perceived. Rigpa is not absorbed into the duality of perceiver and perceived; it is innately stable.

The main point of the training is uncontrived naturalness, which is radically different from our normal habit of thinking one thought after another. To be involved in first thinking of one thing, then another, then a third, is the way to perpetuate dualistic mind. Uncontrived naturalness is not conceptual mind.

How do we deal with all these different thoughts? All thoughts belong within three categories: thoughts of past, thoughts of present and thoughts of future. When beginning to train in meditation, it is not so difficult to deal with thoughts of past and future. Honestly, in rigpa, the thoughts of past have already ceased, and future thought hasn't come yet. The main problem is the involvement in present thoughts. The opposite of uncontrived naturalness is to be caught up in this present thinking, which is always to either affirm something or deny something; to accept or reject. That all is based on hope and fear. As a meditator we may have the idea that there is some nasty dualistic state of mind we need to be rid of, and that there is this excellent or attractive state of rigpa that we need to keep. To involve oneself in accepting and rejecting, holding onto rigpa, the nondual state of mind, and regarding thoughts to be something that need to be deliberately gotten rid of, is definitely not the training in uncontrived naturalness.

All sentient beings are continuously involved in adding one more link, to the chain of the samsaric frame of mind. That is what each thought in every moment is actually doing—perpetuating the samsaric state. How do we end this? This is the real dilemma for a meditator: how to deal with the present thinking that is based on hope and fear, accepting and rejecting.

Really, though, it is not such a big problem. Simply recognize mind essence. In the same moment, the present thought has no foothold, it dwells nowhere; it simply dissolves and is no more. In that moment you don't have to do anything to improve it or make it more excellent. It is already the essence *as it is*. Not having to accept or reject something at that moment—that is uncontrived naturalness.

Train in this uncontrived naturalness as the main core of your practice, again and again. It is not the same as doing a session in which you try to maintain a state for a long time, until you finally dedicate the merit and stand up. That is not what is meant, because we can only do that a couple of times a day. That is called practicing a few times for long stretches. On the contrary, the real practice is short moments repeated many times during the day. These short moments or stretches should be training in uncontrived naturalness.

Here is the method to dissolve any thought. Even the most painful notion is a product of one's own thought, isn't it? One labels 'that over there' as painful, then thinks, "I can't stand to face it, it simply is too much, it is terrible, it is awful, I can't bear it any longer!" This attitude creates one thought after the other, and it is this thought process that becomes overwhelming, rather than the actual painful object. Simply acknowledge that this particular painful thought is just like any other thought. It is not anything other than a thought. The way to deal with a thought is the same, regardless of the content. Simply recognize the identity of the thinker, the essence. In that moment, the thinking cannot remain by itself; it simply dissolves. That feeling of being overwhelmed by other people's pain, this feeling that actually is and always was insubstantial and empty, is now in actuality seen to be empty. There is no *thing* there that actually feels it. It is empty.

This is only good for a few seconds, though. The thought dissolves and there is no problem, but it comes back again as a reoccurrence. The way to deal with this is exactly the same as before: recognize what it is that feels overcrowded or overwhelmed. Again you see that there is no thing there, it is empty. Yet you don't stay empty, you can feel. Repeatedly train in this way.

Recognize the empty cognizance of mind essence once, and it's the same every time you remember it. You acknowledge the same unconfined empty cognizance that was previously recognized. We are not enlightened yet; just because we've glimpsed mind essence doesn't mean that we have reached full fruition. We are still on the path. In other words, we are not fully perfected, not fully accustomed, not inherently stable in mind essence. How to deal with being somebody who is not perfect? Simply train, again and again. There is no other way to deal with it than to become someone who has perfected the practice. Whether the problematic *it* is a feeling or a concept or physical form or condition or sensation, the training is exactly the same. All of these aggregates are indivisible from emptiness from the beginning; simply acknowledge that.

On the other hand, sometimes for a particular type of individual, the pain and suffering of other beings is perhaps too much. Such a person feels that he or she cannot really concentrate on practice. At that time it is best to get yourself together, in other words, recognize mind essence. Sometimes it's not so easy to remember and one gets carried away. Then it is taught that it is very beneficial to investigate; to take a closer look at both the subject and object of the feeling.

For example, let's say one experiences a feeling of being overwhelmed or claustrophobic or crowded in by the pain. Examine both the subject and the object. The object is the feeling, the subject is the "me" who feels it. Allow yourself to take a closer look at this intense feeling. Where is it, actually? Where was it first noticed, and what exactly is the physical location from which it came? Right now, when this feeling is so strong, exactly where is it? When it vanishes at some point, in which direction does it go? To where did it go? Find the exact location. Also investigate the subject that feels it, this mind that is aware and notices. This approach is extremely beneficial. If pain and dread become too much, one should give a close inspection into both the subject and object of the feeling.

Sentient beings do have thoughts, and sometimes our thoughts become overwhelming, too much. That doesn't mean that we should give up at that moment. Of course, when we encounter other beings who suffer, it may seem that we are quite justified in feeling overwhelmed. Actually, though, we have to start somewhere. If you don't have the blessings and the compassionate power to save or benefit others, the place to start is to *at least* to clear up your own confusion. Our own deluded state is close at hand. Being involved in deluded thought has no true substantiality; that is why it is called delusion.

There is honestly no concrete thing called suffering or thought or feeling that you can really pinpoint as being in a particular location anywhere. If there was, we could say it was material, and it wouldn't be called an illusion or a deluded state. It would be real. Can you find the feeling of suffering as a concrete thing anywhere a place where it came out of, a place where it is, and a place where it goes? Is there a solid mind that notices and gets involved in this emotion? Once you discover there is not, there is nothing further to discuss about that.

All the practitioners of the past who investigated this in depth failed to discover an emotion's source, dwelling place, or place of disappearance. The same goes for the personal identity, the self. You have to agree that it is an illusion. This is the illusion of emptiness: every thought is a magical illusion of emptiness. The moment you recognize the experiencer the falsehood is immediately revealed, in that the thought simply dissolves. This is how to begin.

You need to start training. This is of course based upon having recognized the empty, cognizant nature of mind. You need to become adept by training in experiencing the nature of mind again and again. Unless you train, you will never becomes stable, and without becoming stable, the capacity to benefit other beings doesn't manifest.

The more we train in recognizing mind essence, the more the innate qualities arise. These are the qualities of insight, compassion and the ability to benefit others. These intrinsic enlightened abilities start to unfold further and further. At that point, not only is your own confusion cleared up; you will also be able to benefit any person in front of you who is in pain. Not only that, you will be able to simultaneously benefit all sentient beings in the three realms of samsara, even down to the very bottom of the existence, the deepest pit of hell. You can place all of them on the path of liberation in a single instant. All that comes from beginning the training and persevering in it.

Let's say there is a moment when a feeling is simply too much, when what you are experiencing is too painful to face. At that moment, try to remember this while questioning yourself: Where is this feeling of pain right now? Where is it exactly? This overwhelming *thing*, does it have a specific form or a sound, does it smell in a certain way, does it taste in a certain way, is there something I can take hold of? Don't get caught up in the object. What you feel is your mind experiencing the pain; it is not some other thing. Suffering is mental, right? Can you grab the pain? No? That proves it is empty!

To truly have compassion, you need to experience emptiness. Acknowledge that the other person doesn't see emptiness, and therefore suffers. That is where compassion comes from. If you don't realize emptiness and the other person also doesn't, you can pity him, and say, Oh, poor guy, but what is that going to help? You need to train in recognizing mind essence. If there were two people swept away by a raging river and both have no arms, how are they going to help each other? Having insight into compassionate emptiness is like having two arms. Merely superficially thinking Poor guy, poor guy, is all right, but there is no real capacity in that.

There is a supplication we often make which goes, Grant your blessings that we may realize emptiness suffused with compassion! It is this real emptiness indivisible from compassion that has the power to benefit others. Superficially pitying other beings doesn't have any deep power to it. We need to enrich ourselves now, saturate our stream of being with emptiness suffused with compassion and become a master in that. Then you can truly benefit others.

That which does *anything* in this world, that which creates the joys, the sorrows, the indifference, is this thinking mind, nothing other. All the sadness, all the pleasure, and everything in between is a magical trick of this thinking mind. Is there anything other that can create such a show? Everything is mind the maker, the doer and the deed, what is created. Are the deeds, meaning what is made, are they what makes the maker, or is it the maker that creates the deeds? Let's change the words from "doer" and "deeds" into "subject" and "object." The objects are the five elements and the subject is the perceiving mind. Where the perceiving mind moves the attention towards something, does the previously perceived object move after that mind? What should we pay attention to as the thing of chief importance? Isn't it this doer, the mind?

To keep up the subject-object duality and busy your mind with activities is not going to help in the long run. Why keep holding onto perceiver and perceived, subject and object? What happens when you are untainted by outer perceived objects and uncorrupted by the inner perceiving mind? Allow the empty awareness in its nakedness to simply continue. If you allow this, that itself is the mind of all buddhas. Whether you hear about this in a thousand different ways or a hundred different ways, it is simply this.

First you need to understand and get the taste of it. Next, you need to bring it into actuality. On this path you first recognize, then train, developing the strength of it, and finally attain stability. That is what it's all about. Acknowledge this moment of being awake, of being uninvolved in perceived objects, in which the perceiving mind is unoccupied, unemployed, free. Don't be tainted by any emotion. When original wakefulness is fully present, fully actualized, that is the meaning of the word buddha, the purified and perfected awakened state. Growing fully accustomed to and stable in this is itself the path of awakening. First, recognize and acknowledge this, then train in this and become stable; that is enlightenment. Then you have arrived at transcendent knowledge, on the other shore, beyond this shore of dualistic knowledge.

Let me tease you a little. This side of knowledge is called science, being a scientist. Transcending the bounds of knowledge is different, as I explained. How many scientists do you know who have become enlightened? Have you heard of any? Well, if a scientist trains in this, he becomes enlightened. That's pretty neat, isn't it? These days scientists are praised as being the most eminent people in this world, because they make devices through which you can instantly talk to someone on the other end of the world, or you can fly through the skies. Well, with this practice you can go *beyond* being a scientist. Actually, what science can create is pretty amazing, but still, all science is on this side of the shore of knowledge. The profound samadhi means the other shore of knowledge, having transcended dualistic mind.

Right now, if we compare ourselves with a scientist, a scientist seems to be better, right? But once the scientist arrives on the other shore, any mental doings is of no use at all! At that point, as far as we are concerned, it is much better to arrive on the other side at transcendent knowledge. Here's a question for all of you: exactly how much benefit is there from scientific knowledge the moment you are in the bardo? Think about it well. When a scientist is in the bardo he no longer has any gadgets to help him, no spy satellites or jet planes to move around in. In the bardo isn't whatever one created of absolutely no use? Scientific knowledge is not transcendent. The knowledge that we are supposed to train in is transcendent knowledge, prajnaparamita.

Honestly, whatever mundane, unspiritual actions we do show themselves to be a total waste at the end of this life. They are good for absolutely nothing. Any work that one bothers to complete is pointless unless it is connected with a virtuous outcome. We involve ourselves so wholeheartedly in our tasks, with no time to even sit down and enjoy one cup of tea. The sweat from such activity is constantly on our forehead. All that will be absolutely wasted the moment we die. It will be of no use whatsoever.

To understand that whatever we do, whatever we have done, is totally futile; that is true insight. That is real understanding. Nothing other than Dharma has any real value or substance. What is next, then? Apply it! Apply it more and more, and you will capture the stronghold of the view. That is the way to truly understand the Dharma. When we look closely at things around us and in ourselves, we should come to the understanding that everything we have done is basically useless. In realizing I have really fooled myself, there is some understanding to gain. It is not somebody else who fooled me; I fooled myself. In Kham there is a saying: Like having stitched up your own mouth. In other words, you can't eat or drink, so you die of starvation. That is what we have done to ourselves. Nobody else stitched up your mouth; you did it to yourself.

Just between us, this human life with the complete eight freedoms and ten riches, this precious human body, is as valuable as a nirmanakaya manifesting in this world. What we need now is to stop stitching up our own mouths! It is said in many of the guidance manuals that to have the precious human body, not merely a human body, but the precious human body only happens once or twice in a whole aeon. Having achieved this, there is still the risk of returning empty-handed from the island of jewels. This is your choice!

This point of time in the history of humankind is on the one hand a time of immense progress and development, and for many people, of prosperity. We can say that these are happy times. At the same time there is no certainty whether someone alive today will be a corpse tomorrow; any situation can change all of a sudden, so that it's abruptly all wiped away. Such are the times we live in right now. Right now you have some freedom: you are free to choose to practice the Dharma, there is nobody to prevent you. It is all in your own hands. You have the reins, so to speak. This is the time to practice and attain enlightenment!

We should really appreciate this opportunity and stop fooling ourselves. The great masters of the past said, A single breath makes the difference between life and death. If you exhale and don't inhale, your body is a corpse. It doesn't take more than one breath not being inhaled and you are already in the bardo. Each moment we continue to be alive, how amazing!

Notes

1 *Nangjang* training—literally "training in refining experience"—is the personal process of resolving the nature of reality and experience by means of the profound teachings of the Great Perfection. An extraordinary example of this method of practice is found in Dudjom Lingpa's *Buddhahood Without Meditation*. Padma Publishing, 1994.

2 Please understand that we have omitted the detailed pointing-out instruction and left a skeletal resemblance for reference. It is necessary to receive the teachings personally and in their entirety from a qualified master.

3 For details, see *Light of Wisdom*, Vol. II, page 100 onwards.

4 The *Dharmadhatu Kosha* is one of Longchenpa's famous *Seven Treasuries*.

5 The *Lamrim Yeshe Nyingpo* is a teaching given by Padmasambhava and concealed as a terma for the benefit of future generations. It was revealed by Jamyang Khyentse Wangpo and Chokgyur Lingpa after which Jamgön Kongtrül Lodrö Thaye wrote an extensive commentary on it. The English translation is published under the title *Light of Wisdom*.

6 The *Kunzang Tuktig*, the *Heart Essence of Samantabhadra*, is Padmasambhava's condensation of all the Dzogchen tantras into in applicable form suitable to the present day practitioner. It was revealed by Chokgyur Lingpa.

7 The *Barchey Künsel* cycle of teachings were revealed by Chokgyur Lingpa together with Jamyang Khyentse Wangpo and consist of about ten volumes of texts.

8 The *Chetsün Nyingtik* cycle contains the teachings on the Great Perfection from Vimalamitra as given to the great master Chetsün Senge Wangchuk. They were revealed by Jamyang Khyentse Wangpo.

9 *Maza Damsum* refers to the three main protectors of the Dzogchen teachings: Ekajati, Rahula, and Vajra Sadhu.